DECISION AT NAGASAKI - THE MISSION THAT ALMOST FAILED

by

Lt. Col. USAF (Ret.) Fred J. Olivi

with

William R. Watson Jr.

Deluxe Edition

Text-only disk (Mac or PC) is also available

All photographs and other materials

copyright 1998 by Fred J. Olivi,

except their respective owners,

printed by kind permission.

1

To Rich —

Best Wishes For a Happy, Healthy Future?

Fred J. Olivi
Co-pilot B-29
"Bockscar"
Nagasaki Mission
9 August, 1945

DEDICATIONS

To Carole McVey Olivi

Carole McVey Olivi was my wife, classmate and high school sweetheart and Prom date in our senior year at Pullman Tech.

Carole, sharing life with you was one of the greatest joys given to me during my lifetime. I thank the Lord for the 33 years of truly great happiness we shared during our married life. You were a *very* important part and the steadying influence in our happy life together—*you were my life!!*

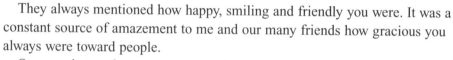

Your patience, kindness, understanding and warm personality in association with other people, through the years, will always be remembered by our many friends and acquaintances.

They always mentioned how happy, smiling and friendly you were. It was a constant source of amazement to me and our many friends how gracious you always were toward people.

Our travels together, on our many trips to Europe, was a great adventure and much joy to both of us. Travelling with you was most rewarding and we never seemed to have difficulties in deciding where to go and what to see.

You were a grand lady and I know my life will not be as happy as it was with you! I'll never forget you and the wonderful, warm, caring, loving person you always were.

I will miss my co-pilot very much!!!

"I Love You, and The Lord Be With You."

Your Freddie

To my Father and Mother, Adorno Olivi and Primitiva (Simonini) Olivi, poor and uneducated Italian immigrants, born in Corsanico (Viareggio) Province of Tuscany, who had the courage and foresight to begin a new life in America in the early 1900's and live the American dream.

To the Pullman Tech High School whose dedicated teachers taught us the training and lessons that proved invaluable and remain with me to this day;

WILLIAM R. WATSON JR.

William R. Watson Jr., born in Minnesota but reared in Illinois, began his career as a writer and editor while in college at DePauw University in Greencastle, Indiana. After military service in Korea, he became a copywriter with the Foote, Cone & Belding advertising agency, and subsequently was a copywriter and TV producer with several Chicago ad agencies. After retiring he became a freelance writer and marketing consultant. One of his magazine articles led to a meeting with Fred Olivi and this book about Olivi's life and wartime experience as the co-pilot of the B-29 aircraft that dropped the atomic bomb on Nagasaki, Japan. Watson resides today in Oak Brook, Illinois.

Table of Contents

Preface

Introduction 7

Foreword "The End of the World" 11

Section One - Growing Up

    Chapter 1   *Pullman, Illinois* 16

    Chapter 2   *The Early Years* 19

    Chapter 3   *The Great Depression* 28

    Chapter 4   *Pullman Tech* .31

Section Two - Army Air Corps

    Chapter 5   *Navy? Army? I Just Want To Fly!* 37

    Chapter 6   *Training, Training, Training* 41

    Chapter 7   *Wendover* 58

    Chapter 8   *"The Pumpkin"* 75

Section Three - The Mission

    Chapter 9   *Flight to Tinian* 78

    Chapter 10   *Keeping the Secret, Secret* 83

    Chapter 11   *Pre-Empted* 87

    Chapter 12   *Get Ready, Get Set* 91

    Chapter 13   *Special Mission # 16* 93

    Chapter 14   *Rendezvous* .118

    Chapter 15   *Kokura* 120

    Chapter 16   *A Thousand Suns Over Nagasaki* 123

    Chapter 17   *May Day! May Day!* 132

    Chapter 18   *It's Over!* 150

Section Four - War's Aftermath

    Chapter 19   *Tinian – After the War* 154

    Chapter 20   *Roswell, New Mexico* 157

    Chapter 21   *Chicago, My Home Town* 162

Section Five - Appendix 167

1 AUG 1995

Message for the 509th Composite Group
50th Anniversary Reunion

It is both a privilege and an honor to convey
my greetings to the surviving members and families of
the 509th Composite Group's 50th anniversary reunion
commemorating its historic
war-ending operations.

The 509th Composite Group holds a special place
in the history of world War II. Formed in 1944, under
the command of Colonel Paul Tibbets, the 509th became
the first nuclear capable air detachment to conduct
operations anywhere in the world. Composed of the
393rd Bombardment Squadron and the 320th Troop
Carrier Squadron, the 509th proved that composite
units could dutifully execute mobile, independent,
and highly classified operations. The 509th successfully delivered the first atomic devices; a mission
which culminated in the surrender of Japan and quick-
ened the end of an already costly war. The efforts of
the 509th saved not only American lives but helped
preserve the American way of life we enjoy today.
Your unwavering dedication and pursuit of excellence
are appreciated by not only myself but by every individual who has served this great country of ours. As
you gather together, I join you in remembering your
colleagues who are no longer with you. I know their
spirit is bright among you .

Please accept my congratulations and heart-felt
thanks for your contributions to the defense of our
nation. Long live "DEFENSOR VINDEX."

William J. Perry

INTRODUCTION

1995 marked a milestone for millions of people in virtually every country on this planet Earth: The commemoration of the end of World War II.

To those of us now in our seventies and eighties who fought in that War, the years from 1940 through 1945 are etched forever in our collective memories. We vividly recall the events that our great-grandsons and great-granddaughters now study in school. Unfortunately, far too often World War II represents "ancient history" to them — a time when everything was so different from what we know today. Just as when we were growing up, World War I seemed so distant.

For many years now, we veterans have been relating our "adventures" to various civic organizations and school assemblies throughout the country. Personally, these visits —especially with the younger generation — have been very gratifying. I am sure other veterans, like me, have welcomed the opportunity to correct a wrong impression or explain what really happened during a particular episode of that terrible conflict..

To this day, two particular episodes related to the end of World War II continue to be extremely controversial: The dropping of atomic weapons on two cities in Japan.

Many stories have been written about the two atomic bomb missions to Japan during the month of August, 1945. (You may recall there was a movie about the mission of the Enola Gay to Hiroshima on August 6, 1945). Certainly, the flight of the first atomic bomber caught the attention of the American public in 1945. Over fifty years later it continues to be the subject of a furious debate at the Smithsonian Museum in Washington, D.C.

Almost forgotten, it seems to me, has been the mission to Nagasaki. In fact, in my opinion, many of the events before, during and immediately after the flight of the B-29, called "Bockscar," to Nagasaki on August 9, 1945, where it dropped the last atomic bomb ever used in the history of human warfare against an enemy's territory, have never been thoroughly aired.

I should know. I was there in the cockpit as one of the pilots.

In fact, I had few specific duties during the mission; therefore, I watched, listened and remembered what was happening around me in the cockpit. As a 23-year old Second Lieutenant, and usually the co-pilot with this crew, I followed orders as momentous decisions were made by my superior officers, most of them

7

only a few years older than I.

For many years, I have been telling my version of that historic mission to high school students, veterans groups, and many fraternal and civic organizations. After hearing my story and seeing my photographs, maps and other documents, many people have urged me to put it all down in writing — to make a permanent record of my recollections about what I heard and saw on that fateful day in August, 1945, an event which helped end World War II, and saved so many thousand American (and Japanese) lives. This book is the result of these requests.

Helping to "jog" my memory is a penciled "diary" I wrote immediately after our return from the mission to Tinian Island. We had been ordered not to write anything during the mission itself in case we were shot down and captured. As far as I know, none of us did, although several "logs" by men who were with me on that troubled flight were published after the war ended. Some are more accurate than others, in my opinion, but like the blind men describing the elephant, men in a stressful situation will see and hear the same event differently. I can only report what I saw and heard.

Many critical decisions were made on a B-29 called "Bockscar" that August day in 1945. There is no argument that there was some "bending" of the rules and orders. But, to this day, I have only the greatest admiration for the men who led our mission. They had to make life or death decisions in just seconds under extremely dangerous conditions. They did their best. No one can ask for more.

On returning to our base on Tinian Island in the Marianas Chain in the Southwest Pacific (Saipan and Guam are the other two principal islands in this Chain), and immediately after we were de-briefed during the early morning hours of August 9, I asked Jim Van Pelt, our navigator, if I could borrow his official logbook. I went to our Quonset hut, and although I was "dead on my feet" after being awake for over 24 hours, I used Jim's logbook to write down the events of our troubled flight on a pad of paper. My penciled notes, depicting the minute-by-minute, hour-by-hour record of our flight as I remembered them immediately after the mission, are an important part of my story. I am pleased to say that my original, penciled "diary" is now in the Malcolm S. Forbes, Jr., collection of historical documents, where it has joined Bob Lewis' flight log of the "Enola Gay's" mission to Hiroshima. (However, Bob Lewis received more money for selling his diary).

In addition, over the years I have acquired many photographs, maps, and other military documents, many only recently de-classified. My "diary" and these documents have helped to refresh my memory and kept me on track while telling my story.

It is my intention to clarify the "who," "what," "how," "where," "when" and "why" about this historic mission. For example, I think it's important to explain how we happened to be flying a B-29 called "Bockscar" on the mission to Nagasaki. Except for that one flight, our crew flew all our missions in a B-29 called "The Great Artiste."

I also want to record for posterity how I, as a very young, first generation

Italian-American employed as a draft-deferred machinist making critical wartime tools with Sciaky Brothers of Chicago, Illinois, a French Company, happened to be in a B-29 on that fateful day.

Until February of 1945, I had never even seen a B-29, much less heard of the 509th Composite Group, one of the most closely guarded secret military organizations of World War II.

Suddenly, I became a participant in making history; some historians have said we changed the course of armed warfare and the conduct of foreign relations. If this is true, so be it. I will always be proud that I had the opportunity to serve my country and be on the mission to Nagasaki. Truly, I was an eyewitness to profound events occurring all around me, events that virtually no one had ever experienced — events that fortunately no one has experienced since August 9, 1945.

Yes, our mission had a lot of problems. It did not go as well as the highly documented and publicized flight to Hiroshima on August 6th, piloted by Colonel Paul Tibbets, Commanding Officer of our highly secret 509th Composite Group. Tibbets' mission was as close to the "textbook" as you get, and was a credit to the skill of Colonel Tibbets and his entire crew.

Three days later, on August 9th, during our mission to Nagasaki, we had serious problems on at least three different occasions. Why we had these crises, and how they were handled, continues to be controversial (and in at least one instance, a mystery) to this day.

At reunions of the 509th I have asked other members of our crew, and members of the other B-29 crews that accompanied us to Nagasaki, about some of these particular events. But they don't remember, choose not to recall what happened, or just do not want to talk about it. This is their privilege and I respect it.

But I remember, because the events really happened. This is one of the reasons I have decided to publish my recollections of that fateful day when we carried the first plutonium A-Bomb — nicknamed "Fat Man" — first to Kokura and then to Nagasaki where it exploded about 1,840 feet above the city. The unholy destructive force of "Fat Man," and "Little Boy" before it on August 6th at Hiroshima, helped convince the Japanese Emperor and other officials in the Japanese Empire finally to accept the American terms for unconditional surrender.

I don't say that our two missions with nuclear weapons ended World War II, but we helped bring it to a close. I don't think there is any doubt of this.

To those who for the past 54 years have criticized the use of nuclear weapons by the United States in World War II, I say:

You must consider the times, and the consequences if we had not used these weapons. Are you willing to accept the fact that thousands upon thousands of American marines, soldiers, seamen, and airmen would have died if this country had invaded the Japanese islands on November 1, 1945? What would you have said in 1945 to these men, their wives and children? Are you willing to say that it was wrong to use every weapon in our huge arsenal because it would kill the enemy, including civilians?

If you say "Yes" to this, then what do you say about the massive bombing of Dresden and Berlin and Cologne, Germany? Many thousands of civilians in these cities were killed by Allied bombers, killed by firestorms that sucked out all the oxygen from the air, suffocating them.

What do you say about the 1,000-plane B-29 bombing missions which burned out the heart of Tokyo and other Japanese cities with thousands and thousands of incendiary bombs?

And what about Pearl Harbor? America did not attack Japan. The Japanese Empire, without any warning, attacked our country and was prepared to invade the Hawaiian Islands until turned back at the Battle of Midway Island in early 1942.

Historians today are arguing these questions. I can only hope that they will not totally re-write history as they tell the stories of Hiroshima and Nagasaki.

I also wonder if the human race will ever learn to conduct international relations without the use or implied threat of nuclear weapons.

Yes, America and the former U.S.S.R. are in the process of disarming themselves, with England and other NATO countries following our lead. But the threat of loosing these awesome and terrible weapons is still with us. Today, reports in the media reveal that it is now possible for almost any technically sophisticated individual to construct a small nuclear bomb and put it in the trunk of an automobile.

* * *

Ours is a dangerous time in the brief history of mankind. As one who saw the mind-boggling destruction of a nuclear weapon first-hand, I cannot fathom why anybody would ever consider using such a weapon again.

General Sherman during America's Civil War was quoted as saying, "War is hell." He was right in the 1860's, and he is right in the 1990's.

It has been said by others more learned than I that in 1945 we "released the genie from the bottle and don't know how to get it back." If this is true, then we on this planet Earth are doomed to experience future horrors that will make the bomb we dropped on Nagasaki look like a 4th of July firecracker.

I fervently hope that history will prove them wrong.

Fred Olivi
Chicago, Illinois

FOREWORD

The End of the World

The long troop train bumped and lurched several times as its brakes finally got the wheels fully stopped on the icy rails. I scratched a small hole in the frost that coated the window and looked out. It was late morning. Through the single-pane glass I could see a badly weathered wooden sign on the side of the railroad station. It read: "Wendover." Our long, overnight train ride was over.

The troop train, crowded to capacity, had left Lincoln, Nebraska, the previous afternoon, paused briefly in Salt Lake City, and then continued through the early morning hours west across the desolate, flat Utah countryside. Our breakfast had been a can of cold "C" rations. None of us had slept more than a few minutes at a time on the hard seats. The date was February 12, 1945.

So what, if the train ride had been uncomfortable, the coach too cold one minute, too hot the next. Soon we'd be back where we belonged — in the air, flying B-24 bombers.

"This is it," I called out to my friends John Lundgren and Dick McNamara. "Wendover! Let's get out of here!"

The three of us had been together since June, 1944, when we had successfully graduated from the Army Air Corps' Advanced Flight Training (Twin Engine Aircraft) base at Lubbock, Texas, and received our Wings and commissions as Second Lieutenants. Subsequently, we were assigned to B-24 transitional training at Ft. Worth, Texas, where we had learned to fly the famous B-24 "Liberator" 4-engine bomber. All of us had qualified to sit in the left seat of a B-24 as Aircraft Commanders, or First Pilots. We were proud. We were "hot" pilots just itching to show how skilled we really were. Like thousands of America's young men we had joined the Army Air Corps to fight the enemy, to do our duty, and be proud of it.

Richard "Dick" McNamara, raised in Olympia, Washington, was as typical an Irishman as I had ever met. Six feet tall, with curly red-brown hair and a gift of gab, he always had a smile and a ready joke for any occasion. Dick was the perfect companion for a quiet Swede like John Lundgren and an aggressive Italian-American like me. John tended to be a "worrier," while I was ready to challenge anybody at the drop of a hat. Dick was the "optimist" who cheered up John and who also kept me from getting into trouble!

I hurried to the vestibule of the dirty, smoke-filled Pullman Coach, eager to climb down from the over-crowded troop train. Thirteen men lined up to get off the train: six co-pilots, one bombardier, one navigator, and five aircraft commanders, including the three of us.

I had been assured by a sergeant in the Personnel Section back at the air crew "pool" in Lincoln, Nebraska that I probably was going to take over the crew of a B-24. He said probably the pilot had become injured or sick, and that I would train with the crew and probably go overseas. I figured that Dick, John and I would wind up as "1st Pilots," each of us in command of a B-24 "Liberator" bomber. This is just what we wanted and were qualified to do.

The sergeant had also told me that most of the B-24 units being formed were going to bases in Italy, which was now in Allied hands. This news seemed to be too good to be true, and on the troop train I daydreamed about the prospect of again seeing my aunts, uncles and cousins in Corsanico and Viareggio, in the Province of Tuscany, north of Rome. Why not? I had enjoyed good fortune thus far in the Army Air Corps and saw no reason why my luck should change. My last trip to Italy had been with my mother in 1928, when I was a six-year-old child.

The train slowly chugged off with its load of soldiers. I stood on the station platform and looked south across the snowy, flat terrain. In the distance, not far from the train tracks, I could see the tall, single tails of several huge airplanes in the distance, just visible over a tall fence! B-24's had two tails.

McNamara made a slow whistling sound as we stood huddled against the wind, and said, "Them's sure funny looking B-24's. Looks like B-29's to me, Fred."

Lundgren and I nodded agreement as we waited on the platform with the other men listed on our "Special Orders, No. 14, dated February 10, 1945."

I thought to myself, "What the hell is going on? Here I am in some God-forsaken hole in Utah, and there's not a B-24 in sight. What's with these B-29's? I'm not staying around this place any longer than I have to. Somehow I'll get transferred back to Texas, where I know they've got B-24's. Besides, Texas is a lot warmer than this freezing hell-hole!"

As we looked at the distant B-29 tails on the horizon, a Major came up, called us to attention, held a roll call and checked our orders individually, looking us up and down while he did so. Once he was satisfied that we were who we said we were, he told us to get on a waiting bus. McNamara and I sat together, Lundgren on a seat across the aisle. Nobody talked. I am sure that all three of us were thinking the same thought: "What's this all about, and how do I get out of here?"

A few minutes later the bus stopped at the main gate. I noticed an unusual number of MP's in the two guard houses, all heavily armed with carbines as well as wearing the usual Colt .45's on their hips. A tall, particularly mean-looking corporal had the bus driver open the door so he could climb inside to look us over. He called out another roll call, and then walked down the aisle, carefully inspecting each of our orders. It was obvious that whatever was going on at this

Wendover Air Base was highly secret. First the Major and now a "gorilla" of an MP.

After the MP was satisfied we were not spies, we were driven on to the base, over a frozen dirt road to a small wooden building. We got off, hauled our luggage inside, and were told by the Major to remove our overcoats and sit down.

We had been seated only a few minutes, when a side door opened and in came a very young Colonel. He was followed by two other officers. We sprang to attention. "At ease, gentlemen," the Colonel said. "Please be seated. Smoke if you want to. I'm Colonel Tibbets, Commanding Officer of the 509th."

We sat down. The young-looking Colonel continued. "I'd like to welcome you to the 509th Composite Group. This is Lt. Colonel Payette, our Intelligence and Security Officer, and this is Lt. Colonel Classen, Squadron Commander of the 393rd Bomb Squadron." The two men, who had seated themselves off to one side, nodded their respective heads as they were introduced. Classen was also very young, probably in his late 20's. Payette was definitely the oldest of the three. He was starting to go bald, looked about 40 and had very cold, black eyes behind his black-rimmed bi-focal glasses. I decided that Payette was one Colonel who I didn't want to have coming after me — for any reason.

Colonel Tibbets stood silent for a moment, looking at us, his gaze moving from one face to another. When his eyes met mine, I looked straight at him. Who was this very young Colonel? He gave the appearance of being very friendly, very open, yet there was a coldness behind those friendly eyes. He looked young enough to have just finished transition training with McNamara, Lundgren and me. He could have been a 2nd Lieutenant, not a full bird Colonel. (I determined years later that he was just 29-years-old when I first met him that cold February morning!)

My thoughts were interrupted by Colonel Tibbets who said, "I suppose you're wondering why you're here? Well, first off, you are now members of the 393rd Bomb Squadron of the 509th Composite Group. Our aircraft are specially-made B-29's. I want to personally tell you fellows that you are being assigned to a highly secret operation, one of the top secrets in the country. Our job is to deliver a brand new weapon which may have the capability of destroying a city. We're still working on it, but it'll be ready soon. What you see here, what you hear here, stays here! Got that? I don't even want you talking about what you see and hear to each other. Understood?"

There was a quiet "Yes, Sir!" from all of us.

Colonel Tibbets wasn't through. "You have been thoroughly investigated by the FBI. We have talked to your neighbors, your grade, high school and college teachers. We know a lot about you. We asked the Air Force for the best, and you're it. I don't think there's any doubt that this unit will be assigned to duty overseas. So, to wrap it up, you're assigned to us now; and you'll start training with us just as soon as you're processed in by our personnel people and assigned to a B-29. I'm sorry that your quarters may be a bit primitive, but they're the best we can do. Oh, yes. You pilots will be assigned as co-pilots. Any questions?"

I had listened attentively to the Colonel, but all of a sudden I realized he was demoting me! Not Fred Olivi, he wasn't! This was a complete surprise. McNamara was sitting on my right. I turned slightly to him, my face growing red with anger; I rose to my feet. McNamara put his hand on my arm as if to hold me down, but I wasn't about to stop. "Colonel," I said, "I guess you know that some of us are qualified to be aircraft commanders and pilots on B-24's. But co-pilots? Isn't this — well, a demotion?"

Tibbets smiled his soon-to-be familiar tight-lipped smile. "Well, yes, that's true, Lieutenant. However, you're not familiar with B-29's," he said. "You've got to go through transition training on the 29, just like you did on the B-24. But since we've already got enough pilots, you will be co-pilots." He paused and looked straight at me. "You're free to leave, if you want to. Colonel Payette will issue you orders back to Lincoln — IF (he really stressed the "IF") that's what you really want. But, before you make that decision, let me make it clear that what we're doing here with the 509th may very well help end this war a hell of a lot quicker. One thing more. We requested pilots with certain levels of character and flying abilities. We chose you. If you decide to stay, I'm sure you won't be sorry. Anything else, Lieutenant?"

For one of the few times in my life, I was speechless. He had really laid into me firmly, but in a nice way. Maybe he was right. Maybe this was where I belonged. Maybe being a B-29 co-pilot wouldn't be too bad. Besides, the secrecy aspect of the 509th intrigued me. What were they up to here on this remote base in Utah? A bomb that could destroy an entire city? Maybe I'd better stay. Besides, if I backed away from this assignment, I might end up in Alaska, or worse.

I quietly sat down. I looked at McNamara. He grinned. Colonel Tibbets stood quietly in front of me. There was a slight nod of his head as if he were saying, "You made the right decision." Thoroughly humbled and a bit confused, I realized that I had almost walked away from something really big.

What I didn't know at the time was that I had just begun what I consider to be the greatest adventure of any 23-year-old Italian-American kid during World War II.

One afternoon, months later on Tinian Island, in September or October of 1945, after the war was over, I was playing handball with Colonel Tibbets. I asked him, "Colonel, I'll never forget that first day back at Wendover in February when you told me I was going to be a co-pilot. I'm really ashamed about what I said. I must have sounded like an idiot. But I still don't really know why I was chosen for the 509th. Why me?"

The Colonel responded with something like this: "Well, Olivi, we contacted Lincoln and told them what we were looking for. We had to have certain characteristics and flying qualifications. Only a very few pilots met our criteria. You did. You got very good marks during your training. As I recall, your training record told us you were a natural flyer; and you met our psychological profile. I think we made the right decision. Agreed?"

I agreed.

SECTION ONE

Growing Up

CHAPTER ONE

PULLMAN, ILLINOIS

If my Uncle Fausto Olivi had settled in New York City in 1894, instead of Chicago when he arrived in America from Italy to seek his fortune, these memoirs of Federico Giovanni Olivi — these days I'm just called 'Fred' — would be a far different tale.

I am sure my father, Adorno Olivi, would not have followed his brother to New York City. He often said Chicago was big enough. I think, deep in his heart, he truly would have preferred to remain in the tiny village of Corsanico, located in the Province of Tuscany, Italy, a few miles from Pisa and the famous "Leaning Tower," and about 150 miles north of Rome. I think he would have been very content to tend his olive orchards which grew on the gentle slopes along the Gulf of Genoa on the Mediterranean. There he would have married his sweetheart, Primitiva, who later became my mother, and raised my brothers Mariano, Emil, and me to be farmers.

But that's not what happened.

Soon after landing in America, Uncle Fausto became very unhappy in "Little Italy" in New York City. He discovered there were few good jobs available. So he continued west to Milwaukee, Wisconsin, where he had heard there was work. In Milwaukee he found a small, but ambitious group of young men and women from Italy who were working along the docks. He found employment and started to learn the new language — English. It didn't take him long to meet and marry a young Italian-American girl who had been born in Milwaukee.

Hearing there was great opportunity at the steel companies in Gary, Indiana, Uncle Fausto and his bride moved to that city just as the riots at the Pullman Car Company, across the border in Illinois, were finally being settled.

It did not take many years for Uncle Fausto to decide that working in the hot steel mills was not for him, even though he made good wages and was able to save money. Being an entrepreneur and a gambler at heart, he discovered a small candy store in Hammond that was for sale. It was an excellent investment, what with the hundreds of boys and girls in that particular neighborhood with a never-ending "sweet tooth."

Within a few years he had become a successful small businessman and wrote back to Italy with glowing tales of the many different opportunities in

America for anyone with a lot of energy and a little luck.

According to Fausto, one of the best ways to make a lot of money in America was to become a landlord. The town in which he chose to start his real estate venture was Pullman, a town of about 8,000 residents, located approximately 15 miles south of Chicago's "Loop" on the far south side. It comprised the area from 103rd street on the north, Lake Calumet on the east, 115th street on the south, and the Illinois Central railroad tracks along Cottage Grove Avenue on the west. This was the Pullman in which I grew up. However, now the Calumet Expressway runs east of the Pullman neighborhood, and the shoreline of the lake has been moved further east.

Fausto wrote my father, Adorno, that a multimillionaire, George M. Pullman, builder of the Pullman Sleeping Car for the railroads, was being forced by the courts to sell the homes and apartments owned by his Pullman Company. In the early 1880's, Mr. Pullman had built the town to house his workers. The courts said such ownership constituted a monopoly.

Pullman built the homes, the church, the schools. Then he rented these homes and apartments at extremely high rates to the firm's workers. But the era of Pullman's "company town" came to an end soon after a terrible strike in 1894, which racked the company. More than 3,000 workers walked off the job on May 11, and the strike spread over 27 states, shutting down the nation's railroads. In 1898, after the strike was finally settled, the Illinois Supreme Court dis-incorporated the town of Pullman, ruling that a corporation could not own a town for its own profit and convenience. Soon after, the Pullman Company began selling off its real estate. Ultimately, the city of Chicago annexed the area.

In 1969, the Pullman neighborhood was designated a National Landmark by the State of Illinois, the City of Chicago, and the U.S. government.

All this, Uncle Fausto wrote my father, meant that opportunity was knocking; and that he, Fausto, had become the proud owner of several 4-flats and other single family homes located close to the Pullman Works. He said that in one of these homes there was a restaurant in the basement. He and his wife were running the restaurant and renting out the house above, but he felt the restaurant needed a full-time manager. His wife didn't like being a cook; and Fausto was busy most of the time looking after his candy store in Indiana and his other rental properties. Fausto needed someone he could trust to operate the restaurant properly. That person, he decided, should be my father.

I learned years later that my father had not been eager to immigrate to America. He was a moderately successful farmer with valuable olive orchards to tend. Most importantly, he had just become engaged to my mother. But after several very persuasive letters from Fausto, my father arranged with a neighbor to look after his farms. In 1900, he bought passage on a steamship and journeyed to Chicago to determine if what Fausto was saying was true. If it was, he planned to send for his fiancée. They would be married in the New World.

The red brick, two story house with the restaurant in the basement that Fausto owned (and in which I was born) is located at 11116 South Langley

Avenue, and just one block from the gate of the Pullman Shops. It still stands shoulder to shoulder with other similar homes along the west side of Langley.

On the east side of the street are several apartment buildings, many of them occupied in the early 1900's by bachelors who worked at the Pullman Shops. My uncle and father knew that most bachelors don't like to cook and therefore tend to eat many of their meals in a restaurant, especially if a good one is close by.

Like so many row homes built in Chicago, and in other American cities during that era, the single family homes on Langley Avenue were constructed with the basements partially raised out of the ground with only three short steps down from the sidewalk to the lower basement level. In order to reach the first floor, there was a short flight of steps up to a small porch which sheltered the front door. A second floor was reached via an inside stairway.

When my father saw the house/restaurant, he had to agree with his brother that this was an ideal location. There was not another restaurant in all of Pullman so close to the Works. The little basement restaurant even had an elegant marble floor, and the kitchen was well equipped with modern stoves, ovens, sinks, and other fixtures. The dining area was small, but could seat approximately 50 people at the tiny tables. With proper management and attention to the quality of the food, they agreed the restaurant was sure to succeed.

To this day, I don't know if it was Uncle Fausto who tried to convince my father to become a restaurateur, or if it was my father who saw a once-in-a-lifetime opportunity to escape the hard drudgery of farming. But father ultimately decided in favor of America, a job in the Pullman Shops, and a home on Langley Avenue in Chicago's Pullman neighborhood. The die was cast.

Father sent for his fiancée, my mother, Primitiva, who arrived in America in 1905, accompanied by her brother as chaperone. Mother always said that her brother had instructions to take her straight back to Viareggio if my father did not marry her immediately!

Primitiva Simonini married Adorno Olivi in St. Anthony's Church on April 15, 1905. The Olivis were in America to stay!

The Olivi family in 1925. From left to right: Emma, Alma, Primitiva, Adorno, Mariano and Emil. I am the curly haired 3 year-old standing in front of my mother, Primitiva.

Chapter 2

THE EARLY YEARS

They told me it was a clear and very cold January day, a typical Chicago winter day with the wind blowing snow from Lake Michigan across Lake Calumet and onto Pullman, Illinois. They also told me I came into the world screaming my little lungs off. The date was January 16, 1922; the location a second floor bedroom in the red brick house located on South Langley Avenue. Wanda Grzybowski assisted my mother during the birth of her sixth child, and third son. Christened Federico Giovanni Olivi, I became "Fradi," which later became "Freddie," and finally just "Fred."

My earliest years are but a dim memory now, but I can still "smell" the baking soda which cloaked my mother as she scurried around the little family restaurant in the basement of the house. She was the chief cook along with my favorite cousin, Angelo Bianchini, in the restaurant while my father worked in the Pullman yards as a switchman on the railroad that moved Pullman Sleeping Coaches between the different car shops.

Primitiva Olivi was, I suppose, exactly what most Americans picture as "the typical Italian woman" — smooth complexion, a familiar Roman nose under dark eyebrows with very dark brown eyes which could sparkle with joy or cloud over in an instant in anger or displeasure. She wore her dark brown hair in a bun which always had loose hair falling into her eyes, causing her to constantly brush the back of her hand across her brow. She was short, about five feet tall, a bit on the plumpish side, but with the strength and endurance of a giant.

I remember my mother as being in constant motion. She was always hurrying from kitchen to the tables, her arms cradling plates piled high with meals, or scurrying from the kitchen where the food was prepared to stir a pot of spaghetti, or roll out pasta, then rush back to serving customers in the little basement restaurant, shouting in Italian one minute, English the next, "Wait a minute! I've only got two hands. Be patient. I'll get there!" Several of my cousins helped as part-time waitresses, but her only steady helper was my sister, who helped cook, wash the dishes and wait on tables.

Mother worked from dawn to dusk six days a week in that restaurant. She was up before the sun appeared to cook and then serve the Pullman workers breakfast at 5:30 am, then dinner at 12:00 noon when the whistle blew at the Pullman shops announcing the noon break, and then again at 4:45 pm when the workers — sometimes with their wives or girlfriends — returned for supper. I don't think she ever got to bed until past midnight.

As a toddler, I was more in her way than I was a helper, although I do remember standing on a chair, helping roll out the raviolis and other pasta dishes. It was fun being the youngest Olivi child, and there is no doubt in my mind that I was a very "spoiled" little boy.

My oldest sister, Emma, was sixteen when I was born; I never really got to know her. She married late in life to an Italian. My oldest brother, Mariano, was more like an "uncle" than a brother. He was thirteen when I was born and subsequently worked in the Pullman Shops with my father. Next in line was my sister Alma. Alma had been born with a twin sister, but this girl died at six months of age. This must have been a tragedy for my parents, although they never talked about the little baby or what caused her death. The closest sibling I had was Emil, who is five years older. The two of us raised a lot of "hell" as young boys. I am not sure whether it was Emil egging me on or my trying to outdo my brother which brought on the spankings. Either way, many were the times when my father had to bring out his razor strap to convince us of the error of our ways. Parental discipline in the Olivi family was swift and sure in the 1920's, but I don't think the red marks on our bare bottoms — which sometimes took a few days to disappear — ever affected our later lives. I know it never stopped me from being the adventuresome individual I turned out to be as I grew older.

Growing up in Pullman, Illinois

1925. Fred Olivi at age 3, with neighbor's collie.

1927. Age 5, all dressed up in my Sunday best.

1927. Age 5, standing in front of restaurant on Langley Avenue with my dishwasher's apron that I wore on occasion when "helping" out.

1928

I was six-years-old when my mother decided to take me with her on a trip to Italy. This was her first trip to her childhood home since 1905, the year she had journeyed across the Atlantic to marry my father. I was so proud and happy that she chose me to join her. I was the envy of all the neighborhood children that summer of 1928 when I told them I was first going to sleep on a train, then go on a big ocean liner, and even pick real grapes growing in the vineyards of that far-away country — Italy!

After an all-night train ride from Chicago to New York, we boarded the Italian liner Roma. My first real adventure had begun. We were accompanied by neighbors, the Fraccaros and the Di'Marias, both with children my age, Marie, Jim and Cordellia.

We left New York for Genoa, Italy, on a bright, clear day, steaming past the Statue of Liberty. The schedule called for a 10-day voyage, but I am sure that before it was over the trip must have seemed like 30 days to my mother. Unfortunately, she was to learn that when you mix a mischievous six-year-old and an ocean liner, the result is trouble with a capital "T."

As I recall, the first day was uneventful. Other than some wooziness from the rolling motion of the ship, I managed to avoid the serious sea sickness which soon afflicted many passengers, including my mother.

By the end of the third day I was beginning to learn my way around the ship, and much to my six-year-old joy, I discovered that Mother was too busy meeting and talking with the other passengers — most of them Italians either returning home from a visit to America, or Italian-Americans on their way to visit relatives — to watch over me every minute. So, for a good part of each day I was left to myself while she visited with other adults seated in the lounge chairs lining the sunny deck. This left me free to race around the deck with another youngster, also six years old and on his first ocean voyage. He was a redhead from California whose name escapes me to this day.

"Red" and I quickly discovered all the secret places where a boy could hide on the ship, how to safely jump over the watertight doorways, and how to slide down the railings. But most of all we loved to stand on the stern and watch the ship's wake following the ship. We never tired of watching the water slide by.

Several days out, the Roma ran into a storm. Not a big one, but there was a lot of wind and rain, just enough to cause the ship to roll and pitch more than normal. The cascading water that crashed over the ship made the wooden deck extremely slippery — like ice on a pond. This was our opportunity for high adventure! Soon "Red" and I had a great game of "tag" going, each trying to avoid the other by jumping in and out of doorways onto the open deck where we could slide to the outside rail. We got soaked to the skin, but never gave it a second thought, although several times we both came close to losing our grip on the railing as the water splashed down the deck. Neither "Red" nor I paid much attention to such a danger. We were having far too much fun!

Our escapade came to a sudden halt when one of the crewmen saw us through a porthole. He rushed out through the doorway into the spraying water, shouting and cursing in Italian, and grabbed us, one with each hand, and dragged us back inside. He asked us our names and where our parents might be located. Then, with the two of us in front, dripping puddles of water with every step, he marched us to the "saloon" where my mother was having tea. The angry crewman explained that he had discovered us on the wet and slippery deck and it was only the by grace of God that one or both of us had not fallen overboard!

I did not see "Red" any more that day. I was in our cabin, lying across my mother's knees, a hairbrush in her hand, receiving one of the most painful spankings I had ever received.

But that was not the first spanking I had received on board the Roma. I think it was on the second day when I discovered that the drink "tea" was distasteful to a little boy who had been weaned on coffee. Shipboard custom called for tea to be served every afternoon at 3:00 pm in the dining room at our assigned table. Usually I went to the dining room with my mother and then ran off to play with the other children, but one day I stayed at the table, sat down, and decided I would try this fancy drink "tea," which I had never tasted. I do not know what I expected, perhaps a taste more like coffee, but the strange and bitter taste of the tea quickly registered on my taste buds. I did not like the taste, so I spit it out! Right on the floor beside the table.

I think, for one of the few times in her life, my mother was speechless. She turned to me in a controlled rage, and speaking very softly in Italian, said something like, "Fradi, how could you? Where are your manners?" She gathered her breath. "All right, since you do not know how to behave, you will spend the rest of the day in the cabin." She rose, put a very firm hand around my upper left arm, and marched me off to our cabin where she spanked me — quite hard, as I recall — then left me to think about manners. I know my manners have improved, but to this day I do not like the taste of tea!

However, during our voyage I did acquire a taste for steak. I discovered that a passenger could order anything at mealtime, including steak for breakfast. So, every morning when they rang the bell signaling breakfast was being served, I would jump out of my bed, pull on my clothes and run to the dining table while my mother was dressing. Once I was at our table, I grandly specified, (as only a spoiled six-year-old can demand), my breakfast steak. I followed that routine during the entire voyage to and from Italy. My taste for steak remains to this day.

Corsanico (Tuscany)

I have many memories of my visit to Italy, the land where my father and mother had been raised, fell in love, and became engaged.

One of the sharpest recollections is about my visits with my Uncle Fausto, my father's older brother, who had returned to Italy in 1922, to manage the Olivi family farm properties. These farms were adjacent to Corsanico, a tiny village located in the hills above Viareggio (in Latin: "The Way of Kings"), which was on the Mediterranean Sea.

In 1920, Uncle Fausto had lost a leg while in America. His horse was startled by a railroad train at a crossing in Hammond, Indiana. When the horse bolted, Fausto was tossed onto the tracks where a box car severed his right leg. Although he recovered and soon learned to walk with an artificial leg, this tragic accident made it very difficult for him to manage his many real estate properties in Hammond and Pullman. Therefore, he returned to Italy and opened a small store in Viareggio. From this location he was able to look after the Olivi family farms. In turn, my father looked after Fausto's properties in America, collecting the rents which he forwarded to Fausto at the end of each year.

Uncle Fausto and I "hit it off" immediately, and I spent many hours with him at his store while my mother was busy with her childhood friends.

It became apparent that the other youngsters in the village didn't want to be friends with me, although I deeply wanted their companionship. Perhaps part of the reason was my cowboy suit which I wore proudly the first few days of my visit. I even had two fake but realistic looking "six-shooters" in leather holsters which I would whip out every few minutes to demonstrate how fast I could "draw." The Italian youngsters had never seen such a costume, and certainly not toy guns that looked like real weapons. First, they were afraid, but soon began laughing at me; and they would not play with me. Truly, I became a very unhappy little boy.

One particular Italian boy's attitude made me feel very belligerent, but I put up with his taunts until he spit at me. That got my attention. I angrily curled my hands into fists and raised them in the classic boxing stance, and told the boy in English, "C'mon!", meaning that if he wanted to fight, I was ready and willing. I took a couple of swings at him, but he turned and ran off.

After that, all the boys in town called me "C'Mon." Every day, they taunted me by calling me "C'Mon" when we passed on the cobblestone streets. I must have chased them a dozen times until a local teacher complained to my mother that the Italian boys were afraid to walk past my uncle's store. I felt vindicated but sad that I couldn't make friends with the other children. Uncle Fausto was sympathetic, but years later my mother told me Fausto had warned her that I would end up in jail one day!

It wasn't only the little boys in Corsanico that I irritated — I even got the attention of the women. When my mother would stop and talk with her friends at the village water fountain, I came up with a stunt which, though unsuccessful, caused me a lot of grief.

Although it was the 1920's, Corsanico did not have modern water mains, so every day the women carried their family's drinking and cooking water from the centrally located well and water pump to their homes in buckets. They carried the round buckets on their heads, which gave my six-year-old mind an inspiration: sneak up on a woman from behind, jump high in the air, and knock the water pails off her head. Needless to say, I proceeded to do that very thing and my mother, after seeing one of my efforts, turned me over her knee, in front of the giggling women who loudly shouted their approval of the discipline.

Her trip somewhat marred by the antics of her youngest child, my mother returned to America and her restaurant. I came home full of tales with which I kept the neighborhood children enthralled for weeks.

Tom Mix

Although my cowboy outfit had not impressed the children in Corsanico, Italy, it did get me a free ride on a horse later that summer. One Saturday my sister, Emma, was asked to take me to Chicago to see the "Tom Mix Wild West Show" at Soldier Field on the lakefront. I suspect that my parents just wanted to get me out of their hair, but whatever the reason, to actually see the most famous movie cowboy of all time was a treat. In addition, somehow my parents had acquired front row seats for Emma and me, right behind the low concrete wall facing a cinder track that circled the grass infield of the famous stadium.

I was all decked out with a big cowboy hat, neckerchief, chaps over my long trousers, two cap pistols in my gun belt, checkered shirt — the full cowboy regalia. I was having a wonderful time when Tom Mix rode his famous horse, Tony, up to where we were sitting. Suddenly, he reached over and picked me up and swung me onto the front of his saddle. It happened in an instant. My sister gasped in surprise and started to reach out to hold me back, but she wasn't fast enough. One moment I was in the stands, the next instant Tom Mix was holding me with his left arm, reins in his right hand. I was holding onto the saddle horn with all my strength. He wheeled Tony away from the stands and into a slow trot. We made one circle around the field. I can't recall if Tom Mix said anything to me during that ride around Soldier Field in front of thousands of clapping spectators. And I don't recall if I said anything to him, but I do remember waving to the crowd.

That bright summer day in Chicago's Soldier Field was undoubtedly the biggest thrill of my life — until August 9, 1945, some fifteen years later.

1928 — My visit to Corsanico, Italy.

Here I am, all dressed up in the uniform of a "Ballila" child soldier. At that time, children were being trained for war in the Italian army by the Fascist dictator, Benito Mussolini. (I liked the uniform, but had no interest in training for war!) My Mother is on the left in the center photograph with my Aunt Mary.

1931 — My cousin, Angelo Bianchini (on the left) with his friend Joe Bacci, after a hunting trip. Angelo was an important factor in my young life as I entered my teenage years.

1936 — My freshman year at Pullman Tech High School. Taken in September in front of the school, from left to right: William Trsar, Endo Panozzo, Ray Poenie, Francis Nietupski, and me on the far right.

1940 — My cousin, Angelo Bianchini, with his wife, Bernice, and daughter, Jean, in front of the Pullman rowhouse at 113th and Langley Avenue. Angelo and Bernice owned the Jolly Inn — a neighborhood restaurant famous in the area for fried chicken and Italian cuisine.

Chapter Three

THE GREAT DEPRESSION

While the 1920's had been a glorious time to be young and full of mischief, the 1930's, and the onslaught of the Great Depression, saw the Olivi family in Pullman face a far more difficult time. It seemed that every year gave us challenges none of us had ever expected, nor were prepared to handle. No family was. We had to learn to cope, or perish as a family unit.

Like most of the other children who grew up in that era, I was expected to help the family by earning as much money as I could, and to that end I developed several "careers" as I grew into a young teenager.

One of my most important sources for money came from selling newspapers. Paul Dikos, my neighborhood boyhood friend and fellow "junker," was my partner. (More on "junking" later in this chapter.) Every day during the summer months, and on school vacation days, Paul and I stationed ourselves at 4:45 pm outside the 111th Street gate at Stephenson Avenue in front of the Pullman Shops selling the Chicago Daily News and other evening newspapers to the Pullman workers on their way home.

Later in the evening, Paul and I would run over to the Illinois Central Railroad station at 115th street and Cottage Grove Avenue to pick up the next day's "early bird" edition of The Chicago Tribune. The IC Trainman would toss the newspaper bundles out from the baggage car as the train roared past us. Although the newspapers were wrapped with heavy twine, they often broke open, spilling the newspapers which then blew all over the tracks and station platform in the fierce turbulence caused by the fast-moving train.

Paul and I also had a regular route delivering newspapers to merchants along South Michigan Avenue, west from the IC Station to 115th Street & Michigan Avenue, then north to 111th Street, where we had a wooden newspaper stand on the northwest corner. We sold papers at this location every evening until about 10:00 pm, and then walked the one and a half miles to our homes on Langley Avenue.

Paul and I also had another favorite, but somewhat dangerous occupation — "junking." We scoured the neighborhood alleys for old newspapers, copper, brass, aluminum and lead. What we collected we sold to the local ragman, "Cockeyed Jake," who got his name because one of his eyes was always turned upwards.

"Jake" met us at 6:30 pm on Saturdays. He had a rickety wooden wagon which was pulled by two very skinny white horses. "Jake" rode in the wagon seat which was in such bad repair that he was forced to brace himself to keep from falling off. He was a gruff sort of fellow, probably in his mid-fifties, with a shiny gold front tooth.

I believe now that "Jake" was probably an honest man at heart, but back then I only knew him as a gruff, bad-tempered old man with whom I had to "negotiate" every item. "Jake" knew all the tricks, and it was a great education for a teenager to deal with him. One of our gambits was to wet down the newspaper in the middle of the stack, adding a few pounds, and hopefully try to get more money for the added weight. But Jake knew all the tricks of the trade and we never could get the better of him during our negotiations. I don't think we ever fooled Jake. He caught us every time, laughing with a bit of a sneer and flashing his gold tooth, he would say, "Thought you could put one over on old 'Jake,' did 'ya? Well, not today, lads, not today."

Most of the metal we sold to "Jake" came from digging in the Pullman dump where the old Pullman Sleeping Cars went to their final resting place. Paul and I knew these cars had been stripped in the Pullman Yards, but there was always some metal that had escaped the men in the Yards before the cars were pulled to the junkyard and abandoned.

We did our scavenging at night, loading our loot into gunny sacks, always keeping a watchful eye out for the Chicago police. The police were our nemesis, and, since we were stealing private property, we knew we would be arrested if caught. Many times we had to quickly hide our heavy, metal-laden gunny sacks and hightail it through the "jungle" of Pullman cars, crawling under and around the rusting cars which stood side by side on the railroad tracks. Our big advantage was that we knew the territory better than the policemen. We never did get caught! But we sure got the hell scared out of us several times. I have to admit that selling what we could salvage in copper, brass, and aluminum was very lucrative for a 12-year-old boy.

Although I wasn't paid in cash, one of my favorite "careers" during the summer months during the Depression was helping "Red, the Peddler" sell fruits and vegetables throughout the Pullman neighborhood. My payment was all the fruit I could eat (and hide away to take home at the end of the day).

"Red" was a very smart entrepreneur. He had a bell on this fruit truck and as he drove up and down the streets of Pullman, he rang it, alerting housewives of his arrival. But rather than have the women come down from their homes or apartments to place their orders, "Red" utilized the services of several other young boys and me to act as "runners." The routine was as follows: The housewife would shout out her order, "Red" would put the proper fruits and vegetables into a paper sack and hand it to one of us boys who would carry the bag to the lady at her doorway, take her payment back to "Red," and then run back to the customer with her change.

It was during my first summer when working for "Red" that I learned to enjoy over-ripe, speckled bananas!

As the Depression steadily grew worse year after year, the tiny family restaurant's business dropped off to a trickle of customers. Finally, my family closed it down in 1931. Unfortunately, most of the men who had been loyal customers for years lost their jobs at the Pullman Shops and could not afford to eat in a restaurant, no matter how inexpensive. In fact, many workers simply packed up their families and moved away after losing their jobs at the Pullman Works. I lost a number of childhood pals in this manner.

A significant and very sad event occurred in 1936 which changed the Olivi family. My father died after a brief and painful bout with cancer. We slowly recovered from this tragic loss, but our family income dropped substantially. Life became exceedingly difficult for the Olivi family. Now, we were truly poor.

With the death of my father, my older brother, Mariano, who somehow had kept his job at the Pullman Works, as the eldest son became "head of the household." I was in high school and only able to contribute a few dollars every week to the family coffers. My brother, Emil, was moving ahead with his education, hoping to get into college and study dentistry.

Mariano's small salary became the Olivis only dependable source for money.

The winds of change were upon us.

Chapter Four

PULLMAN TECH

In 1936, the same year my father died, I entered a high school known officially as The Pullman Free School of Manual Training, better known in the area
around Pullman as Pullman Tech. Although the building still stands, the school no
longer exists, so perhaps I should describe how and why it came into existence.

George M. Pullman, when he created the town of Pullman, also decided
there should be a free "technical" high school for his worker's children — primarily the boys, although girls (including my Prom date, Carole McVey, whose
grandfather worked at Pullman, and who years later became Mrs. Fred Olivi), did
attend special secretarial classes. Pullman decreed that his school would train students in the technical and manual arts, preparing them for work in his Pullman
Railroad Sleeping Coach Shops.

In order to be accepted, a student at Pullman Tech had to have a father,
mother, brother or some other family member who at one time worked at the
Pullman Shops. There was no rule that a graduating student had to work for
Pullman, but most did.

Pullman Tech is where Mariano had gone to high school, with my brother, Emil, following some ten years later. My sisters did not attend since none of
them were interested in becoming secretaries.

Pullman Tech was not a fully accredited high school for college or university study. It didn't offer foreign language courses and other "college prep"
studies. This fact came home to me during 1935, when my brother, Emil, who had
just graduated from Pullman Tech, told my mother and father of his dream to
become a dentist. But such a career was out of the question. There was no money
to send him to college. What little money we had was for food. Father and Mother
were sorry, but Emil had to go to work at the Pullman Shops.

However, one of the teachers at Pullman Tech, a Mrs. Hoover, became
aware of Emil's goal, and approached my parents with the idea of sending Emil
to Fenger High School. Fenger was a public high school run by the Chicago Board
of Education and located a few miles west of Pullman Tech, where he could obtain
the necessary credits in about a year for admission to a pre-dental education at
DePaul University. If Emil was willing, and if my parents would agree, she would
pay for his education. Mrs. Hoover believed Emil had the ability and tenacity to

achieve his goal. I think it was also agreed that he would have to pay her back once he became a dentist.

My father, who was quite ill at this time, questioned how we would live. Someone had to make enough money to support the family. It was at this time that my eldest brother, Mariano, showed his true colors.

Mariano agreed to support the family so Emil could live at home, attend Fenger and then DePaul. In the summertime Emil would work at the Pullman Shops.

At first, my mother didn't like the idea, but ultimately my father and she agreed to Mrs. Hoover's proposal. Emil went to Fenger for a year where he attended the required classes which enabled him to enter DePaul University, the first Olivi to obtain a college education.

I entered Pullman Tech in the fall of 1936, after taking a battery of difficult tests which determined whether or not I had the ability and aptitude to successfully pass the type of technical courses offered at the school. Pullman Tech did not have to accept me, no matter who my relatives were. I had to demonstrate and prove my own innate ability to master the subjects. Also, in 1936, my father died of cancer.

During my freshman year, in addition to a heavy load of math and science courses, I was exposed to all the vocations taught at Pullman Tech — machine shop, electrical, drafting, architecture and an automobile repair course in which welding was part of the curriculum. I spent ten weeks getting acquainted with each course.

At the beginning of my sophomore year I was asked to select which vocation I wanted to pursue. I chose machine shop, principally because I believed a career as a machinist would bring me a good income; also, I had always liked to make things with my hands, beginning when I was about 10-years-old and began to build model airplanes.

In fact, model airplanes and aviation in general, always fascinated me as child. I made models of just about every airplane that flew in World War I. I think Baron Manfred von Richthofen's Fokker Triplane, the triple-wing airplane in which he shot down so many Allied planes, was my favorite. It was a "neat-looking" aircraft to my young eyes, and his title, "The Red Baron," always fascinated me. (Today, I have a Fokker Triplane painted on my garage door). Of course, I also built models of the British Sopwith Camel and the French Nieuport and Spad aircraft. Some of my earliest model airplanes are still with me, stored in my basement or in what my wife calls the "war room," which also is filled with books, maps, and other documents relating to World War I and II.

I will be eternally grateful to the wonderful, dedicated teachers at Pullman Tech. They worked me hard, and they opened my eyes. I was challenged to do my best, all the time, every time. There were no excuses for poor study habits or poor grades!

I participated in all the high school sports except baseball, and was a "letterman" for three years in football as a halfback. It was on the football field that

I met the one individual (other than my parents), who had the greatest influence on me at Pullman Tech — Coach John Cummings. He had such an impact on me that his influence continues to this day.

Coach Cummings was a hard taskmaster and disciplinarian who believed in doing everything right up to the best of your ability. Beware if you didn't take things seriously while participating in a sport coached by Mr. Cummings.

I learned this the hard way as a freshman. One afternoon, I was "horsing around" during practice when Coach Cummings spotted me. He came over and stopped all activity while he started to discipline me in front of my teammates. He loudly berated me, kicking me in the seat and slapping my helmet to get his point across. He did not physically hurt me, but my ego sure was wounded. I was a sad, 140-pound football player for several days afterwards, but I resolved that I would not disobey his rules again.

I never forgot that lesson on the practice field. As I look back on my days as a player under Coach Cummings, I am happy that he was so tough on me. More than any other person, he taught me the fundamentals of living, as well as the fundamentals of football. He treated his young athletes like men, not boys. He accepted no excuses. Your performance was what counted. I carried that lesson into my adulthood.

I can still remember him yelling at us during one game, "I don't want to see your blocking and tackling, I want to hear it!"

Coach Cummings didn't just coach the football team. He also taught mathematics; and in the classroom he was the same, tough, demanding person.

I remember one day when my friend, Frank Nietupski, was struggling to solve a math problem at the blackboard. Cummings gave Frank a few hints, but Frank just couldn't go any further. He turned around, dejected and defeated. Coach Cummings walked over to Frank; and, accenting each word by poking his index finger into Frank's chest, he growled, "You better damn well learn your lessons, Mister, because you can't keep your feet under the old man's table all your life! And that goes for all of you, understand?"

I understood, and I will never forget those words of Coach Cummings — and their deeper meaning. If I was going to succeed in life, I couldn't expect others to carry me. It was going to be up to me, alone.

And you know, Coach Cummings was right!

I graduated from Pullman Tech in June of 1940 and immediately went to work in the Pullman Shops as a machinist. As I recall, I was working "piece work," making parts for the Pullman Cars. I earned about $40.00 to $50.00 a week.

After I had been working a few weeks, my brother, Mariano, decided that he would no longer support our family. My brother, Emil, was now a Navy Midshipman in a government sponsored dental school program at DePaul and was unable to take over Mariano's role. Mariano decreed I should now become "head of the Olivi family," and become the sole source of income for my mother and sister, Emma, who had developed severe arthritis in her feet. Standing long hours on the marble floor in the basement restaurant had partially disabled her and she was unable to find work.

At the time, I found it difficult to understand Mariano's actions, but today I realize Mariano was right. It was time for him to move on with his life. He had an excellent job at the Pullman Shops, was married, lived in a house down the street, and was raising his own family. It was time for me, the youngest son, to step up and accept financial responsibility for the Olivi household.

It was 1940, and we all knew that America's entry into the war was imminent. Every day brought news of the fighting in Europe and the threat of war in the far-off Pacific.

As I mentioned earlier, Emil had joined the Navy in 1940, when he learned the Navy would pay for his education through dental school. On graduation, he was commissioned a Lieutenant (JG) and served as a dentist in the China - Burma - India theater during the War.

I registered for the Selective Service "Draft" in June 1940, as soon as I finished high school. Immediately I was classified as an essential worker because the Pullman Shops were now producing airplane wings, tail sections and other wartime products. Because I was a skilled machinist, working in a factory on critical wartime production, the Draft Board decided not to draft me into the military forces. In 1940, I was not too unhappy about the Board's decision. My mother was very happy that her "little boy" was not going to become a soldier!

But none of us in our wildest dreams could have anticipated December 7, 1941. Pearl Harbor had an impact on each and every member of the Olivi family. And we were no different than thousands and thousands of American families.

Our lives changed — forever!

1940 — Taken in the spring. I'm wearing my "letter sweater," and shown here with my mother after I had been awarded a Pullman Tech letter for playing varsity football.

1940 — Someone took this shot of Ivan Janota and me. Ivan was my best friend in high school and remained so after graduation when we both worked in the Pullman shops. Ivan shared my love of aviation and we both hoped to be aviators.

1941 — High School Sweetheart, and Senior Prom Date and Future wife, Carole McVey with Fred Olivi going to a movie in Chicago.

1941 — High School Classmates From left to right: Fred Olivi, Carole McVey, Ivan Janota

SECTION TWO

Army Air Corps

Chapter Five
NAVY? ARMY? I JUST WANT TO FLY!

After December 7, 1941 — Pearl Harbor — the Olivi family lost contact with our relatives in Italy. We could only hope that we would see them again when the war ended, which we all hoped would be soon now that the United States was in the conflict. None of us talked much about having relatives on the "wrong side" in a war.

I remember, years earlier, when Mussolini was coming into power in the 1930's, he asked Italians in America to send back their gold rings and watches to be melted down in order to help fund the Italian war effort in Ethiopia. My father, a loyal Italian all his life, asked my mother if she would be willing to part with her jewelry. I vividly recall her answer, "No! The Olivis are now Americans!"

We knew that over in Italy my Uncle Fausto was looking after my father's two farms and collecting the rents. My father had been doing the same thing regarding Fausto's real estate holdings in Pullman. When my father died in 1936, my mother continued to collect the rents; during the War, the money bought us groceries.

My work in the Pullman Shops became a daily routine. By the Fall of 1941, the Shops had been converted to 100% war production; and I was now making aluminum spot welding machines for a French company, Sciaky. This company had an invention which had been smuggled out of that country to America just before the Germans defeated France. The invention was a fantastic new machine which could weld lightweight aluminum for aircraft wings.

The work wasn't very exciting, but I was making some contribution to the war effort, and I was bringing home over $50.00 a week to my mother. A fantastic sum of money at that time.

But I wanted to fly!

Perhaps it was the Naval recruiting posters, maybe it was the idea of landing and taking off of a carrier on the high seas, maybe it was because the Navy seemed more "glamorous." Maybe it was because the Navy promised, "Join the Navy; See the World!" Whatever the reason, I wanted to be a Navy pilot. Second choice was the Army Air Corps.

I wasn't alone in this desire to fly an airplane. My best high school friend, Ivan Janota, also worked in the Pullman Shops as a welder. When we were at

Pullman Tech, Ivan and I had taken a streetcar out to an airfield on 87th Street and Cicero Ave. and both of us had enjoyed the thrill of a 15-minute ride in an open cockpit, two seat, bi-plane. Cost: $2.00. This experience led us to the Chicago Municipal Airport (now Midway) where half-hour rides cost $3.00. Ivan and I were "hooked" on flying.

If you've ever piloted a small airplane seated in an open cockpit, you know the thrill of feeling yourself being lifted off the ground, the air rushing by your face. Rather than looking through a window (as on our modern airliners), you see firsthand how small, yet somehow close, everything looks from 1,000 feet in the air. There is nothing like the feeling of having "control" over your own destiny, and the apprehension, however slight, when you make your first landings. It's like eating candy; once you start, you don't want to quit.

Meeting Ivan was one of the best things that happened to me when I began attending Pullman Tech in 1936. After a rocky first start and encounter, we became the best of friends, playing football together for four years and continuing our relationship after graduation. In addition to our love of flying, we both liked dancing to the big bands of the late 1930's and early '40's. We often double dated and went to the Trianon and Aragon Ballrooms in Chicago to dance to the music of Dick Jurgens, Griff Williams and Freddy Martin.

Our friendship continued after the war, but in 1978, Ivan died of a heart attack, five years after undergoing heart by-pass surgery. He was one of the first to try the new operation and a true pioneer.

Losing my best friend was devastating to me and it took some time for me to adjust to life without Ivan.

During lunch breaks at the shop, and after work, Ivan and I held long conversations about how we hated the repetitive nature of the work and how much we desperately wanted to get into the war as flyers.

One day we decided the quickest way for us to become pilots was to travel to Canada and join the Royal Canadian Air Force. I approached my mother with the idea, which she immediately squashed. Ivan didn't have much better luck with his parents. Ivan later joined the Marines and served in the South Pacific.

I probably would have worked in the Pullman Shops for the duration of World War II, except for two reasons. One, my sister found a job where she could sit, and she spent the remainder of the war years as a clerk in the tool shop at the 103rd Street Pullman Shop. Here, they made wings and tail sections for the C-47, the military version of the Douglas DC-3, and undoubtedly one of the finest airplanes ever built. Her income was a big boost for the Olivi household.

The second reason was I learned from another worker at Sciaky that it was possible to send a military allotment to a parent or family. This "allotment" idea had never occurred to me before. I discovered that the U.S. Government would send $150.00 a month to my mother as an allotment. (My pay in the Army would be $21.00 a month.) It was like a flash bulb had gone off and my problem would be solved and my responsibilities taken care of!

At first, my mother gave me a firm, "No!" when I brought up the idea;

but I kept after her until her resolve weakened. I think it took about two months for her to agree that I should go downtown to Chicago and investigate the possibilities.

That's why, on a Saturday morning in October 1942, I boarded the Illinois Central train in Pullman for downtown Chicago where the recruiting centers were located. I got off the train at the Randolph Street station, intending to take a bus on Michigan Avenue north to the Navy recruiting office. As I recall, the Navy office was located at the corner of Wacker Drive and Michigan Avenue. But as I came up the steps from the train station onto Michigan Avenue, my eyes saw a huge sign on the front of a building, advertising that the Army Air Corps recruiting office was located in the building and, more important, they needed pilots!

I think I figured I would check out both the Army and Navy, and since the Army Air Corps office was just across the street, I might as well start here.

Whatever the reason, I was soon undergoing a very complete physical, far more thorough than any I had had when playing football. Then came the "mental tests." To my dying day I will thank the teachers at Pullman Tech who taught me mathematics, civics, English, and most of all, how to think! Without the training I received at that school, I know I would have never passed those first Army Air Corps tests!

But I did! By the end of the day I was sworn in, and told to go back home and wait for a call to active duty and Basic Training. The recruiters told me I might have to wait a month or so, but that I should not worry — I was IN!

The "few months" turned out to be four months, and I went back to my job at Sciaky, racing home every afternoon to see if there was any mail from Uncle Sam. Finally, in February 1943, that special letter arrived. I had orders to report to Sheppard Field in Wichita Falls, Texas, for Basic Training. My mother and sister cried, but I was ecstatic, the happiest 21-year-old on Langley Avenue.

I was going to be a pilot! That I had not even talked to the Navy really never entered my mind.

Evergreen Park, Illinois, March 1966 — Testimonial dinner for Pullman Tech High School Football Coach John C. Cummings.— Committee Members from left to right: Fred J. Olivi, Harvey Hincker, Dr. Emil J. Olivi

August, 1944 — On leave after gaining my commission as a Second Lieutenant in the Army Air Corps following graduation from Pilot School in Lubbock, Texas. Here, I'm back home in Pullman with my high school sweetheart and prom date, Carole McVey, who years later became my wife.

Summer, 1944 — Before shipping overseas, my brother, Emil J. Olivi, is shown here with our mother in front of the family home on Langley Avenue. Emil, a dentist, was a Navy Lieutenant (JG) during World War II, and served in the China-Burma area with a Navy weather detachment SACO that provided the Army Air Corps with reports of weather conditions over the Japanese Empire.

March, 1966 — At Chicago's Martinique restaurant, we held a testimonial dinner for the man who helped shape so many young lives as football coach and teacher at Pullman Tech, Coach John C. Cummings. Coach Cummings undoubtedly was the strongest influence on me during my teens as I entered adulthood. From left to right: Coach Cummings, Olivi, Mrs. Cummings, their son Grant.

March, 1966 — Martinique Restaurant, Evergreen Park, Illinois
Members of Pullman Tech's Football teams, that played on various teams through the years in high school, honoring Coach John C. Cummings. Testimonial Dinner was attended by the following:
L to R -

1. Rinaldi, J	*7. Coach Cummings*
2. Velo, F.	*8. Bonior, J.*
3. Okleshen, G.	*9. Goldie*
4. Hincker, H.	*10. Dr. Emil Olivi*
5. Olivi, Fred	*11. Marynowski*
6. Veroni, B.	*12. Holba*

Chapter Six
TRAINING, TRAINING, TRAINING

Sheppard Field

Basic training at Sheppard Field in Wichita Falls, Texas, was, at least for me, like training for the football team back at Pullman Tech — very physical. Because the hot Texas summer months were past, there were only a few extremely hot days when we began our Basic Training in February 1943. I had few difficulties getting into the type of physical condition the Army wanted. In fact, the Army instructors were easier on me than Coach Cummings!

Living in a barracks with 50 other guys was a new experience, but we got along quite well. The food was tolerable. The discipline, KP and guard duty became part of the routine. I think most of us — me, for sure — knew there would be an end to the drudgery. We just had to "tough it out." Sadly, there was no flying during our Basic Training. It seems they just wanted to shape us into the type of Cadets desired by the Air Corps.

East Central State Teachers College

When we completed Basic Training, we were told the Army Air Corps had too many young men "in the pipeline" headed for Primary Flight Training. So, in April 1943, about 300 of us were shipped up to East Central State Teacher's College in Ada, Oklahoma, for five months of college classwork designed to prepare us for the Classification Tests in San Antonio, Texas.

We were the first contingent of Aviation Students to be sent to this lovely, small town in Oklahoma. The majority of male students had gone off to war, and the towns' people and coeds welcomed us with open arms. We were assigned quarters in two dormitories that had been cleared of other civilian students.

Our classwork consisted of mathematics, some physics and chemistry, aviation theory, introductory navigation, and other subjects that I just can't recall over fifty years later. I do remember that we had to study very hard every night in order to keep up with the textbooks and quizzes.

The food was great and our living quarters were quite spacious with each one having his own desk.

Best of all, each of us got ten hours' flight time in a Piper Cub airplane. After a few rides with my instructor, I became extremely comfortable in the new environment. Although I never was allowed to fly "solo," I felt as if I had been flying all my life, and I still have my log book as a memento of those first hours in the air.

Our college professors and military instructors kept us on a rigorous schedule that kept us hopping more than ten hours a day. I should add that the regular students did not share our classes, but we did get to see the girls on the weekends. I have to admit that I had a great time at East Central State Teacher's College. I learned a great deal, met many fine people, and almost hated to leave that September, when the six months were up and we were transferred to the San Antonio Aviation Cadet Center for Classification.

Note: Our 343rd College Training Detachment is unique, in that we have met in each of the last nine years to meet and keep our friendships intact that began 56 years ago in Ada, Oklahoma. We enjoy our CTD gathering and to the best of my knowledge no other similar Training Detachment can make that statement.

Classification

As I look back on it, the weeks I spent in San Antonio, Texas, on "The Hill," as it was called, were my real introduction to the Army Air Corps. I was now 21, and felt I could handle anything they handed out. However, nothing had prepared me for the rigorous classwork and testing I now had to undergo.

For nine straight weeks there was a constant stream of technical courses, mental examinations, and physical exams. At the very beginning of this Pre-Flight School, I was told that if I did not pass every class I would be assigned further training as an enlisted airman and become a member of an aircraft crew — probably as a gunner — definitely not as a pilot!

It seemed that every day there was a new type of test, invented by some guy who really knew how to create impossible questions. It now became apparent to me that the preparation I had received at — of all things — a technical high school was exactly the kind of education that might get me through all the rugged tests. I had an excellent background in mathematics and science. I knew how to analyze a problem and logically figure out the correct solution. I had been taught how to think! Even my work as a machinist in the Pullman Shops turned out to be helpful.

However, nothing at Pullman Tech had ever prepared me for the course and tests in Morse Code. This was not a class in what I always had understood to be telegraphy — a sending/receiving machine that sent out electrical dots and dashes, with the operator then writing down the letters as he heard them. Rather, we had to recognize the dots and dashes visually as they were "sent" to us with a blinking light bulb, and to write down the appropriate letters of the alphabet immediately. The blinks that meant "dots" were a fraction of a second shorter than the blinks that signified "dashes." I found it almost impossible to distinguish between the two.

Our final test was a series of five groups of five letters in each group. There was absolutely no room for error. I had to get them 100% correct or fail, and never have the opportunity to become a pilot.

I don't think I've ever studied so hard for any test. I can't recall his name, but one of my fellow Cadets spent hours with me, sending me the letters of the alphabet, five letters at a time, with a flashlight. Over and over, I strained my eyes, trying to decipher the blinks. I could get most of them, but "most" was not acceptable. I had to get them all!

On the day of the final examination, I really thought that I would never be able to identify the flashes, but I resolved to do my best and to just trust "fate" to take over.

We sat in a circle, each of us at a school desk. In the middle of the room was that damn bare light bulb. The instructor darkened the room and started sending the five groups of five letters. The test was completed and I turned in my paper and left the room feeling very dejected. I was sure I had failed.

When the papers were returned to us the next day, I discovered — much to my amazement — that I had accurately identified all twenty-five letters. I passed!

When the nine weeks ended, I learned that I was qualified to be a pilot or a bombardier, but not a navigator. We were asked to choose one. I quickly selected "Pilot." There was nothing now standing in the way of me going on to Primary Flight School!

I should add that approximately 30% of my fellow Cadets "washed out" during this "classification" routine — some during the course of the nine-week schedule, others at the end of the classification period. Some had a hidden physical disability that the doctors discovered while we underwent agility exercises and tests. Others couldn't pass the critical visual or hearing exams. When it came to the "mental" exams, several college students, a few of them with four-year college degrees, failed to qualify as a pilot, navigator or bombardier. I wondered about <u>my</u> chances of passing these tests!!

Flight Training : Primary ... Basic ... Advanced

In January 1944, I was assigned to the Primary Flight Training School at Parks Air College in East St. Louis, Illinois, where I finally got the opportunity to learn how to fly something larger than a Piper Cub. Our planes were durable, mono-wing PT-19's. I think some are still flying today at air shows across the country.

We learned basic navigation and map reading, studied cloud formations and the effect of wind, and all the aviation basics. I soloed in eight hours. It was a glorious time in my life!!!

There was only one problem: I finally was close to home — Pullman was only 250 miles away — but I never got a pass!

In March, I was assigned to Basic Flight Training at an airfield in Independence, Kansas. We were trained to fly much more powerful airplanes, primarily the 450 horsepower BT-13's, BT-14's and BT-15's.

For the first time I was introduced to instrument flying and found it a real challenge to fly "blind" while trusting the little instrument dials on the cockpit panel. In addition, I was introduced to flying at night, which is a very different situation from flying during daylight hours. Night flying — then and now — is only different, not difficult, and soon I was as comfortable gazing at the stars above as I was looking at the highways below.

At some point during the training, I remember my instructor asking me if I intended to fly single or multiple engine airplanes — my choice. I almost said "Single Engine," which would have meant additional, specialized training as a fighter pilot. But I said, "Multiple," because it occurred to me that I might want to become an airline pilot after the war was over. As it turned out, I qualified for both, but stuck with my choice of "Multiple Engine Aircraft."

In June 1944, as the American troops crossed the English Channel, I was assigned to Advanced Flight Training (Twin Engine), at Lubbock, Texas. I remember many conversations in the barracks during which we Cadets wondered if the war would end before we got a chance to show what we could do. I think the consensus was that, while the war in Europe might end fairly soon, the fight against the Japanese Empire would take a long time because Japan was still entrenched on islands all over the Pacific. All of us believed we would have the opportunity to fly combat missions — some time in the future, in some distant land. We left the exact location to "Fate."

My training on multiple engine aircraft was an extension of what I had learned during my Basic Flight training, the difference was just the extra engine. Controlling two engines presented no problems for me. I was having fun!

We trained in the AT-17, an excellent twin engine aircraft that could take a lot of punishment and was very forgiving when you made a slight error. Our cross country flights were a real challenge to our navigational abilities.

By the end of July I had successfully passed all my "check rides," including my difficult instrument check ride, and on August 4, 1944, I was commissioned a Second Lieutenant in the Army Air Corps and received my Wings.

I thought all the hard training was over and from now on it would be easy. How little I knew about what the Army had in store for me!

After the commissioning ceremony, my name was posted on a list of seventeen pilots who were being assigned to "Transition" training in Ft. Worth, Texas, on the B-24, four-engine bomber. Only seventeen were selected for this training that we were told would definitely lead to combat. The other new Second Lieutenants who had completed "Multiple Engine" training drew assignments to fly training missions for navigators and bombardiers.

Once I had my orders, I got a seven-day leave and journeyed home to Pullman to see my family. My mother, Mariano, and Emma all cried when I walked in the door at 11116 Langley. I'm sure I also shed a tear or two. I had been gone from home for over a year, and I certainly wasn't the same Fred Olivi. We had a lot of catching up to do!

Naturally, many of the neighbors had to stop by and see how much I had changed now that I was an officer and a pilot. I think they were impressed. Most of the young men in our neighborhood were serving in the infantry as privates and corporals, not as officers.

My sister told me before I left home to report in at Ft. Worth that some of the neighbors had asked her privately why I was still in the United States, and why I wasn't overseas helping end the war by dropping bombs or doing something besides going to school? She never did tell me her reply.

The B-24 "Liberator" Bomber

When I returned to Ft. Worth, it was somewhat like "going home." I had spent so much time in the state of Texas that I almost considered myself a Texan!

After I reported in and was assigned to my quarters, I went out on the flight line and got my first close look at the big B-24. It was over 66 feet long, had a wingspan of almost 110 feet, and rose more than 17 feet in the air on its tricycle landing gear. It was the most immense flying machine I had ever seen, and I wondered how I would ever learn to fly such a giant.

Joining me in Ft. Worth were my long-time companions Dick McNamara and John Lundgren. We had become close friends during our days at the Advanced Flight Training in Lubbock, Texas. Although we didn't share the same quarters, we spent most of our free time together, seeing the sights in Ft. Worth and dancing at the canteens. We never expected to be together, flying B-24's, (and we never expected to be assigned to the 509th Composite Group at the end of our "transition" training).

Perhaps I should explain the term, "transition" training. In the Army Air Corps of the 1940's, when you were transferred from flying one type of aircraft to another, you first went through what they termed "transition" flying. That is, you learned your new aircraft from the ground up. This meant that in addition to learning how to fly your new aircraft, you went to "ground school," learning everything there was to know about that particular airplane. It was solid, thorough training, and I am sure the Air Force today utilizes the same type of training.

After several weeks of "ground school," we were split into groups of two. Each group was assigned a flight instructor and a B-24.My group's flight instructor was Lt. Ditty V. Allen from Texas. We took turns sitting in the left seat, the pilot/aircraft commander's seat, the instructor sat in the co-pilot's right hand seat. Our first lesson: taxi up and down the runway without using the brakes!

Since the B-24 was powered by four Pratt & Whitney engines, each developing about 1,200 horsepower, we quickly discovered that it was quite difficult to control all that horsepower and the momentum it generated using only the four throttles.

I'll never forget that first day in the B-24 when my instructor told me, "Your turn, Lieutenant. Take it down the runway, slowly." I gently pushed the four throttles forward. It seemed to me that this wasn't going to be too difficult. Then he told me, "Now, turn left onto that taxi-way. No brakes!" I eased off on the left throttles, gave more power to the right engines, turned the wheel and the B-24 started to roll off the taxiway onto the grass. Instinctively, I hit the brakes! The B-24 began to bounce up and down as its brakes stopped the three wheels.

"Not that way, Olivi!" the instructor shouted. "Use the throttles, just the throttles. No brakes! No bouncing." I'm glad I couldn't see the other fledgling B-24 pilot sitting behind me. I am sure he was silently laughing, just as I had when I watched him on his first taxi. His name was Olearzyk, from New Jersey.

I turned the B-24 back onto the taxi-way, perhaps using too much power, but I did it without using the brakes. It was obvious to me that the slightest touch to the brakes would cause the B-24 to bounce up and down, as if it were on a trampoline. We moved forward about 200 yards to where another taxi-way intersected the one on which we were practicing. "OK, turn right," the instructor said. I eased up on the two right throttles, gave the ones on the left a bit more power, and turned the wheel. Like a giant goose, waddling down a strip of concrete, the B-24 slowly made the turn. Not smoothly, but turn it did — without bouncing!

Each day got better. Soon we three "hope-to-be" B-24 pilots had all accomplished what had seemed to be the impossible: we could maneuver the airplane on the ground without the brakes. Next, we were permitted to take it into the air!

Flying the B-24 was a pleasure. It had a lot of horsepower and responded to the slightest touch. Take-offs and landings were never difficult. Before we knew it, we were practicing formation flying with other "transition" pilots, and going out on day-long cross country flights guided only by a radio beam. This was "heady" stuff, and I loved every minute of it. Surprisingly, flying the most versatile bomber in the Army Air Corps air armada came quite easy to me.

I continued my transitional training through the months of September and October and graduated in November as an "aircraft commander." This meant that I was qualified to be the First Pilot and sit in the left seat in any B-24.

I was finally ready, qualified and trained to fly, and command, a B-24 in combat!

Lincoln, Nebraska

After a very short trip back home to Pullman, I reported in at the Air Corps Crew Classification "Pool" in Lincoln, Nebraska. From this headquarters, crew assignments were made up and men shipped to different air bases in all parts of the country. Normally, about 35 pilots, bombardiers and navigators would be on a single shipping order, not necessarily as members of the same crew, but as individuals who would be used to "fill out" crews on a particular aircraft.

I don't know how many officers and enlisted men were present when I reported in on December 9, 1944, but there must have been thousands. The air base was "crawling" with men like myself who had nothing to do but wait. I checked the bulletin board at least twice a day to see if my orders had come through and my name had been posted, telling me how, when and where I was to report for further duty.

McNamara, Lundgren and I loafed, played cards, went to the movies and were bored. Every day after breakfast there was a formation at 9:00 am. As our names were read off, we shouted, "Here!" or "Yo!" or "Yeah!" Then we'd head back to the barracks to wait until the next day, when we followed the same routine. After several weeks, I decided the waiting for my name to appear on Orders was too much. So I came up with a great idea. It involved my going "AWOL" — Absent Without Leave — which carried a very harsh penalty if I got caught. But I figured I would not get caught, if my plan worked as well as I expected.

It worked like this: McNamara or Lundgren would answer when my name was called at the 9:00 am formation, and I would take the Burlington Railroad's Zephyr train to Chicago, where I would stay until "Mac" telephoned me that my orders had been issued. It was a fool-proof scheme, if they didn't go looking for me at the Base, and if "Mac" would answer to my name when it was called.

Actually, my escapade went better than expected. I spent about four weekends in Chicago unofficially. I had a grand time! And it was not until February 7, 1945, that I got an urgent telephone call from "Mac" telling me, "Get your butt back here, Olivi, you're on Orders!"

I grabbed my gear and headed for the Union Station, where I got a seat on the Streamliner train to Lincoln. Once back on the base, I joined the others in my group and went to the personnel office where we were issued Special Orders 41 on February 10, 1945. Destination: the 509th Composite Group at Wendover, Utah.

I bought "Mac" and Lundgren each a very expensive bottle of Scotch as my "Thank you" for covering for me. They deserved even better.

There were thirteen of us on Orders to the 509th. Listed as B-17 co-pilots were 2nd Lieutenants Norris, Briggs, Griffin, Adams, Dickman and Flight Officer Deahl. Flight Officer Castater was a B-29 navigator, and F/O Ormond was a B-24 bombardier. Listed as a B-24 aircraft commander was 1st Lieutenant M. J. Lyons. Also on the list were 2nd Lieutenants Richard McNamara, John L. Lundgren, Robert McNeice, and Fred Olivi.

At about 6:00 pm, after a quick meal in the mess hall, we were herded into buses and delivered to the Lincoln train station where a drab-looking troop train waited.

I guess I had hoped that the Army Air Corps would fly us to our next assignment, but no such luck. Just a dirty old troop train. There were no berths,

just rows of mohair seats that smelled of grease and smoke. The three of us —
McNamara, Lundgren and I stowed our gear and grabbed seats, "Mac" and I on
one side, Lundgren across the aisle.

I don't recall exactly what we talked about. Each of us was deep in his
own thoughts. Some guys read, others wrote letters to wives, girlfriends, or the
folks back home. I looked out the window most of the time, and tried to sleep. I
finally dozed off about 1:00 am as the train ate up the lonesome track across the
rolling hills of Nebraska, through the mountains of northern Colorado, and onto
the flat, desolate plain of Utah.

The train paused for a few minutes in Salt Lake City. Some of us got out
and stretched our legs, never straying too far from the train. I think a lot of guys
headed for the mailbox.

1943 —*I began my flying career with the 343rd College Training Detachment at East Central State Teachers College in Ada, Oklahoma. My first 10 hours of flight instruction were in this Piper Cub airplane, (and I still have my flight log). Today, the college is known as East Central State University.*

31 Aug. 1943 — College Student/Aviation Students at Sweet Shop at East Central State College.
L to R: College student, Harris Bass, Fred Olivi, Ben Jones

1943 — One of my roommates at East Central State, Guenther Luckenbach, (on the right) and I posed for this picture as we got ready for PT (physical training), which apparently involved a softball game!

1943, Ada, Oklahoma — Aviation students waiting our turn for flight instruction in a Piper Cub (not plane in background). Standing in the back are (L to R) Olivi and McCabe. Kneeling are (L to R) Herring, Charles Meketa and Vander-Meer.

1943, Ada, Oklahoma — More PT. In the back row (L to R), Aviation Students Westphal, Favor and Meketa. In the front row (L to R), Goldgehn, Cunningham, Olivi and Smith.

May 1990, Ada, Oklahoma — At a reunion of the 343rd College Training Detachment, I posed for this picture with my college roommates who survived the rigors of advanced training to become pilots.
(L to R) Guenther Luckenbach, who became a Lieutenant flying B-24's, Art Cunningham, a Lieutenant who flew B-17's, and me, a Lieutenant who flew B-24's and B-29's.

August 1943, East Central State Teachers College
Ada Oklahoma — Flight ready to march to class

November 1943, San Antonio, Texas — A
weekend pass in San Antonio while in Pre-
Flight found me with Cadet Charles Meketa,
strolling the avenue.

March 1944, Parks Air College in East St.
Louis, Illinois — Here I am on the flight line
during my Primary Flight Training. I loved it!

1944 — My class aviation cadets, Class 44G, at Primary Flight Training, Parks Air College, East St. Louis, Illinois. I'm bare-headed, kneeling in front. Only one other Cadet wasn't wearing his helmet (he's standing on the left in the photo). I wish I had written down all their names.
Standing - L to R - Rigsby, Charles Meketa, Petrekis, _____, Olsen, Phillips, _____, _____,
2nd Row - L to R - George Meketa, Nelson, _____, Paul, _____,
Kneeling - L to R - _____, , Olivi, _____, Hester, _____,
Front Row - _____

1944 — Cadet Olivi in cockpit of PT 19 ready to take off for training flight

L to R - 1944 — Cadets George Meketa and Fred Olivi after flight training session at Parks Air College

1944 — Independence, Kansas, Basic Flight Training, Class 44G
L to R - Aviation Cadets By BT-13 Aircraft

1. Olivi

2. Chuck Meketa

3. Phillips

4. George Meketa - In cockpit

5. Pierce

6. On Wing - Olsen and A.B. Paul

Aviation Cadets
Class 44G at
Basic Flight
Training Base at
Independence,
Kansas - April,
1944
2nd Row Sitting,
L to R -
Cadet Olivi,
Cadet Paul

May 1944, Independence, Kansas — I'm in Basic Flight Training, learning to fly the BT-14. In this photo, Cadet A. B. Paul (left) and I and waiting for the flight instructor.

Another photo with Cadet Charles Meketa (on wing on BT-14) during our Basic Flight Training.

June 1944, Lubbock, Texas — I'm in Advanced Flight Training, Class 44G. During our free time, three other Cadets and I found a lake. (L to R) Meketa, Olivi, McLaughlin and Sinnot.

July 1944, Lubbock, Texas — This photo was taken of our Training Class 44G as we trained to fly multi-engine aircraft. In the front row (L to R) are Cadets Newly, Nicholai, Nielson and O'Brien. Standing in the rear (L to R) are Cadets Olsen, Olivi, Instructor Lt. Carson, Instructor Lt. Dean, Cadets O'Kelley and Newey. O'Kelley was my flying partner and we often flew together on our training flights.

August 4, 1944 — We made it! This is Class 44G following our graduation from Advanced Training Class and we're now Second Lieutenants in the Army Air Corps. I'm kneeling in the front row, second from the right.

The official insignia of the 393rd Bomb Squadron - 509th Composite Group stationed at Wendover AFB, Wendover Utah in 1945

Chapter Seven

WENDOVER

The 509th Composite Group

Although earlier I had had reservations about being a co-pilot on a B-29 instead of a pilot on a B-24, I quickly put my brief "run-in" with Colonel Tibbets behind me, hoping Colonel Tibbets would do the same. (He did).

One thing for sure, Colonel Tibbets knew what he was doing when he hid his operation at such a lonely airbase on the barren Bonneville salt flats in the northwest corner of Utah. Wendover Field was perhaps the most isolated place I'd ever seen, obviously a great location if you wanted absolute "physical" security, which Tibbets knew he had to have in order to maintain the secrecy of the 509th Composite Group. For example, we could tell our families only that we were based at Wendover Air Base, located near Salt Lake City. We could say we were flying B-29's, but nothing else. Not where we flew, not when we flew, nothing about our training. Reinforcing the rules were weekly lectures on security. Soon, it was routine not to talk — even to your crewmates — about what you were doing.

I read after the war that about 30 special, undercover security agents were assigned to the 509th by General Leslie Groves, commanding General of the ultra-secret "Manhattan Project" that developed the A-Bomb. They were assigned to infiltrate every phase of the 509th — actually to spy on us. I don't know who these guys were, but I'm glad I kept my mouth shut!

According to stories being circulated when I arrived there in February 1945, comedian Bob Hope had called Wendover "Leftover Field," and singer Bing Crosby had said it was "Tobacco Road with slot machines." I don't know about the accuracy of either comment, but there were slot machines aplenty in the one-and-only gambling casino straddling the border of Utah and Nevada. And Wendover did seem to be an airbase so remote that no one could possibly have wanted it, so it was easy to joke that Wendover was "left over."

I hasten to add, however, that the people of Wendover treated us royally. I think pre-war Wendover had a population of about 200, although I'm sure that number increased briefly during 1945, because of the 509th. I recall there were a couple of restaurants, several rustic bars which featured dance floors and music, and the State Line Hotel and Casino which was in Wendover, but across the state line in Nevada. The Hotel had a Western Bar and Casino operation and was a popular place to spend a few idle hours. I do remember that there were a lot of slot machines along the Nevada border, in gas stations, bars, restaurants, the hotel — everywhere, including the men's room!

McNamara, Lundgren and I were quickly processed through the 509th's personnel department and assigned to our living quarters, "Mac" and I to one place, Lundgren to another.

Colonel Tibbets had said our quarters might be a bit "primitive." He was right. Not only were they primitive, they were almost "unlivable" tar paper shacks, more suited to house cattle or sheep than officers in the United States Army Air Corps!

These 10-man, one-story wooden buildings were constructed about a foot off the ground with two-by-four frames, sheathed with thin plywood, and covered with tar paper. Inside there were five small cubicles, two men to each. An upper and lower bunk bed filled up most of the space in each cubicle; the ceiling was so low that the man sleeping in the upper bunk could barely sit upright.

Potbellied stoves burning soft coal stood at each end of these architectural nightmares. An enlisted man was assigned to keep them going 24 hours a day. I soon discovered, however, that the fierce winds blowing across the salt flats regularly blew out the fires, causing soot to fill the shack. I lost track of the number of cold mornings when I had to shake out my bed linen with soot all over the covering blanket.

The tarpaper shacks had only one advantage: they were located close to the officers' club and the mess hall!

The next day we drew our assignments, with both "Mac" and I assigned to specific B-29 crews. Lundgren was not assigned to a crew, but was listed as a "spare pilot" and reported to the Headquarters Company. We still saw him frequently because he became involved with the "briefings" we had before every flight, both in the United States and overseas. I am not sure whether or not he was ever assigned to a regular crew.

The 509th Composite Group was unlike any Army Air Corps organization I had ever heard of. Only fifteen B-29's made up the 393rd Squadron, five airplanes each in Flights designated as "A," "B" and "C." Three other B-29's were added to the squadron just prior to the time we left for Tinian Island. In addition to the bomber squadron, the self-contained 509th also had its own "airline" — the 320th Troop Carrier Squadron. It was not until after the War that I learned of the special role played by the 320th, flying scientists between Wendover and Los Alamos, and transporting essential engineering equipment from all over the United States to Wendover. This squadron flew seven C-54 four-engine transport planes and was affectionately called the "Green Hornet Airline."

Also making up the 509th was the 390th Air Service group, the 603rd Air Engineering Squadron, the 1027th Air Matérial squadron, and a very special unit called the First Ordnance Squadron. I remember that there was a constant stream of strangers at Wendover. These men were "inspecting" the B-29's, working with the engineering and ordnance people. Exactly who they were and what they were doing was not my business. I figured I would be told in the future, IF they wanted me to know.

The aircraft crew to which I was assigned was in Flight "C." The pilot was First Lieutenant Charles D. Albury of Miami, Florida. McNamara was assigned to a B-29 piloted by Robert Lewis. (More on "Mac's" role as a co-pilot later in this narrative).

I've often thought about how Fate — some call it "luck" — has played such an important part in my life. If I had been assigned to one of the other fourteen B-29's, I would not have had the opportunity to go on the mission to Nagasaki six months later.

After we had been introduced, Albury told me that, following normal transition in the B-29, I would get checked out and acquainted with the aircraft. I would be splitting my time between ground school and actually learning how to fly the B-29. He would be my instructor. Albury said he hoped I was a fast learner; he wanted to get me out on practice missions as soon as possible. He also indicated I was the last to "fill out" his nine-man crew. I did not ask — nor do I know today — if I replaced another pilot, and if so, who he was. Some things you just didn't talk about back in 1945.

I came to know Don Albury quite well during the next few months and grew to admire and respect his ability to fly. Albury always asked someone to do something, never used his rank and position to order it done. Members of the crew respected Albury and we trusted him. Most important, we all liked him.

The months of March, April and May flew by. My transition training on the B-29 went smoothly. After just a few "check rides," Albury had me handling our takeoffs, "shooting landings," feathering engines while in flight, and learning many things about the aircraft and its operation.

However, training to fly the B-29 was a constant learning process as we practiced dropping our mysterious single bomb, a bomb we called the "Pumpkin," or the "Gimmick," or the "Gadget."

I also flew several training flights with Dick McNamara in his assigned B-29, which was piloted by Bob Lewis. (This was the same B-29 Colonel Paul Tibbets later flew to Hiroshima with Lewis as his co-pilot).

Lewis gave us our first lessons on how to "fly the step." This was a delicate maneuver in which the B-29 was put into a very gradual downward path. The idea was to use the least amount of fuel to attain maximum mileage. It sounds easy, but in reality it wasn't. Too steep a glide path and the B-29 tended to put itself into a shallow dive. Not enough glide and fuel consumption soared. Both "Mac" and I had many hours of training in this maneuver until we mastered it. (The "step" was practiced by all pilots and co-pilots — which turned out to be a "lifesaver" for our B-29 on August 9th).

There was another mid-air maneuver that Albury had me practice time after time; and if you didn't do this one right, you could tear the tail off a B-29. The maneuver was a violent turn and dive.

Albury surprised me by executing this hazardous and tricky maneuver on one of my first training flights, telling me to pay close attention because the 155 degree diving turn he was going to execute was "S.O.P." (Standard Operating Procedure) when dropping "The Pumpkin."

He called over the intercom to the rest of the crew, "Hold on, Boys. Here we go!" Albury suddenly dropped the left wing and swung the B-29 into a sharp turn and dive. I felt the centrifugal force push me against the side of the aircraft as it banked and picked up speed.

At first I thought, "He's banked too hard. This plane wasn't designed to take this kind of stress. He'll kill us all." But as Albury brought the nose of the B-29 up and straightened out the flightpath, I saw he was laughing. "Crazy maneuver. But this ship can take it, Olivi, as long as you don't push it too far."

Then Albury told me the reason for the dangerous, violent turn. We had to put as much distance between the B-29 and "ground zero" where the bomb would explode. The idea was to do it in as little time as possible. It took me quite a few training sessions before I felt comfortable taking the B-29 into this dangerous maneuver. But I soon gained confidence, always remembering not to exceed the 155 degrees.

The Crew

Albury quickly introduced me to the other eight, sometimes nine, members of his crew. We trained together at Wendover, went on leaves to Salt Lake City together, and became — in my opinion — very close. Each knew he could depend on the others, no questions asked.

Much later, I think it was late April or early May, I was introduced to the "9th" permanent member of our crew: Aircraft Commander, Major Charles Sweeney of North Quincy, Massachusetts.

Sweeney was the new Squadron Commander of the 393rd Bomb Squadron, moving to that position from commander of the 320th Troop Carrier Squadron (C-54's). Lieutenant Colonel Tom Classen, formerly Squadron commander, was promoted to Deputy Group Commander of the 509th, directly under Colonel Tibbets.

I didn't meet Major Sweeney until he showed up one day to fly our B-29 on one of our training flights. He sat in Albury's lefthand pilot's seat. Albury moved over to my righthand, co-pilot's seat. I stood and sometimes sat, perched on the step leading up to the deck where the Navigator and Radio Operator had their stations. Sometimes Albury and I switched, and thus I got my flight training from both pilots!

Actually, I was pleased and somewhat proud to have the Squadron Commander himself select our crew as "his own." Sweeney had 13 other crews to choose from since Tibbets had already selected his, headed up by pilot Bob Lewis and co-piloted by my buddy, Dick McNamara.

As the officer in charge of the entire squadron, Sweeney could choose which crew he wanted to fly with! With rank goes privilege.

I don't know what the odds are against having two brand new co-pilots assigned to the only two B-29 crews that dropped A-Bombs on Japan, but somehow, through some strange quirk of Fate, "Mac" and I beat the odds!

Our Navigator was Captain James F. VanPelt, Jr., of Oak Hills, Virginia. Jim was very much a gentleman's gentleman — quiet, unassuming and very bright. After the War he became a surgeon. Jim died in 1994.

The Bombardier was Captain Kermit K. Beahan, of Houston, Texas. Kermit had many hours of combat experience in Europe. When Tibbets formed the 509th, he asked for (and got) several men transferred from Europe to his new command — Beahan among them. He was good, and I soon came to marvel how he could hit a 500 foot circle from 30,000 feet!

Kermit and I became very good friends at Wendover and enjoyed each other's company. I remember vividly our automobile rides into Nevada, with Kermit driving like a wild man. I especially remember our weekend, three-day leave to Salt Lake City, where this "wild Texan" and I had a great time.

Kermit was a good-looking Texan with a Texan's gift of gab. He loved to boast about his female "conquests" to anyone who would listen. Almost every night he regaled us with stories of the girls he romanced in Wendover, across the state line in Nevada, and back home in Texas.

It was Kermit's reputation that gave us the idea for a name for our B-29, although it was not until after our August 9th mission to Nagasaki that we were permitted to have a design painted on the nose. The name the crew picked: "The Great Artiste." I don't recall who came up with the exact name, but it fit Kermit to a "T." He was an artist! Sadly, Kermit died in 1990.

Our Flight Engineer was Master Sergeant John D. Kuharek, who hailed from Columbus, Nebraska. An Army Air Corps career man, Kuharek had served in Europe as a B-17 flight engineer. He had lots of experience and really knew what made a B-29 engine "tick." Kuharek always impressed me as someone I could depend on. He was a very quiet, "unflappable" kind of guy, older than most of us in the crew. As I recall, he was to become eligible for retirement from the military only six years after the war ended.

The sixth man in the forward cabin was the Radio Operator, Sergeant Abe M. Spitzer, from the Bronx in New York City. Like Kuharek, Spitzer was older than most of the crew and really knew his business. A thoughtful, quiet man, Spitzer at times became "spokesman" for the enlisted men in our crew. Abe died several years ago in an auto accident.

In the pressurized rear cabin, there were only two men: the Assistant Flight Engineer and observer, and the Radar Operator. Later in this narrative, I will explain how and why additional men rode along on our August 9th mission to the Japanese Empire.

The Assistant Flight Engineer, who also served as the pilot's "eyes" from his position behind the wing, was Sergeant Raymond C. Gallagher from Chicago,

Illinois. I believe Gallagher was originally trained as a gunner, but when the central fire control system and machine gun turrets were removed from our special B-29's, he stayed on as Kuharek's Assistant Flight Engineer and Observer.

The role of "observer" was very important because it was difficult to see the engines from the pilot's and co-pilot's seats without turning almost 180 degrees. Since both pilot and co-pilot were extremely busy during takeoffs and landings, he reported the position of the flaps, and monitored the four engines from his vantage point.

Ray Gallagher was a very special person on our crew because he possessed our "good luck charm" — a little doll named "Marianne." His niece, Margaret, had given it to him when he was on leave. No one made fun of "Marianne." If the doll was important to Gallagher and reminded him of home, that was good enough for all of us.

I occasionally see Ray these days. He lives not too far from me in Chicago. Sadly, he is not in good health, but he still has "Marianne" with him. I hope the little doll continues to bring him good luck.

1945 — Tinian. Sergeant Ray Gallagher was the Assistant Flight Engineer and Scanner (responsible for visually checking our four engines and watching for enemy aircraft from his vantage point in the rear compartment of our B-29). (Photo courtesy of Leon Smith)
The doll, called "Marianne," was Ray's good luck charm and he would not fly without it. The doll accompanied us on every flight. In fact, Ray once left "Margaret" in the barracks and we delayed our take-off while he retrieved it. To my knowledge, no member of the crew ever chided Ray about his good luck charm — it was working for all of us!
(Photo courtesy of Ray Gallagher)

Joining Gallagher in the aft cabin was our Radar Operator, Sergeant Edward K. Buckley, who came from Lisbon, Ohio. The highly sophisticated (for its day) radar equipment on our B-29 consisted of the AN/APQ-13 radar bombing/navigational aid which was housed in a retractable radome located between the two bomb bays. (Much more about our radar equipment and the critical role it played during our August 9th mission later in this narrative). Buckley became a veterinarian in his home town after the war, and died in 1981.

All by himself in the rear of the B-29 was Tail Gunner Sergeant Albert T. "Pappy" De Hart of Plainview, Texas. "Pappy" died several years ago.

These nine men made up the flight crew. I am sorry that I don't recall all the names of the men who made up our ground crew. They kept us flying at Wendover Field, and at Tinian Island. I, for one, will be eternally grateful.

The B-29

In the "transitional" ground school, I found out why they called the B-29 the "Super Fortress." It was immense, the largest bomber in the world. The B-29 was over 99 feet long. The B-24, which I thought was big, was 66-feet long. The wingspan was over 141 feet, the tail rose almost 28 feet into the air. It was big, but it also was crowded, especially in the forward compartment.

The plane carried over 7,000+ gallons of aviation gasoline — approximately a railroad tank car load — and had a range of over 3,000 miles. The bulk of this fuel was carried in the wing tanks, but our B-29's were fitted with two additional 300-gallon tanks in the rear bomb bays. The B-29 flew easily at 30,000-plus feet and had a cruising speed of 220 miles per hour — although we flew at well over 290 miles per hour on occasion.

Another feature on the B-29 that I really appreciated was a pressurized cabin. Actually, the B-29 was composed of three pressurized sections with the forward cabin connected to the rear cabin by means of a tunnel running over the two un-pressurized bomb bays. This tube was about 36 inches in diameter, just large enough to crawl through if you had to, but small enough to deter frequent visits between the two. The tail gunner had his own small, completely separate pressurized cabin at the rear of the plane. I did not miss the heavy flight suit and cumbersome oxygen mask required in the B-24.

On several occasions we flew very long distances. These flights of about 3,000 miles each were designed as "navigational" missions for Jim Van Pelt, our Navigator. I recall one of these training missions took us east to Chicago, Illinois, then southeast to the Carolina coastline, and finally back to Wendover. On another night "navigational" mission, we flew westward to Oregon and out over the Pacific ocean, then southwest to a specific point, turned east until we reached the California coast, and then north back to Wendover. These training flights were a great challenge to all of us, and I thoroughly enjoyed them.

In addition, we practiced bombing by radar. I was unfamiliar with radar bombing, so these training flights held a certain fascination for me.

This will not be a "technical description" of a radar "run," but hopefully it will give readers a general idea of how we did it back in 1945.

First, the pilot brought the B-29 onto a certain compass heading at a designated altitude. A special radar scope in the Navigator's compartment then began tracking the target on the radar scope. This radar scope was synchronized electrically with the bomb sight, which fed the exact ground speed and release time to the Navigator. In addition, the Radar Operator in the rear compartment was involved. He coordinated the radar images and fed important data to the Navigator during the radar-controlled bomb run.

Although the Bombardier relinquished control of the bomb drop to the Navigator during a radar "run," it was always possible for him to take back control, should that be desirable or necessary.

On August 9th, all our training with radar bomb "runs" paid off.

I think it was in late March when we were ordered to fly to Offutt Field at Omaha, Nebraska, where we exchanged our aircraft for a brand new one. Its serial number was 44-27353. The 509th insignia, a huge arrow pointing forward in a circle, was painted on the tall tail later, after we had reached North Field on Tinian Island. The B-29's were made by Martin Aircraft under license from Boeing Aircraft.

Up to this moment, Albury and I had flown training missions at Wendover in any B-29 that was available and assigned to our crew. We switched from plane to plane. It did not really make much difference to us which one. Actually, as I look back on it, I think we pretty much "used up" our first B-29's by flying so many training missions.

But now we had our own B-29. When I went out on the flight line with Albury to look it over, I immediately saw that, in addition to new and special engineering features I had been studying in Ground School, these B-29's even looked different. Other than two .50 caliber machine guns in the tail, there were no gun "blisters." Only observation ports protruded from the fuselage on each side, behind the wing. These B-29's were sleek, obviously designed for extra speed and altitude. I remember Albury commenting that he had heard these fifteen B-29's had been altered to meet Colonel Tibbets' specifications. I was gaining even more respect for the Colonel!

In addition to the lack of gun turrets, this new B-29 of ours had several very significant engineering features, including blade cooling cuffs directing additional air onto the four Wright R-3350-57 engines and special Curtiss electric reversible propellers. As far as I know, these were the first reversible propellers ever installed on any combat aircraft in World War II.

We flew it back to Wendover and went out on several "shake-down" training flights. I particularly liked the reversible propellers.

The new B-29 was a signal — our "tip off" that something was going on, that our days at Wendover were almost over. Now we knew for sure that our intensive training was coming to a end. The war in Europe was over. And, although we didn't talk about it much, every member of our crew knew that our next base would be in the Pacific.

Mission: Help destroy the Japanese Empire.

This is from the material we gave the media before our 49th Anniversary Reunion that was held in Chicago, Illinois. I include it here because it provides some statistical data on a B-29 "Super Fortress" Bomber.

509th COMPOSITE GROUP

Committee Members:
Raymond C. Gallagher
Frank Griffin
Frank W. Norris
Fred J. Olivi
Robert J. Petroli
Robert H. Wasz

Fred J. Olivi
2535 West 117th Street · Chicago, Illinois 60655 · Telephone: 312-881-0233

B-29 "BOCKSCAR"

"Bockscar", the plane that dropped the second atomic bomb on Nagasaki, Japan, 9 August 1945, ending WWII, was one of 15 special bombers assigned to the highly trained and ultrasecret 509th Composite Group of the 393rd Bomb Squadron, based in Wendover, Utah.

The specially modified B-29 was built by the Glenn L. Martin Company at Omaha, Nebraska and picked up by the crews of the 393rd Bomb Squadron assigned to fly the planes to their overseas base in the South Pacific.

```
Wing Span      =  141 ft.
Length         =   99 ft.
Height         =   27ft. 9 in. (Top of Tail Fin)
Powerpack      =  Four (4) R-3350-57 Fuel Injection Wright
                  Cyclone 18 Cylinder Radials, each with a pair
                  of General Electric B-11 Superchargers to
                  give 2200 brake horsepower at takeoff.
Propellers     =  Four (4) Blade (16 ft. 7 in.) Curtiss Electric
                  with reversible pitch.

Maximum Range  =  4100 miles.
Maximum Speed  =  375 MPH @ 25,000 ft.
Cruising Speed =  200-250 MPH.
Fuel Capacity  =  9548 Gallons with extra tanks in rear bomb
                  bay.
Ceiling        =  35,000 ft.
Armament       =  Two (2) Twin 50 Caliber Machine Guns in the
                  tail.
Radar
  Equipment    =  AN/APQ 13 Radar Bombing Navigation Aid with
                  retractable radome located between the two
                  bomb bays.
```

All 393rd Bomb Sqd. planes were stripped of all other armaments and gun turrets except for the tail guns, and used their stripped down condition to avoid Japanese fighters over the Empire. The cabin was pressurized for the comfort of the crew members operating the bomber at high altitudes. This eliminated the necessity of the crew using oxygen masks while flying at high altitude during the mission over the Japanese Empire. The stripped condition of the aircraft enabled them to fly higher, faster, and farther to avoid interception.

1945 — Wendover AFB, Wendover Utah. The Remote Training Base of the 509th Composite Group, 393rd Bomb Squadron located 125 miles west of Salt Lake City in the middle of the Salt Flats. Note the vintage cars parked outside the building.

1945 — Wendover Air Force Base, Utah. Here I am, probably on my way to pick up a pass for the weekend.

1945 — Wendover. As the newest arrivals, Lt. McNary (on the left) and I were assigned to a temporary building that was covered with tar paper. This made for very cold nights during the late winter days when the wind blew in from the mountains. In addition, the building was impossible to keep clean.

1945, late Spring at Wendover — This photo was taken at the swimming pool where we practiced "ditching" from a B-29. In the rubber raft with me are (L to R) Capt. Jim VanPelt, Sgt. Abe Spitzer, me, Capt. Don Albury.

1945 — Wendover. This is a photo of the original crew of B-29 "V-82", taken in the U.S. before
we flew to Tinian Island. This is the B-29 that was nicknamed "Enola Gay" just prior to its historic flight to Hiroshima, Japan on August 6th. Several men in this photo were replaced for the
Hiroshima mission, although they saw action on missions before and after the Hiroshima flight.

In the "original crew", in the back row (L to R) were Wyatt Duzenbury, Flight
Engineer; Dick Nelson, Radio Operator; Bob Shumard, Ass't Engineer/Scanner; and George
Caron, Tail Gunner. In the front row (L to R) were Rider, the Navigator, (replaced by Ted Van
Kirk; Williams, the Bombardier, (replaced by Tom Ferebee); Bob Lewis, Pilot, (replaced by
Colonel Paul Tibbets who became Aircraft Commander, with Lewis moving to Co-Pilot); Joe
Stiborik, Radar Operator; McNamera, Co-Pilot, (replaced by Lewis).

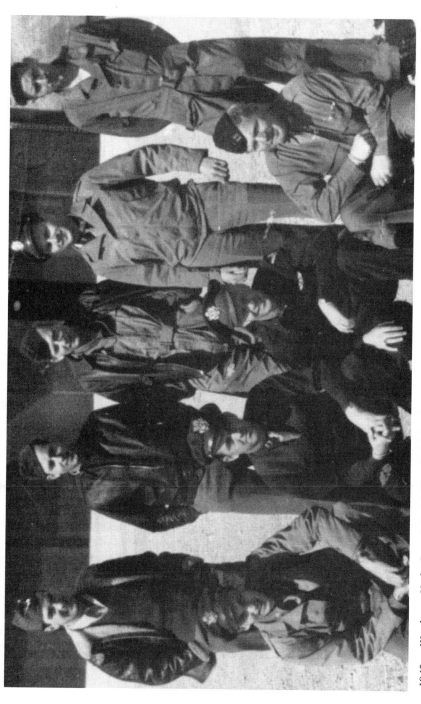

1945 — Wendover, Utah. Crew A-5 of B-29 called "Spook." The crew was headed by Lt. Colonel Tom Classen, Deputy Commander of the 509th Composite Group. L to R, front row: Lt. Col. Classen, Capt. Wright, Lt. Kemner, and Capt. Chapman. Back row, L to R: Cpl. Weller, Cpl Caylor, S/Sgt. Lewandowski, Lt. Rowe and T/Sgt. Strickland. (Photo courtesy of Army Air Corps)

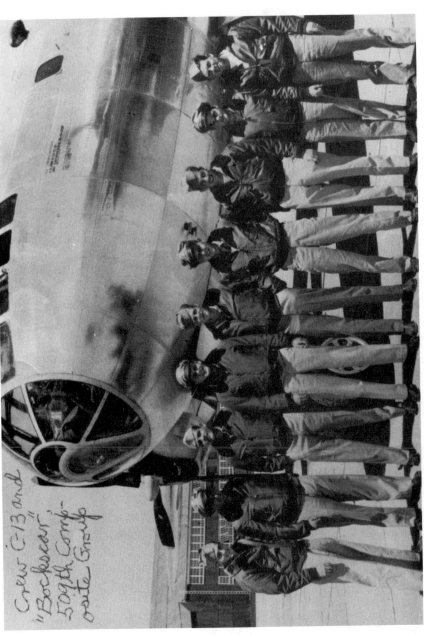

Crew C-13 and "Bockscar", 509th Composite Group

Crew C-13 of the B-29 named "Bockscar." This crew, switched aircraft with our crew and flew our B-29, "The Great Artiste." They carried instruments that were dropped over Nagasaki on August 9th. L to R: Sgt. Curry, Lt. Levy, Sgt. Stock, Capt. Bock, Sgt. Belanger, Lt. Godfrey, Sgt. Barney, Lt. Ferguson, and M/Sgt. Arnold. (Photo courtesy U.S. Army Air Corps)

Assigned Aircraft

393rd Bombardment Squadron (VH)
509th Composite Group
313th Bombardment Wing
20th Air Force
United States Army Air Forces
Tinian Island North Field - July/August 1945

B-29 Aircraft Serial Number	Victor No.	Aircraft Name	Crew No.	Aircraft Commander
36-MO-44-27296	84	Some Punkins	B-7	James N. Price
36-MO-44-27297	77	Bockscar	C-13	Frederick C. Bock
36-MO-44-27298	83	Full House	A-1	Ralph R. Taylor
36-MO-44-27299	86	Next Objective	A-3	Ralph N. Devore
36-MO-44-27300	73	Strange Cargo	A-4	Joseph E. Westover
36-MO-44-27301	85	Straight Flush	C-11	Claude R. Eatherly
36-MO-44-27302	72	Top Secret	B-8	Charles F. McKnight
36-MO-44-27303	71	Jabit III	B-6	John A. Wilson
36-MO-44-27304	88	Up An' Atom	B-10	George W. Marquardt
40-MO-44-27353	89	The Great Artiste	C-15	Charles D. Albury
40-MO-44-27354	90	Big Stink	C-12	Herman S. Zahn
45-MO-44-86291	91	Necessary Evil	C-14	Norman W. Ray
45-MO-44-86292	82	Enola Gay	B-9	Robert A. Lewis
50-MO-44-86346	94	Spook - Smith	A-5	Thomas J. Classen
50-MO-44-86347	95	Laggin' Dragon	A-2	Edward M. Costello

Note: The crew/aircraft combination shown above was the normal arrangement. Variations often occurred.

SPECIAL BOMBING MISSIONS ON JAPAN

509TH COMPOSITE GROUP

JULY-AUGUST 1945

MISSION NUMBER	DATE	AIRCRAFT	TARGET	BOMBS
1	JULY 20	3	KORIYAMA	PUMPKINS
2	JULY 20	2	FUKUSHIMA	PUMPKINS
3	JULY 20	2	NAGAOKA	PUMPKINS
4	JULY 20	3	TOYAMA	PUMPKINS
5	JULY 24	3	SUMITOMO	PUMPKINS
6	JULY 24	4	KOBE	PUMPKINS
7	JULY 24	3	YOKKAICHI	PUMPKINS
8	JULY 26	4	NAGAOKA	PUMPKINS
9	JULY 26	6	TOYAMA	PUMPKINS
10	JULY 29	3	UBE	PUMPKINS
11	JULY 29	3	KORIYAMA	PUMPKINS
12	JULY 29	2	YOKKAICHI	PUMPKINS
13	AUG 6	7	HIROSHIMA	LITTLE BOY
14	AUG 8	3	OSAKA	PUMPKINS
15	AUG 8	3	YOKKAICHI	PUMPKINS
16	AUG 9	6	NAGASAKI	FAT MAN
17	AUG 14	4	NAGOYA	PUMPKINS
18	AUG 14	3	KOROMA	PUMPKINS

Chapter Eight

"THE PUMPKIN"

At no time during our training at Wendover did anyone tell us how much explosive power there was in a fully-armed "Pumpkin." But we were ordered not to take any chances, thus the 155 degree turn and dive.

Most of us called the giant bomb in our bomb bay "The Pumpkin," but it was also known to many in the 509th as "The Gimmick." Some fellows just called it "The Weapon."

I do not know who gave the "Pumpkin/Gimmick" its official name "Fat Man," but "Fat Man" entered all the history books as the name of the Plutonium (Atomic) Bomb we dropped on Nagasaki, Japan. I still think "Pumpkin" is a better description; it looked like a squat, misshapen pumpkin, and for our practice bomb runs to Muroc Lake, California, it even was painted a mustard yellow.

"The Pumpkin" was unlike any bomb I had ever seen. It was over five feet in diameter, over ten feet long, and had a huge square tail assembly. In fact, it was so big and heavy that just loading it into a B-29 was a major operation. First, the "Pumpkin," in a heavy-duty cradle, was wheeled to a shallow pit. After the bomb was positioned over the pit, a hydraulic lift on which was mounted a special cradle rose to accept the bomb. The bomb then was lowered into the pit. With its engines turned off, a B-29 was very carefully pushed backwards until the forward bomb bay was directly above the bomb sitting in the pit. The hydraulic lift then pushed the "Pumpkin" up into the B-29 where it was suspended, barely clearing the sides of the bomb bay. I think it took more time and a larger crew to load a single "Pumpkin" bomb than it did to load dozens of normal bombs into a B-29.

Even the way it was suspended in the bomb bay was unique. Instead of a normal bomb rack the "Pumpkin" was held in a special "cradle."

I was told after the War that in 1944, Colonel Tibbets sent his bombardier, Major Tom Ferebee, to England to bring back the special mechanism used by the Royal Air Force to hold 2,000 pound "Blockbuster" bombs in its "Lancaster" bombers. I don't know if the story is true, but it makes sense.

During the months of March, April, May and June in 1945, we flew many training missions, dropping our "Pumpkins" from 30,000 feet onto a 500-foot diameter target area in the Muroc Dry Lake area in California. Most of the time, these "Pumpkins" were filled with 10,000 pounds of an explosive called Torpex.

On some flights, the "Pumpkin" casing was filled up with concrete. Either way, these single bombs were so heavy that the B-29 "jumped up" as the bomb was released.

During one of these training flights, I remember Beahan cursing as we watched our "Pumpkin" begin to tumble before we lost sight of the bomb as it streaked toward the ground. He knew he had made a "perfect drop" with his Norden Bomb Sight, but the bomb was "unstable" and fishtailed. It missed the target area by a wide margin.

Unknown to us at the time, engineers and other special technicians from Los Alamos, New Mexico, were on the ground and were carefully monitoring the "flight" of our gigantic "Pumpkins." It was not until after the war that I learned there was a design problem with the tailfin assembly on the early "Pumpkins," but the engineers finally solved it.

I hasten to add that none of us in the 509th, other than Colonel Tibbets himself, knew anything about the "final insides" that our pumpkin-shaped bomb was designed to carry. I never heard the word "atomic" used; and I wonder how many of us would have understood the meaning of the term, much less understood how anyone could make an atom explode.

It was not until after the War that I discovered that the "Pumpkin," aka "The Fat Man" — the bomb we dropped on Nagasaki — was totally different than the "Little Boy" atomic bomb dropped on Hiroshima. It looked different, used a different kind of atomic explosive device, even was exploded in a different fashion.

All we knew at Wendover was that the ultimate "Pumpkin" would be a very powerful and very big, strange-looking bomb.

Our job was to deliver it to an assigned target, not ask questions. We just flew our training missions, and practiced, and practiced that 155-degree escape maneuver!

SECTION THREE

The Mission

Chapter Nine

FLIGHT TO TINIAN

Soon after we picked up our new B-29 in Omaha, and flew it back to Wendover, we gave it the nickname, "The Great Artiste." We were told, however, that we could not have any artwork painted on the nose.

But I'm getting ahead of my story.

In April, we finally learned where we were headed when orders came through transferring the 509th's ground support squadrons to Tinian Island in the Marianas Group of Islands in the Pacific. It would be just a matter of time before we, too, headed out.

During late April and into May there was a gradual "staging" of these support units. They quickly packed up their tools and assorted equipment and boarded troop trains for the West Coast where ships waited to transfer them to Tinian. However, the ground crews assigned to our B-29's remained behind to service the aircraft. We were told our ground crew would fly with us to Tinian.

I had read in the newspapers about Tinian, and the other B-29 bases on Saipan and Guam. The stories about how these strategically-located islands were taken by American forces in 1944, after bloody battles, made fascinating reading. It was reported that a few Japanese were still hiding in the hills, and I wondered if I would see any of them. It was no secret that the 20th Air Force, now based on these islands, was bombing the hell out of Japan. The newspapers and news reports on the radio kept all of us in the military aware of the war effort in the Pacific. We were tightening a noose around the neck of the Japanese Empire, as island after island came under American control. Japanese cities were now open to attack from the air; our B-29 bombers from Tinian, Saipan and Guam were systematically destroying them, one by one.

America was finally winning the war in the Pacific.

There was a lot of "red tape" and paper work before we transferred overseas, and we had to undergo another round of "shots" to protect us from every disease known to mankind. I don't think any of us objected. We were too excited and eager to put our training into real action against the enemy. Make no mistake, we wanted to get overseas and looked forward to flying combat missions against the Japanese Empire.

In early June, our crew received its orders to fly to Tinian. Our flight plan first took us to Mather Air Force Base in California, where we were scheduled to spend a few days processing our paperwork for overseas duty and refueling. The next day we would head for John Rogers Field in Honolulu, Hawaii, where our B-29 would be checked over and again refueled. Then we would head southwest across the Pacific to Kwajalein Island for another brief refueling stop; and finally, on to our destination, North Field on the island of Tinian.

We went through the customary briefings for weather, fuel consumption and navigational check-points along the way. We also had several training sessions on "ditching procedures," although I think we all knew that our chances of survival were minimal if we ever crash landed in the ocean. In addition, we were issued weapons and the appropriate ammunition — Colt .45's for officers, .30 carbine rifles for the other men in the crew.

The addition of the ground crew as passengers on our flight to Tinian presented a real problem. As the biggest airplane in the world, the B-29 was a sophisticated bomber, not a transport airplane. It was designed to carry about ten men, not fifteen or twenty. The plane's designers had utilized every nook and cranny for equipment essential in combat, and I am sure they never gave a thought to putting additional passengers into the plane.

Even without passengers we were crowded. In the nose, the bombardier was squeezed into a very small space, surrounded with delicate equipment, including the Norden Bomb Sight, a small table, and various controls. On the flight deck, the pilot and co-pilot's seats were surrounded with instruments and controls. Behind the co-pilot, facing the rear of the plane, the flight engineer had a small seat in front of all his controls where he could monitor the fuel supply and adjust the engines for maximum performance. Behind the pilot, the navigator also had a small chair and table for his charts, maps and radar scope. Next to the flight engineer, the radio operator had his own small table and chair in front of his radio equipment. The removal of the forward gun turret opened up a little room, but not much. However, there was some open space in the rear cabin area, primarily because the gun turrets and machine guns had been removed. Even so, space was at a premium because of the radar operator's enclosed space housing his delicate radar equipment.

Actually, the cramped condition in our B-29 reminded me of an episode in the Marx Brothers' movie comedy, "A Night At The Opera." In one scene a hotel room is filled, wall-to-wall, ceiling-to-floor, with people. Every time the door opened, a body tumbled out into the hall.

Our situation was not that severe, and it wasn't funny. The men from our ground crew had to find a place to sit, stand or lie that would not interfere with movements of the flight crew. Some of the men took turns napping in the tunnel, most just sprawled on the floor, their heads on parachutes or "Mae West" life jackets. I'm not positive, but I think it was the first time some of the ground crew had ever flown in a B-29!

With Major Sweeney in command and seated in the pilot's seat, we "buzzed" Wendover Field for the last time and headed to Mather Air Force Base in California. (I believe the base no longer exists). Flight time was a little over two hours. We were joined by three other B-29's, also heading to Tinian, but we didn't fly in formation — just in the same vicinity in the air.

It was at Mather Field that I first learned what it meant to be the only Second Lieutenant among higher-ranking officers. I was put in charge of security for "The Great Artiste" whenever it was on the ground. Since we were scheduled to spend the night at Moffet, this meant I was responsible for protecting our B-29. The enlisted men in our ground crew were assigned to guard duty.

I was new at this role as "Officer of the Day," and very awkward when I had to inspect their weapons; however our sergeants helped me work out a reasonable schedule. Checking on the men throughout the night also meant I didn't get much sleep. The Second Lieutenants on the other B-29's had the same problem during our flight to Tinian. We were fliers, not infantry soldiers. Ordering enlisted men to do anything always made me uncomfortable, but somebody had to do it.

This kind of armed security for our ultrasecret, modified B-29's at one of our own military bases, in our own country, may seem strange, but before we left Wendover Colonel Tibbets had issued strict orders that no unauthorized person was to get near one of his B-29's. And only members of the 509th Composite Group were so authorized!

I think this was one of the reasons why our ground crew flew with us. In addition to serving as armed guards, they did the refueling and were available for essential maintenance, should it be needed. No one else was allowed to even touch one of our B-29's.

"Authorized persons only" also meant generals! It didn't happen during our stopover, but a day or two later. One of the 509th's B-29's, on its way to Tinian, was parked at Mather Air Base. It was early evening, and most of the crew was eating dinner in the base "mess hall." The commanding general of the base, who had heard about these strange-looking B-29's without gun turrets refueling at his base, decided he had to see one up close. He drove out to the flight line in his personal Jeep to inspect the plane.

The enlisted man on guard duty, actually just a member of the ground crew for that particular B-29, stopped the general from approaching. The enlisted man had his orders. The general was not a member of the 509th, and he definitely did not have the proper clearance.

After some very heated words, the general told the airman that he, the general, was going to go aboard the B-29, and the airman better get out of the way. The airman pulled back the bolt on his carbine and got ready to fire, taking aim at the general's chest. He pleaded with the general to stop, saying he would shoot if he had to. The general finally did stop, but promised the airman, "I'm going to nail your rear end on a wall. You haven't heard the last of this!" He got into his Jeep and roared off, swearing he was going straight to Tibbets.

Tibbets <u>did</u> hear about this encounter, and told the general the airman was just following orders. When the general asked if the airman actually would have pulled the trigger, Tibbets said something like, "General, I do not have a single doubt that the airman would have fired if you had kept moving toward the B-29."

I don't know who the enlisted man was, but he sure knew the rules and how to follow orders.

That was the kind of security expected from all of us in the 509th! Thank goodness the general did not pick on our B-29. I'm positive anyone in our ground crew would have reacted the same way, but I'm glad we missed the experience.

We took off for Hawaii the following day, climbing to 20,000 feet, our assigned altitude for the trip. After Jim Van Pelt had us on the right heading, Major Sweeney turned the controls over to me while he took a nap in the tunnel. Actually, there wasn't much to do besides stay alert. We had "George" doing the flying for us.

"George" was our name for the automatic pilot, an essential control on long flights. "George" kept us right on line, at our normal cruising speed of 220 miles per hour.

To those of us in the flight crew, this was just another routine flight, longer than most of our training flights, but nothing out of the ordinary. We all had our assigned tasks to perform, and thus several crew members were occupied — Van Pelt was undoubtedly the busiest with his navigation, while Spitzer had to be on the alert all the time, radioing our position at designated times to "picket ships" which monitored our flight across the Pacific. The knowledge that the U.S. Navy was keeping track of our plane was very comforting.

Flight Engineer Kuharek was very busy monitoring the performance of our four engines and keeping track of our fuel supply. Albury and I were in close contact with Van Pelt in order to keep "The Great Artiste" flying in the right direction.

In the rear compartment, our ground crew had nothing to do but look out the two observation ports at the puffy clouds between us and Pacific below. Or they slept, or played poker, or told jokes, or wrote letters in which they couldn't reveal anything that was going on! It must have been a very boring flight for them.

After 9-1/2 hours of flying over nothing but water, our navigator, Jim Van Pelt, hit the Hawaiian Islands right on the nose. What a welcome sight!

We landed at John Rogers Field, where we were scheduled to spend two days, to give the ground crew enough time to give our engines a thorough inspection. I set up a schedule for guarding "The Great Artiste," then Kermit Beahan, Don Albury and I took a taxi to Honolulu and the Moana Hotel on Waikiki Beach. We each got a room. Cost $3.50 a night. I must have spent an hour soaking in the fancy bathtub before we went out for dinner, and then to a service club where we danced with the U.S.O girls until past midnight. The next day we toured Honolulu.

In a few days Kuharek, satisfied that our B-29 was in tip-top shape, gave the OK to continue our flight.

We took on a full load of fuel, got clearance from the control tower, and headed west for Kwajalein Island in the Marshall Island group. We were scheduled to refuel at this island, although we probably had enough fuel to reach Tinian, if we "pushed our luck."

Kwajalein, on a map, is just a tiny dot surrounded by nothing but hundreds of miles of ocean. Finding it was a real test of navigation for Jim Van Pelt. But just as he had "nailed" Oahu in the Hawaiian Islands, Jim directed us straight to the coral atoll, which rises only a few feet out of the Pacific Ocean. It was virtually invisible from the air and must have been very difficult to spot from a ship.

The atoll was controlled by the U.S. Navy and used primarily for refueling Navy airplanes and ships enroute to the South Pacific. It was a lonely place, even more isolated than Wendover!

We identified ourselves, got clearance from the control tower, and landed. We were scheduled to spend the night on Kwajalein before proceeding to Tinian Island. The next morning we took off for Tinian, some seven hours flying time away.

After seven hours, Tinian Island appeared on the horizon. Our new home-away-from-home rose out of the Pacific to welcome us.

We had been in the air for twenty hours and had flown over 6,000 miles across the Pacific without a "hitch." The Japanese Empire was only 1,500 miles away!

Chapter Ten

KEEPING THE SECRET, SECRET

ATOMIC MIGHT

The Japs well knew, - they had been warned
Of the Allied might that was being formed
But they chose to die for the Rising Sun
And proudly stuck to their ill made gun.
But a thunderous blast, a blinding light,
Brought the 509th atomic might.

It was the 6th of August, that much we knew
When the boys took off in the morning dew,
Feeling nervous, jumpy, sick and ill at ease
They flew at the heart of the Japanese,
With a thunderous blast, a blinding light,
And the 509th's atomic might.

Below like a miniature checker board
Lay a Japanese town in one accord,
Unknowing the might that lay in store
It went to the shelters, the rich and poor,
That's when the thunderous blast, and blinding light
Came from the 509th's atomic might.

From out of the air the secret fell
And created below a scene of hell,
Never before in times fast flight
Has there been displayed such a sight,
As the thunderous blast, the blinding light,
Of the 509th's atomic might.

From ear to tongue, from tongue to press
The story spead, - stupendous - nothing less!
From pole to pole, around the earth,
Folks knew now of our powerful worth,
With the thunderous blast, the blinding light,
Of the 509th's atomic might.

Oh, God! – that when this War doth cease
And again we turn our thoughts to peace
That you will help us build, - not devastate,
A life of love and truth, - not hate,
Without the thunderous blast, the blinding light,
Of the 509th's atomic might.

Sgt. Harry Barnard

This poem, which appeared in the base newspaper soon after the 509th was in place on Tinian, was typical of the "friendly curiosity" we met almost every day. Mostly, we just smiled and didn't even try to answer all the questions. We had been prepared back at Wendover, as evidenced by the incident at Mather Air Base, to keep our mouths shut and to do what we were told to do without asking questions. The rumors never let up until after August 6th, when the whole world found out what the 509th really was doing!

As we circled Tinian, waiting for clearance to land, I found myself staring at the four 8,500 feet long parallel runways at the northern edge of the island. We had heard about these engineering marvels, constructed out of coral by the Navy Construction Battalions (SeaBee's), in less than a year. (Tinian had fallen to the Americans in August 1944). But I could hardly believe my eyes at the immensity of the project. Oriented east to west, the runways seemed to cover thousands of acres, and ran from shore to shore. We landed and took off over water at North Field; there were no other options. And just across a three mile strait lay the island of Saipan, also with long runways and hundreds of B-29's.

Tinian Island covers approximately 42 square miles and is about 10-1/2 miles long and four miles at its widest point. One of the Navy SeaBees must have been from Manhattan, New York, because the main north-south street was named "Broadway," and I have to agree: the shape of Tinian Island did resemble the island of Manhattan.

In addition to North Field, there were runways located in the middle of the island, designated as West Field. The whole island was alive with B-29 bombers, and North Field had become the largest and busiest airfield in the world. I don't know how many B-29's used Tinian as home base, but there were hundreds and hundreds lining the perimeter of the air base.

The 509th Composite Group occupied a small area immediately adjacent to North Field. In comparison with the other groups, we took up hardly any space. Our engineering, radar, communications, fueling units, armament and living quarters were situated very close to a compact square in which our fifteen B-29's were parked.

In the same compound, in a highly secret area surrounded by barbed wire fences and tall canvas walls, there were several Quonset huts, guarded 24 hours a day. *(I did not have the clearance to visit these buildings, and it was not until long after the War that I learned the two atomic bombs were assembled in these buildings which were air conditioned).* In addition, the pits for loading a "Pumpkin" into our B-29's were located at the airfield on Tinian.

I don't remember who in our advance party from Wendover reserved the Quonset huts we used as living quarters, but we appreciated the effort, although we did have to live in tents for the first week or so.

Happily, Dick McNamara and I were assigned to the same Quonset, which housed pilots, co-pilots, bombardiers and navigators from both Albury's and Lewis' B-29's, and other flight crews from the 393rd.

Officially, as far as the Army Air Corps was concerned, the 509th was attached to the 313th Bomb Wing of the 21st Bomber Command, headed up by General Curtis LeMay. The 21st was part of the 20th Air Force Command. Colonel Tibbets was the one who had to keep it all straight. We just followed orders and flew the aircraft.

The isolation of our group from everyone else in the 313th, our aircraft with gun blisters but no guns, our unique tail insignia — a black arrow in a circle — and our failure to take part in any of the normal combat bombing missions soon had the 509th marked as a "special" unit.

For example, during our indoctrination period with the 313th Wing, I was "quizzed" by a couple of co-pilots who wanted to know why our B-29's lacked gun turrets, and what kind of bombs we were going to drop, and how soon we would start dropping them? I think I finally said, "Look guys, I just can't answer your questions. Ask Colonel Tibbets!" That answer didn't satisfy them; but to tell the truth, I didn't know much more than they did!

There was nothing we could do to stem the rumors circulating on the island about the 509th. It seemed that everything we did provoked comment. Even "Tokyo Rose" welcomed the 509th to Tinian. I don't know how the Japanese found out about our arrival, but they did. Most of us guessed that Japanese soldiers hiding in the hills must have radioed the information back to Tokyo. We never did answer that particular riddle.

In some ways, I think the 509th made it easy for everyone to speculate. For example, in early August, the tail insignia on "The Great Artiste," the black arrowhead in a circle, was replaced.

At the same time, the letter "A" went on tails of several other B-29's, while the letter "N" in a triangle, and the letter "P" in a square went on still others. These markings were supposed to identify the 509th B-29's as being part of other groups already based on Tinian, but the flight and ground crews around North Field knew the truth — we didn't belong to anyone!.

In many ways, I think we sympathized with our questioners. We had it pretty easy. They were flying missions day and night, carrying incendiary and high explosive bombs to Japanese cities where they faced fierce anti-aircraft fire and swarms of Japanese fighters. So, when we went off on our training and secret bombing missions, one B-29 at a time, they had good reason to wonder where we went and what we were doing.

The first week on Tinian, we attended a Lead Crew Training "ground school" run by the 313th to learn the proper take-off and landing procedures at North Field, and to demonstrate our competence to fly a B-29. This did not take long. We learned that Colonel Tibbets had taken a "hot shot" pilot of the 313th up and demonstrated our 155-degree turn and dive.

Our first training mission was to the island called Truk. This small island in the Marianas had been by-passed when U.S. forces captured Guam, Saipan and Tinian, and was still occupied by the Japanese army. Since it was only four hours away from Tinian, Truk became the "target of choice" for our B-29 crews. Another island, called Rota, was also used for our practice missions.

Truk was bombed daily on scheduled dates almost around the clock, and surprisingly, they fired back at us. This was my first experience with ack-ack, which didn't even come close as we made our bomb run. But at last we had dropped a "Pumpkin" — loaded with 10,000-pounds of Torpex explosive — on the enemy. Although we were fired at, the mission did not count toward the total of 35 missions we needed to complete our combat tour in the Pacific.

After several other training flights, on July 23rd we were given the assignment to actually bomb a city in Japan with a "Pumpkin"! Target: Fukoshima.

Our briefings for this first mission, which consisted of several B-29's, each with a different target city, were fairly routine. We learned that we would fly singly, as we had trained to do at Wendover, and without fighter escort. We were routed to pass near Iwo Jima and then head straight to our target, where Kermit Beahan would drop our "Pumpkin," set to explode about 1,840 feet, plus or minus, off the ground.

We took off shortly after midnight and quickly reached our assigned altitude of 9,000 feet. We were to stay at this height — flying unpressurized — until we reached Iwo Jima, then climb to our nominal bombing altitude of 30,000 feet. I don't know about the other members of the crew, but I was excited, and perhaps a bit apprehensive. This was not going to be a "practice/training mission." This one was for real.

But I had not figured on Fate. As we neared the Japanese coastline, one of our engines began to overheat. Albury decided to abort the mission. Kuharek was told to "feather" the engine. Slowly, "The Great Artiste" began to swing around. I remember I suggested to Albury that since we were going to abort the mission to Fukoshima, why not find a "target of opportunity" — any target — and drop our "Pumpkin."

Albury said, "No. We bomb Fukoshima, or bring it back." I was disappointed, but he was in command. Once his decision was made, that was it. We returned to Tinian, flying almost seven hours on three engines.

The next day, civilian engineers from the Wright Cyclone Engine Factory *(it was not unusual during World War II to have civilian experts available at all our airbases),* swarmed over the engine, trying to determine why it had over-heated. Finally, it was decided to re-create the incident in the air with the civilian engineers on board. We took off and flew for several hours, but the technicians could find nothing. It was just another unexplained "Gremlin."

However, the incident did not prevent us from participating in two more missions to the Japanese Empire before the end of July. On these two occasions, everything went as planned, and Kermit had the satisfaction of dropping his "Pumpkins" right on target! Follow-up aerial reconnaissance revealed our 10,000-pound "Pumpkins" had done a lot of damage.

Between missions, we swam at the Officers' beach, went to the movies, played softball, and generally loafed. July was a great month to be in the 509th.

Then on August 4th, we were told that seven B-29's, led by Colonel Paul Tibbets, would participate in a highly secret mission to the Japanese Empire. Take-off would be early the morning of August 6th.

Our "playtime" was over.

The 509th was about to change the course of the war!

Chapter Eleven

PRE-EMPTED

The August 4th announcement that finally the 509th was going to deliver its secret bomb — this time the "real one" — came as a bombshell to me personally.

I was happy and proud when it was announced that Sweeney, Albury and the rest of my crew had been selected to accompany Colonel Tibbets on his historic mission, but I was struck speechless when I was told by Albury that I had been "preempted" from the mission. "Preempted" was just a polite, military way to say, "Someone else is taking your place." However they said it, it hurt. This was the mission for which we had all trained. To be told I was not going was a great shock.

Albury told me he was sorry, but there was no room for me on "The Great Artiste" because it was scheduled to carry a number of scientists, plus their special instruments to measure the bomb's blast. Someone had to to stay behind on Tinian. Me!

And I wasn't the only co-pilot staying behind. My friend, Dick McNamara, the regular co-pilot of the "Enola Gay" was told he was not going on the mission. His place would be taken by Bob Lewis, normally the pilot, who would serve as co-pilot for Colonel Tibbetts. Actually, "Mac" thought it was kind of ironic. We had trained together, flown together, played together, and together had been assigned to B-29's in a very elite, secret organization. And now we were "pre-empted" together!

There was no surprise in the 509th when we learned that Tibbets would be the lead pilot. Everyone in the 509th — from the first day we starting training at Wendover — expected Colonel Tibbets to be in command of the B-29 carrying the FIRST SPECIAL bomb the scientists had been working on in their isolated compound. However, I don't think any of us expected there would be six other B-29's participating in the mission.

While our crews were being briefed in secret sessions during the next two days, "Mac" and I went swimming and generally loafed. Albury, Van Pelt and Beahan didn't say much about what they were learning at these briefings. Security and "tight lips" were still the order of the day with men of the 509th. We had to learn "though the grapevine" about the assignments for the six B-29's accompanying Tibbets.

Sweeney was to accompany Tibbets to the target where "The Great Artiste" was to drop special instruments hanging from parachutes at the same time Tibbets dropped his bomb. Our aircraft was rigged with various devices to record what the instruments sent out, and the information was to be evaluated by the scientists.

Captain Marquardt in his B-29, Number 91, would also accompany Tibbets to the target, also carrying a number of scientists and observers. After the bomb exploded, these scientists, with their special cameras, were to take photographs and record the event.

Three other B-29's were scheduled to serve as "weather" planes: the B-29 number 85, piloted by Major Eatherly, was to report weather conditions at Hiroshima; Major Wilson in B-29 number 71 was to do the same at Kokura; and Major Taylor in B-29 number 83 was to report back on Nagasaki.

Another B-29, piloted by Lt. McKnight, was directed to fly to Iwo Jima, land, and be readily available should it be needed as a backup plane for Tibbets.

Also, I believe it was just before this historic mission that Colonel Tibbets had the distinctive "arrow in a circle" insignia on all our B-29's removed. The new insignia on Colonel Tibbets' aircraft was a circled "R." The ground crew who did the repainting said they figured the Colonel wanted the Japanese to think if a plane was shot down or captured, it was just another B-29 from other units based on Tinian, not from the 509th. It didn't take long before everyone on North Field knew about the new markings. They were impossible to hide.

I think "Mac" took the sad news of our "preemptions" better than I. He was philosophical about staying on the ground while his crew flew off with its "Special" cargo. I was angry at first, and "Mac" listened to my unhappy mutterings. Thank goodness I did my belly-aching in private.

Perhaps "Mac" had been informed long ago that he might be "pre-empted" when Colonel Tibbets took the FIRST "Special" Bomb to the Japanese Empire. I'll never know because "Mac" died in 1978, and we never talked much about either the Hiroshima or Nagasaki missions after the War ended.

I got over my disappointment when I finally realized that, even if I didn't get to go on this particular mission, I still had been chosen to serve in a very special organization. There was some solace in this fact.

"Mac" and I didn't witness the kleig lights, newspaper photographers, and general excitement the night of August 5th and early morning hours of August 6th. I recall that we went to a movie, then to the Officer's Club, and "hit the sack" at our regular hour.

The next morning at breakfast, and all through the day, everyone worried and prayed for a successful conclusion to the mission. I may not have been on board "The Great Artiste", but I sure prayed for the safe return of my friends and fellow crewmates.

From noon on, we scanned the sky for the B-29's that had gone to Hiroshima. Shortly after lunch the three weather planes landed. And just before

3 pm, Tibbets landed the "Enola Gay, " followed by "The Great Artiste" and "No. 91."

I don't know how many of us there were out on the tarmac welcoming home the crews, but it looked like hundreds to me. There were more generals than I had ever seen, and even one admiral, all clustered around Tibbets after he had parked his B-29. The photographers had a field day. Tibbets was decorated with the Distinguished Service Cross, our second highest military medal for meritorious service.

I didn't get much of an opportunity to talk with any one from "The Great Artiste" that afternoon. After the ceremonies concluded, the three crews were hustled off immediately for a debriefing with Col. Payette, the intelligence officer who handled all our debriefings.

Later that evening, after dinner and at the Officer's Club, I finally got a chance to ask Albury and Beahan about the mission. I think Beahan's first words went something like, "Fred, you won't believe how big a bang that s.o.b. made. I've never seen anything like it. Even after we circled the city, we still couldn't see anything except clouds of dust."

At last, the wrap of total security was being lifted. There was a lot we still didn't know and were not supposed to know. But now we knew why there were many civilians tucked away in their isolated and heavily guarded area in our 509th compound. But they didn't talk much, even after Hiroshima.

Members of the three crews could talk openly about the mission. They were full of comments about what it felt like when the shock wave hit the plane, and how they reacted to the bright light that filled the B-29. I think the one comment that was on everyone's lips went like this: "The Japs have got to surrender now. No one can withstand the ultimate bomb!"

Yes, now we knew. Our "Pumpkin" — now generally called "The Fat Man" — was an atomic bomb. I know I did not know exactly what that meant, other than somehow we Americans had figured out a way to split atoms. I seriously doubt that anyone in our crew, other than perhaps Jim Van Pelt who had studied a lot of science in college, had the foggiest notion what was involved to get an atom to split.

The next day, August 7th, a beer fest with free beer was held for the entire 509th so everyone could celebrate the successful mission to Hiroshima. I remember Colonel Tibbets made a speech, thanking everyone for their cooperation, and how every one of us had helped make the mission possible. There were several other speeches, which I hardly remember, and later in the day on our short wave radios, we all heard President Truman announce to the entire world that an "atomic bomb" had been dropped on the Japanese Empire!

I was having a great time at the party, trading my free bottles of beer for soft drinks, when Don Albury walked up and took me aside. He said he had something private to discuss. *(Believe it or not, I do not drink. Never have. No real reason, just never acquired a taste for alcohol, I guess).*

When we were alone, Albury told me "The Great Artiste" was scheduled to deliver the second A-Bomb, probably on August 9th, and did I want to go along? Sweeney would be the aircraft commander, and Albury would be the pilot, but Sweeney and Colonel Tibbets had said I could go — if I wanted to, as co-pilot.

I think I just looked at him with dumb amazement. Of course I wanted to go — but who? why? how? what had happened?

Albury explained when he learned from Major Sweeney that "The Great Artiste" had been selected for the mission, he asked Sweeney, "What about Olivi? He could be a third pilot. We'll have room since we won't have all those scientists with their heavy equipment on board."

Sweeney said it was OK with him, but he'd have to ask Tibbets. When asked, Tibbets said he had no objections and gave his permission. If I agreed, I was to show up at a preliminary briefing the next day at 9:00 am.

"Preempted" one moment, an "extra pilot" the next. That's the Army. Always the unexpected. Fate was being good to me once again.

Chapter Twelve
"GET READY ... GET SET ..."

I was elated, to say the least, to learn that I was to be a member of the crew which had been selected to drop the second A-Bomb on the Japanese Empire. Being a "third pilot" sure beat being left on Tinian for the second time.

In fact I guess I fairly "bubbled" with the good news. There was only one thing that truly bothered me: I was going while my good friend, Dick "Mac" McNamara, would again be left home on Tinian. "Mac" congratulated me on my good fortune, but I know he was disappointed.

Our first briefing was on August 8th, and it was then that I began to realize the immensity of the weapon we now called "Fat Man." I learned the bomb dropped on Hiroshima had had an estimated explosive force of 20,000 tons of TNT. Twenty-thousand tons! Our "Pumpkins" held about 10,000-pounds of Torpex. That figured out to just about five tons — a mere firecracker by comparison.

I learned our mission originally had been scheduled for August 11th, but the meteorologists had been predicting bad weather over the Japanese Empire during that time period, so this second A-Bomb mission was moved up to August 9th. This was OK with me. I was eager to get going. It was important to let the Japanese know we had more of the devastating bombs that we dropped on Hiroshima. The second bomb to be used on Nagasaki three days later on August 9th was proof.

The re-scheduling of our mission to an earlier date also brought about a change in aircraft. This switch created a great deal of confusion, especially in newspaper stories filed immediately after our mission — and even in official Army documents published after the war.

The reason for switching aircraft was actually quite logical. In order to drop instruments over Hiroshima, special electronic equipment had been installed in the bomb bay of "The Great Artiste" to measure radiation and other data occurring at the time of the A-Bomb's explosion. When it became apparent that it was going to take at least a day to re-install the special "hanger" essential for carrying the "Fat Man," a quick decision had to be made. We couldn't wait. Colonel Tibbets and his superior officers decided that the crew of "The Great Artiste" would carry "Fat Man" in another B-29 called "Bockscar," named for its pilot,

Captain Fred Bock. Bock and his crew would fly our B-29, "The Great Artiste," and drop the instruments. This decision made a lot of sense. A simple switch of crews from one B-29 to another. It happened all the time in the 509th, depending on available aircraft for scheduled missions.

On August 8th, I got my first close look at America's second atom bomb when members of the flight crew were invited to sign our names, or some sort of personal message, on "Fat Man." The huge bomb had just been pulled out of the highly guarded assembly area and was ready to be slowly moved to the special loading pit. I had seen "Pumpkins" up close before, but this one somehow looked different. It was painted a dull, mustard yellow and looked ominous as it sat on its cradle. I know I was in awe of the fact that inside the ugly-looking bomb was something that would split atoms. How it worked was (and is today) beyond me. But I had heard enough about Hiroshima to know that this bomb also was history-in-the-making.

There was a lot of "brass" in attendance, and I think almost everyone wrote something on the bulbous-shaped bomb. I can't recall what I wrote, probably just my name. But a few used very descriptive words in their messages.

We walked along as the "Fat Man" was slowly pulled to the loading pit. I watched as "Fat Man" was lowered into the pit, and "Bockscar" was backed over the pit, using its reversible propellers. Then, very slowly, the world's second atomic bomb was lifted up into the bomb bay. You couldn't help but feel "goose bumps."

During the day of August 8th, the weather reports kept us all worried. Weather over Japan had not improved and the forecast for the next several days was a "maybe, if we're lucky." But late in the day we learned that weather over the Japanese Empire had improved. We were told to get some sleep and to report at midnight for our final briefing.

The mission was on.

Chapter Thirteen

AUGUST 9, 1945

"SPECIAL MISSION #16"

This morning at 03:48 we took off from North Field, Tinian, to drop another atomic bomb on the Japanese Empire. This is the second atomic bomb dropped in four days — the Japs should catch hell again!

Our target is Kokura on the main island of Kyushu — Nagasaki secondary.

This is the very first entry in a penciled diary I wrote immediately upon returning to Tinian after our mission on August 9, 1945.

I was exhausted after being awake for over 24 hours, but I was determined to chronicle, as best I could, the events of the day; hour-by-hour, minute-by-minute. We had been ordered <u>not</u> to write anything during the mission, but no one told us not to write <u>after</u> the mission. So I did.

To help insure accuracy, I asked Jim VanPelt, our Navigator, if I could borrow his log book which was the "official" record of the historic flight of the B-29, numbered V-77, and better known as "Bockscar."

Jim said, "OK, but don't lose it!"

What follows in this chapter are my word-for-word entries in my diary. After each entry, I will try to detail what I was thinking and/or doing at that particular moment during the mission.

I realize it will be difficult <u>not</u> to embellish these notes with knowledge I gained **after** the mission. Hindsight is always 20/20, and there have been many accounts of "Mission #16" on August 9, 1945, that had Kokura, Japan, as its primary target but was forced to fly on to Nagasaki. Some are more accurate than others. Some are highly critical of actions taken by my superior officers on this ill-fated mission. Some accounts have been written by men who were <u>not</u> in the cockpit area where momentous decisions were being made. Several authors interviewed members of our crew in order to get information. I know I have been interviewed many times during the past 50 years, and several times have been misquoted. So be it.

It is not my objective in this chapter — nor hopefully in any chapter in these memoirs — to second-guess any of the decisions made in 1945. Rather it is my intent to add to my diary entries only what I saw and heard, not what I thought I heard or saw back in 1945. Obviously, in 1997, as I write this book, I now know a great many details about what occurred before, during and after our mission — details I didn't know in 1945. Any reference to my current knowledge will be clearly identified.

Now, back to my diary.

12:30 AM

Briefing as scheduled — no opposition expected.
Reached planes at 01:00,
August 9 prior to take off.

During our briefing I met three men who were to accompany us on our mission. All were strangers to me, and I learned each was to play a critical role during our mission.

Navy Commander F. L. Ashworth was introduced as "Weaponeer," and identified as being in charge of our atomic bomb, "Fat Man." Assisting him was Army officer Lieutenant Philip Barnes, who was identified as being our "Electronics Test Officer." The third man was Lieutenant Jacob Beser, who was identified as the "Radar Countermeasures Officer."

I had no idea what a "Weaponeer" was, or what he had to do with "The Fat Man." Barnes' job at least sounded familiar, although I didn't know why we needed a "test officer" on board. I think I hoped they had done all the testing before they put the bomb on the aircraft.

I had seen Beser several times before, both at Wendover and on Tinian, but never had been told what he did. He always flew with other crews, and had his own restricted area in which he worked and kept his equipment. All I knew about Beser was that each time he flew he had some sort of special electronic equipment he installed in that particular B-29. His was a very hush-hush operation and how he used his secret equipment was never revealed to me — until our briefing the night of August 8, 1945. Even then, all I was told was that he had radar-jamming equipment which would monitor Japanese radar that might interfere with "The Fat Man." The "why" we needed such sophisticated radar equipment was unknown to me until after the War.

In addition, a civilian was introduced during the Briefing. This gentleman was William Lawrence, a reporter for the *New York Times*, and he was to be a passenger on "The Great Artiste," which was being flown by Fred Bock on this particular mission. This was not unusual, given the fact that it was no longer a secret that America now had an atomic bomb in its arsenal. In fact, I felt good — sort of proud — that a newspaper man was going to accompany us on this mission.

The other B-29's selected for "Special Mission #16" included a photo aircraft to take pictures of the atomic bomb's explosion. This was piloted by Lieutenant Colonel Jim Hopkins, our Group Operations Officer. Hopkins replaced Norman Ray, who normally piloted that crew's plane but had an emergency appendectomy and could not fly the mission. Hopkins and Bock would go with us to Kokura.

Something very unusual occurred at our briefing, something I'll always remember: Colonel Tibbets gave us a choice. I recall he said something like, "If any of you don't want to go on this mission, where there's no doubt we will be bombing civilians with this new atomic bomb, just say so. If you feel uncomfortable about this, you're free to step down. No action will be taken against you. If that's the way you feel, we'll respect it."

I can't speak for any other member of the three crews selected for this mission, but I was surprised. Never before in my military career had any one given me the opportunity not to go on a mission.

All of us knew about the fire bombing of Tokyo. We knew from our daily briefings about the bombing of Cologne and Dresden where thousands of civilians had died. No one took Colonel Tibbets up on his offer. Rather, I think all of us hoped this second atomic bomb would end the conflict sooner. In itself, that was enough reason to go.

Captain Ralph Taylor was chosen to fly to Iwo Jima and stand ready should his B-29 be needed as a replacement for our B-29, "Bockscar." Captain George Marquardt was to fly ahead of us to Kokura and report weather conditions over our primary target city. Capt. Charles McKnight was to do the same at Nagasaki, our secondary target city. These three B-29's left Tinian on schedule, about 12:30 in the morning of August 9th.

Only two real surprises, at least to me, came out at the briefing. Because of bad weather our rendezvous location was moved from Iwo Jima to the island of Yakushima, just off the south coast of the main Japanese island of Kyushu. And the altitude at which we were to fly to the Japanese Empire had been raised 17,000 feet from the normal 9,000 feet. A different rendezvous didn't seem to present any problems, but the higher altitude meant greater fuel consumption. I don't think any of us gave much thought to these changes. It was just part of our job to adjust. In addition, I knew we would be carrying an extra 640 gallons of fuel in two tanks located in the rear bomb bay. This extra fuel also helped balance the aircraft, offsetting the weight of the "Fat Man" in the forward bomb bay.

During the briefing I learned Kokura was our primary target, with Nagasaki as the alternate. Unlike Colonel Tibbets' mission on August 6th, we had no third alternate target.

I do remember Colonel Tibbets being very specific about two things during our briefing. One: Wait only 15 minutes at the Yakushima Island rendezvous location before flying to our target, and Two: Drop "Fat Man" visually. Kermit Beahan, our Bombardier, had to see the target to insure accuracy during the bomb run. The orders were very specific.

After the briefing, we headed for the Mess Hall and the usual pre-mission breakfast. I think I ate a pretty good meal, considering my excitement.

Then, we got on a truck which delivered us to the flight line where "Bockscar" sat, dimly silhouetted in the glare of headlights from jeeps, trucks and other vehicles that were constantly moving around the aircraft. From what the other members of my crew told me, I gathered that this send-off was definitely not as well-attended as the one to Hiroshima three days earlier. There were a few Army photographers taking pictures, but nothing like the flood lights and hoopla that surrounded Colonel Tibbets and the "Enola Gay." And this is the way it should have been. That was the first atomic mission. Ours was just number two. Now everyone knew what to expect. No reason to get excited.

As the co-pilot (actually, the third pilot), I did my "walk-around" of "Bockscar" and performed my usual pre-flight check of the aircraft, its control surfaces, bomb bay doors, wheels and tires — the normal thing I always did before a mission. That done, I went over to a jeep that was parked nearby, sat down and waited for Major Sweeney to give the word to climb aboard.

On the other side of the aircraft, about twenty-five yards away from where I waited, I noticed Sweeney talking in an animated fashion to Colonel Tibbets. This didn't seem unusual since Sweeney was the kind of Irishman who liked to "talk" with his hands. Several times, Sweeney also conferred with Sgt. Kuharek and Jim Van Pelt, and they kept referring to charts and other records. But this, too, didn't appear unusual. There were always last minute changes on almost any mission. At least once Jim Van Pelt came over and discussed with me our new route and altitude to the Japanese Empire. Very normal. However, it did seem Sweeney, Tibbets and the others were taking a very long time to reach a decision about whatever they were discussing. In fact, their discussion lasted longer than normal. This was unusual, and I began to wonder if our mission was to be "scrubbed."

I found out hours later in the air over Japan what they were discussing. Their decision almost caused us to fail in our mission. More on this later.

Finally, after what seemed an eternity, Sweeney yelled it was time for us to get going.

03:48

Take off with 7,250 gals gas — no apparent trouble — but we sweated it out, and I mean just that. All hell will break loose if we lost an engine on take off — we may as well kiss the world goodbye!

Weather is bad so we're climbing up to 17,000' (feet) to clear it instead of the usual 9,000'. Cruise control chart not set up for 17,000 feet — so that means we'll use a hell of a lot more gas than the usual amount at 9,000'.

Looking back on that fateful take off, I recall hearing an unusual "thump" — a loud bang — just as we lifted off the runway. Sweeney and Albury do not remember it, but they had their hands full, so I can understand their not hearing anything but the roar of the engines. Me, I was standing between them, looking and listening, and I <u>know</u> I heard something. I thought we had blown a tire.

Sweeney held "Bockscar" on the runway a long, long time, taking full advantage of every precious foot.

We were heavy. Almost too heavy, I thought. And one miscalculation, or an engine failure, would be a one-of-a-kind disaster. We had been told at the briefing that our "Fat Man" atomic bomb, riding just five feet behind us in the bomb bay, was safe but armed! The final touches were to be completed in the air by Commander Ashworth after we were well away from Tinian.

BUT —!

I couldn't help but wonder if "Fat Man" would detonate by itself if we crashed? I didn't know anything about atoms, nuclear energy, or radiation. I <u>did</u> know from talking to members of my crew that this new bomb was more powerful than any of them had imagined. From what they told me, it became obvious that "Fat Man" had enough explosive power to blow up Tinian Island — certainly all of North Field!

In the back of my mind, and I am sure in the thoughts of others in "Bockscar" that night as we gathered speed, were the times we had witnessed other B-29's, heavily loaded with mines used to seal off Japanese waterways and harbors, lose an engine on take off and explode on the end of the runway. Such an unholy sight was not easily forgotten as we roared down one of North Field's 8,500 foot runways toward the dark sea and almost pitch black night sky.

As first the nose wheel came off the concrete and then the main landing gear broke contact with the ground "Bockscar" was filled with a collective sigh of relief. Our first big obstacle, take-off, was behind us. We settled in and started to make the aircraft ready for our long mission — longer than we expected!

We had passed our first crisis. We were on our way to Kokura, Japan, our primary target.

Our Navigator gave Major Sweeney a heading, and Sweeney slowly began to climb to 17,000-feet.

I think it was about 04:00 (4:00 am), that Commander Ashworth opened the small hatch to the bomb bay and crawled inside. I recall that he was in the bomb bay about 15 or 20 minutes. Lieutenant Barnes stood by, but poked his head inside several times to talk with Ashworth. I asked Barnes what they were doing and Barnes replied they were changing the "green plugs to red" before the B-29 was pressurized. I wondered aloud if this meant that "Fat Man" was now set to explode, and I recall either Ashworth or Barnes replied "Yes, if it goes below 5,000 feet, it'll detonate." WE WERE A FLYING BOMB!

With that comforting thought, Barnes turned to the black box that had been placed on the table beside Abe Spitzer, our radioman. This box had lots of dials and lights and one big red bulb that slowly blinked on and off. Barnes sat on a small stool beside the table, and from that moment on, never took his eyes off that flashing red light until we dropped "Fat Man" almost six hours later. Commander Ashworth also kept looking at the slowly blinking red light, but he also moved around talking to Sweeney, Albury and Van Pelt.

When I asked Barnes what the blinking red light meant, he replied, "Well, as long as this red light flashes real slow, like it's doing right now, everything is OK in the weapon. But if it starts to blink real fast, that means trouble."

I didn't want to know more, so I stopped asking questions.

04:40

Stopped climbing. Level at 17,000 feet. Some of these damned cumulus and thunder clouds are rough as hell! But "George" will win through.

Soon after Major Sweeney brought "Bockscar" up to 17,000-feet, he turned to me and said, "OK, Olivi. It's all yours. Take it to Yakushima. I'm going to get some sack time."

Sweeney climbed out of his left-hand seat and headed for the tunnel and his nap. I sat down and took over the controls. Beside me, Albury already was starting to doze in the right-hand seat.

In my diary I referred to "George," the name we gave to our automatic pilot. "George" was a great help on long missions and kept us pretty much headed along the designated compass heading which came from our Navigator, Jim Van Pelt. Although "George" did most of the flying, at least one pilot always had to watch the instruments and be ready to take over manual control of the aircraft in the event of an emergency.

The fact that Sweeney asked me to take over the controls at this early phase in the mission was not unusual. On several other flights he had done the same thing, which gave him the opportunity to crawl into the tunnel and "cat nap." Since I was the extra pilot on board, I considered it part of my job to "rest" the other two pilots, especially since they needed to be fully alert when we reached our target.

Our altitude of 17,000-feet put us right in the middle of thunder storms, which made for a bumpy ride. The lightning flashes illuminated the sky around us and were a pretty sight — until we had to fly through one. Then "Bockscar" got tossed around. This was not unusual. We had all flown through severe thunder storms before, although I doubt that Commander Ashworth and Lieutenant Barnes were enjoying our "roller coaster" ride through the inky night sky.

05:30

This route straight through to the Ryukus sure is long — and tiresome! The usual way by Iwo is much better, and something to look forward to.

Chuck and Bee (Sweeney and Beahan) are sleeping. God, I'm so tired I can barely keep my eyes open. Wish I could sleep, too, but flying through these cumulus clouds sure wakes you up in a hurry. Poor Jim (Van Pelt), he's in the same boat as I. He sure works hard at his navigating — I take my hat off to him.

My diary entry does not mention the "St. Elmo's Fire" we encountered on our way to Japan. It was spectacular, and one of the best displays I had ever seen. The "Fire" danced along the tips of the propellers and along the wings, and gave an eerie glow as we bumped along through the cumulus clouds. There was no danger to our B-29 from this phenomenon, and it helped keep me awake as I fought off drowsiness caused by the constant hum of the engines.

I don't know how many of the crew were able to sleep that night. I suspect that many of them in the rear compartment were able to doze. In the forward section, Sweeney, I'm sure, was able to doze off. I knew that Beahan could sleep under any condition. Albury, sitting beside me, nodded off several times, but I think he was more awake than asleep. Certainly Van Pelt, Spitzer and Kuharek stayed awake — they had essential jobs to perform. And I'm sure that Ashworth and Barnes, maintaining their vigil over the blinking red light on their special black box, never slept. At least, I hoped they were awake.

1945 — Aerial view of Tinian Island. In the foreground is the largest air field in the South Pacific during World War II —North Field. Dominating the photo are the four parallel runways, each 8,500 feet long, running east and west, virtually from one side of the island to the other. The long length of these runways made it possible for our B-29's to carry maximum bomb loads on the missions to the Japanese Empire.

1945 — An aerial view of the 509th Composite Group's site on Tinian Island. The headquarters building is in the center with the living quarters, mess halls, engineering and maintenance shops around it. (Photo, courtesy of Professor Anderson Giles, University of Maine).

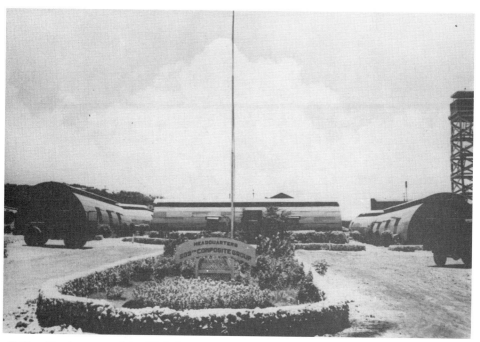

1945 — Headquarters of the 509th Composite Group was in this Quonset hut.

May or June, 1945 — When we first arrived on Tinian we lived in and worked out of canvas tents, like this one that housed Operations for the 320th Squadron, better known to all as "The Green Hornet Line." I was amazed at how quickly the Navy Seabees constructed our Quonset huts.

Another view of the area on Tinian occupied by the 509th Composite Group. While not spacious, the Quonset huts were very comfortable.

This photo is a "straight-down" overhead view of the two atomic bomb loading pits on Tinian Island. On the left (1) is the pit used for loading "Little Boy," the bomb dropped on Hiroshima. On the right (2) is the pit used for loading "Fat Man," the bomb dropped on Nagasaki. (Photo courtesy of Professor Anderson Giles, University of Maine).

Tinian 1945 — Assembling area of atomic bombs in air-conditioned quonset huts of ordnance group.

1945 — North Field, Tinian Island. Lt. Fred J. Olivi, Co-pilot on B-29 "Bockscar" standing in front of "Enola Gay" aircraft that dropped the first atomic bomb on Hiroshima, 6 August, 1945.

COL. THOMAS J. CLASSEN, DEPUTY COMMANDER - 509th COMPOSITE GROUP

His varied Air Force career began in June 1940. Following graduation at Kelly Field, Texas, he was a flight instructor at Randolph and Goodfellow Fields for a year. Shortly after the advent of World War II, he was assigned to a B-17 group in the Hawaiian Islands; then into action in the Solomons. There in the course of one year, he participated in 49 combat missions. While on duty in the South Pacific, he was awarded the Distinguished Service Cross, Distinguished Flying Cross and Cluster, Air Medal and Cluster, and the Purple Heart. It was during this tour of duty on a search mission, looking for the Japanese fleet in the intense aerial war in the battle for supremacy of the Solomon Islands that he earned his medals.

The mission required 66 days to complete and included a 45 minute air battle against 8 Japanese zeros, two of which were shot down by his crew. At the end of this action, their position was about 800 miles northeast of Guadalcanal. The airplane was in bad shape with seven guns out of commission, two dead engines, and three wounded crewmen. It had to be ditched. After a successful ditching and entering the rubber life boats, they floated for 16 days until they reached the Cartaret Islands.

Making friends of the island natives, they tried building native boats to reach safety, with the help of the natives.

After contacting two Australian coast watchers who notified Guadalcanal that they were alive, arrangements were made to rescue the aircrew by a PBY and fly them back to Guadalcanal. Thus the 66 day mission ended after a period full of apprehension and lessons learned the hard way. It was an experience to be long remembered and not easily forgotten!!

1945 — North Field, Tinian Island. Major Charles Sweeney, Commanding Officer of the 393rd Bomb Squadron, 509th Composite Group, at the controls of a B-29. Sweeney was Aircraft Commander of the B-29 "Bockscar" on the mission to Nagasaki on August 9, 1945. (Photo courtesy of Leon Smith).

1945 — Tinian. Here we are, the pilot and co-pilot of Crew C-15. Captain Don Albury and I posed for these photographs in the B-29 we called "The Great Artiste" shortly after arriving on Tinian. Don is shown here in the pilot's seat, I'm in the righthand, co-pilot's seat. During the mission to Nagasaki on August 9, 1945, we flew the B-29 nicknamed "Bockscar." Albury moved to the co-pilot's position when Major Sweeney became pilot/Aircraft Commander. I stood between them, just behind the box of control switches. (Photos courtesy of Leon Smith)

1945 — Tinian. Captain James VanPelt, Navigator of Crew C-15, at his desk just behind the pilot's seat. As is evident in this photo, space was at a premium in a B-29 and Jim was surrounded with emergency equipment, books of maps, and other switches and controls. (Photo courtesy of Leon Smith)

Capt. Van Pelt, our navigator, almost was responsible for dropping the second atomic bomb, "Fat Man", by radar over Nagasaki, on 9 August 1945, instead of Capt. Beahan, our crew Bombardier. The 7/10ths to 8/10ths cloud coverage over the city, and our critical gas supply, left our crew with the only possible solution of dropping the plutonium bomb and making it a complete mission. Had radar been used, we would have been acting against orders given to us at the briefing – "drop the bomb visually only". To this day I wonder what would have happened to us on our return to Tinian Island if this had happened!

1945 — Tinian. Captain Kermit Beahan, Bombardier of Crew C-15, standing in front of his tent before our Quonset huts were ready. Kermit became one of my first friends and a great pal when I arrived at Wendover. I always considered him to be one of the best bombardiers in the 509th. Captain Beahan was credited by Commander Ashworth for saving the Nagasaki Mission by dropping the "Fat Man" A-Bomb visually as ordered at the Briefing. After sighting the target through cloud coverage Capt. Beahan had 40 seconds to set up the Norden Bombsight and drop the bomb successfully and help shorten and win the war in 1945.

1945 — Tinian. Master Sergeant John Kuharek was the Flight Engineer of Crew C-15. Here he is in front of the myriad dials and controls that kept our four engines humming. John served in the Military before Pearl Harbor in 1941. Kuharek knew his job very well and was one of the earliest Flight Engineers in the early B-29 program. A _good_ man to have on your crew taking care of the engines! (Photo courtesy of Leon Smith)

1945 — Tinian. Sergeant Abe Spitzer was the Radio Operator for Crew C-15. He's shown here at his crowded desk on the right side of the aircraft, just behind the Flight Engineer. The round shape just behind Spitzer was the hatch door to the front Bomb Bay. The "Fat Man" Atomic Bomb was carried there and dropped on the Nagasaki Mission. (Photo courtesy of Leon Smith)

1945 — Tinian. Sergeant Ed Buckley was the Radar Operator for Crew C-15. Located in the rear compartment of our B-29, in this photo he is checking out the APQ 13 Radar. He and Capt. Van Pelt, the Navigator, almost dropped the "Fat Man" bomb by radar on the city of Nagasaki!
(Photo courtesy of Leon Smith)

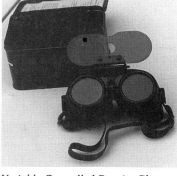

Variable Controlled Density Glasses worn by both crewmen of the Enola Gay and Bockscar on their respective atomic bomb missions against Japan.

1945 — Tinian. Staff Sergeant Albert Dehart, Tail Gunner for Crew C-15. Dehart controlled the only guns carried by the specially modified B-29's in the 509th Composite Group. In order to conserve weight, all other weapons and gun turrets had been removed except for the twin .50 caliber machine guns in the tail position. (Photo courtesy of Leon Smith)

North Field, Tinian, sometime during 1945. Olivi standing in front of our B-29, "The Great Artiste."

Officer's Beach, Tinian, 1945. The island had great beaches, and I was joined in the sand by (in the middle) Lt. Beebe, Engineering Officer of the 509th, and (foreground) Lt. Williams, Bombardier of the original crew of the "Enola Gay" with Capt. Lewis as the Airplane Commander.

Jim Van Pelt, our Navigator, in front of "The Great Artiste." I believe this photo was taken some time after our mission to Nagasaki.

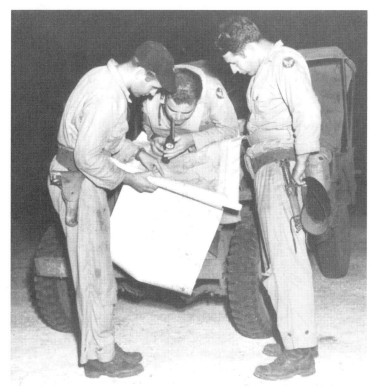

August 8, 1945, after midnight — I'm on the right in this photo taken in the early morning just after midnight before we left for Japan. I was checking over our flight maps with Captain Jim Van Pelt our Navigator (standing on left), and Major Charles Sweeney, Aircraft Commander (sitting on hood of Jeep). (U. S. Army Air Corps Photo)

August 8, 1945 — Waiting in the pitch black night for the OK for "Bockscar" to take off were: (sitting on jeep at left) Lt. Jacob Beser, Radar Countermeasures; (on jeep in center) Lt. Commander (U.S. Navy) F. L. Ashworth, Weaponeer, who armed the atomic bomb after we were airborne; (standing in foreground) David Lawrence, a reporter from the New York Times who witnessed the explosive power of "Fat Man" as a passenger on "The Great Artiste;" and (sitting in the jeep) Colonel Paul Tibbets, Commanding Officer of the 509th and pilot of the "Enola Gay" on the Hiroshima mission. (U. S. Army Air Corps Photo)

August 9, 1945 — Before take-off for Nagasaki. (L to R) Major Sweeney AC - Nagasaki A - Mission; Colonel Tibbets AC - Hiroshima A - Mission; Captain Van Pelt - Navigator of "Bockscar" the Nagasaki Mission. (Photo courtesy U.S. Army Air Corps.)

August 9, 1945 — North Field, Tinian. Crew members of "Bockscar" before take-off on Nagasaki Mission.
(L to R) Buckley, Spitzer, Capt. Van Pelt, Lt. Olivi. (Photo courtesy U.S. Army Air Corps.)

Left to right, Captain Kermit Beahan, Bombardier on Nagasaki Mission, is joined by Lt. McFall of the 509th Headquarters, prior to take off for Japan. (Photo courtesy U. S. Army Air Corps)

August 9, 1945 — North Field, Tinian. Enlisted crew members of "Bockscar" before take-off on Nagasaki Mission. (L to R) Spitzer, Buckley, Kuharek, Dehart, Gallagher. (Photo courtesy U.S. Army Air Corps.)

B-29 PLANES AND CREWS
NAGASAKI
AUGUST 9. 1945
MISSION #16
OPERATION CENTERBOARD II

BOCKSCAR, 35-M0-44-27297, V-77	STRIKE AIRCRAFT
COMMANDER	MAJ. CHARLES W. SWEENEY
PILOT	1ST LT. CHARLES D. ALBURY
CO-PILOT	2ND LT. FRED J. OLIVI
NAVIGATOR	CAPT. JAMES F. VAN PELT. JR.
BOMBARDIER	CAPT. KERMIT K. BEAHAN
WEAPONEER	CDR. FREDERICK L. ASHWORTH USN
WEAPONS TEST OFFICER	LT. PHILLIP M. BARNES
ECM	LT. JACOB BESER
FLIGHT ENGINEER	M/SGT. JOHN D. KUHAREK
ASST. FLIGHT ENGR.	SGT. RAYMOND G. GALLAGHER
RADIO	SGT. ABE M. SPITZER
RADAR	S/SGT. EDWARD R. BUCKLEY
TAIL GUNNER	SGT. ALBERT T. DeHART

GREAT ARTISTE, 40-M0-44-27353, V-89	INSTRUMENT AIRCRAFT
COMMANDER	CAPT. FREDERICK C. BOCK
PILOT	2ND LT. HUGH C. FERGUSON
NAVIGATOR	2ND LT. LEONARD A. GODFREY
BOMBARDIER	1ST LT. CHARLES LEVY
FLIGHT ENGINEER	M/SGT. RODERICK F. ARNOLD
ASST. FLIGHT ENGR.	SGT. RALPH D. BELANGER
RADIO	SGT. RALPH D. CURRY
RADAR	SGT. WILLIAM C. BARNEY
TAIL GUNNER	SGT. ROBERT J. STOCK
SCIENTISTS,	LAWRENCE H. JOHNSTON
OBSERVERS	WALTER GOODMAN
	JESSE KUPFERBERG
OFFICIAL N.Y. TIMES REPORTER	WILLIAM LAURENCE

BIG STINK, 40-M0-44-27354, V-90	PHOTO AIRCRAFT
COMMANDER	MAJ. JAMES I. HOPKINS, JR.
PILOT	2ND LT. JOHN E. CANTLON
NAVIGATOR	2ND LT. STANLEY G. STEINKE
BOMBARDIER	2ND LT. MYRON FARYNA
FLIGHT ENGINEER	M/SGT. GEORGE L. BRABENEC
ASST. FLIGHT ENGR.	SGT. THOMAS A. BUNTING
RADIO	SGT. FRANCIS X. DOLAN
RADAR	CPL. RICHARD F. CANNON
TAIL GUNNER	SGT. MARTIN C. MURRAY
SCIENTISTS,	WILLIAM G. PENNEY (BRITISH)
OBSERVERS	GRP. CAPT. G. LEONARD CHESHIRE RAF (BRITISH)

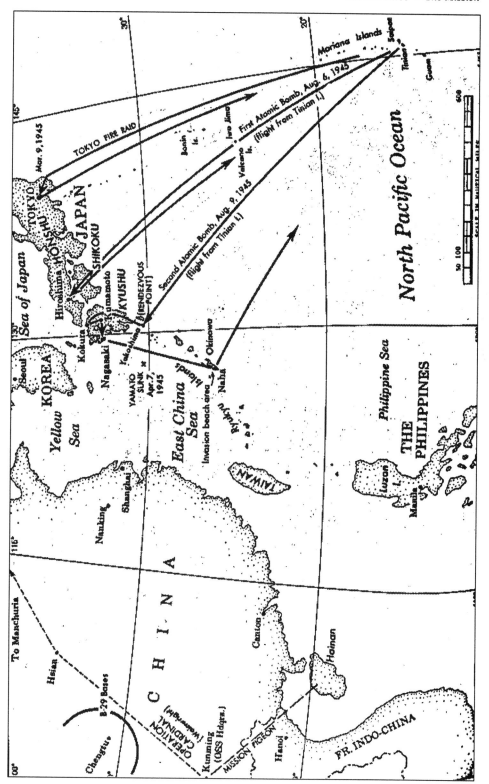

1945 — North Field, Tinian Island. Lt. Morris R. Jeppson, Weapons Test Officer and assistant to Navy Captain Parsons Weaponeer on the B-29 "Enola Gay" Hiroshima Mission.

1945 — North Field, Tinian Island. Lt. Phillip Barnes, Weapon Test Officer, monitored the little black box hooked up to the "Fat Man" Bomb in the front bomb bay of the "Bockscar" on the Nagasaki Mission. He never left his responsibility through out the mission. Photo courtesy of Leon Smith.

In 1993, while visiting the Air Force Museum in Dayton, Ohio, I posed beside an exact replica of "Fat Man." I'm 5'10" so you can see how huge this weapon was. (Photo courtesy of Ray Simak, U.S. Air Force, Ret)

Chapter Fourteen

"RENDEZVOUS"

09:10

Reached rendezvous point at 09:10, Aug. 9. Bock is in sight and is joining up. Hopkins nowhere in sight. We'll circle rendezvous for 15 minutes — he may come.

I'm sure everyone was fully awake by the time we reached our rendezvous location — Yakushima Island. The weather was excellent, with the sun was coming up behind us.There was clear visibility with scattered, puffy white cumulus clouds scattered like cotton balls across the sky below us.

Jim Van Pelt had hit our rendezvous right on the nose, which was excellent navigation through the stormy night from Tinian, now 1,500 miles away. I was then— and am today — amazed at how our navigators could guide a B-29 over all that ocean to an almost invisible island. Remarkable!

Sweeney took over the controls and flew us up to our assigned bombing altitude of 30,000-feet. I stayed out of the way, mostly standing between Sweeney and Albury. There was a great deal of activity at this time in the cockpit. Kuharek was fine-tuning the four engines for this altitude and Van Pelt was giving new headings. Although we were on strict radio silence, Spitzer was busy scanning his radio. We didn't want to miss any messages about weather conditions over Kokura and Nagasaki from McKnight or Marquardt, who by this time should have been in position over those cities.

"Bockscar" was put into a gentle circle around the tiny dot below that was Yakushima Island. In about three or four minutes, "The Great Artiste" appeared off our wing. It was very strange to see our own B-29 beside us.

Every member of the crew not busy with other duties, including Commander Ashworth, took up a vigil at every available window looking for Major Hopkins in the photographic aircraft.

The harder we looked, the more exasperated we became. The minutes went by — five, ten, fifteen. Still no Hopkins. And we could not break radio silence to locate him!

I remember Kuharek talking to Sweeney and Albury about this time, but this was not unusual since the Flight Engineer had to keep the aircraft commander up-to-date on gasoline consumption, engine performance, and the general status of the aircraft.

With "The Great Artiste" at our side, we orbited Yakushima. Again and again. And then again! Every one on "Bockscar" had heard Colonel Tibbets' orders: Wait fifteen minutes. No longer than fifteen minutes. Then head for the target.

During this circling, I don't recall exactly when, we received radio messages from both McKnight and Marquardt. Both Kokura and Nagasaki had cloud cover, but the visibility was sufficient for visual bombing. The report for Nagasaki also said we might expect increased cloudiness as the day went on.

09:50

Hoppy still hasn't arrived. We can't wait any longer. Our gas is going fast at this altitude and pulling this power setting (38-23-1/2). Going to IP with Bock.

At last, after more than 45 minutes, Sweeney swung "Bockscar" in the direction of Kokura. Major Hopkins was out there somewhere in the bright sunlight, but we never saw him.

To this day, I don't know why Hopkins never showed up. One story has it that he was above us at 35,000 feet, but at that altitude he would have run through so much gas he would have been unable to hold such an altitude for an extended period of time. Therefore, I tend to discount this particular version of the "missing third aircraft" of our mission.

No one wants to talk about it today at our reunions, and certainly it is not for me to challenge Hopkins' ability as a pilot or the expertise of his navigator. Both were superb at their jobs.

However, all I know is that two of us found the proper rendezvous island off the coast of Japan that early August 9th morning, and flew together to Kokura.

Although I and undoubtedly most of the other members of the crew didn't know it at the time, the extra thirty minutes in orbit around Yakushima cost us clear, visual bombing conditions over Kokura, our primary target. During those critical minutes, the sky over Kokura, which Captain George Marquardt had radioed was "clear, with broken light clouds," became obscured by smoke and cloud cover.

These were the crucial fifty minutes (50) that saved Kokura from destruction and placed Nagasaki forever in the history books.

Chapter Fifteen

"KOKURA"

10:20

Hit IP on nose — Jim is doing a good job, but our gas is still something to worry about — weather report from weather ships claims clear weather.

10:40

Target in sight but 7/10 clouds coverage — Bomb must be dropped visually but I don't think our chances are very good.

11:30

Made 3 runs on Kokura but couldn't drop our bomb. These damn clouds sure are making us sweat. Some flak — no fighters — as yet. Gas damn low! Going on to our secondary - Nagasaki — our gas warrants one run visual or radar — it's now or never! Less than two hours of fuel left.

The hour we spent over Kokura, trying to drop "Fat Man," seemed to last an eternity.

When we arrived at our IP (our "Initial Point" for a bomb run), it did not take long for all of us to realize that dropping "Fat Man" visually with the Norden Bomb Sight was going to be a problem. In addition to heavy ground haze there was a great deal of smoke covering the city.

It was only after the mission that I learned the smoke came from fires burning in the city of Yawata, located several miles west of Kokura, and known as the Pittsburgh of Japan. Yawata had been fire-bombed earlier and was still ablaze. A slight breeze carried smoke from these fires right over the heart of Kokura. Apparently, the breeze came up after our weather plane left the area, because they never mentioned anything about smoke.

As we got into our first run, bomb bay doors open, Bombardier Kermit Beahan kept muttering about not being able to see the ground. Finally, about halfway through the run, he called out, "No drop. No drop!" The bomb bay doors banged shut.

Sweeney swung "Bockscar" around in a half-circle, opened the bomb bay doors, and started a second bomb run along a different heading. As we started the run, I noticed a few puffs of black smoke in the air below our 29,000 foot altitude. Anti-aircraft guns! The ack-ack exploded well below us, but I hoped the Japanese gunners didn't get lucky. Again, about halfway through the run, Beahan said, "No drop. No drop."

As Sweeney once again began to circle our B-29, there was a great deal of animated conversation in the cockpit area regarding what to do next. Our Flight Engineer, Kuharek, seemed to disagree with what Sweeney was planning, and even Navy Commander Ashworth got into the discussion. I didn't hear every word, but what I heard disturbed me — a lot!

It was then that I first learned what had kept us on the ground so long back at Tinian. Either Sweeney or Kuharek, I don't recall which, started talking about the fuel booster transfer pump not working. I was familiar with this machinery. It was the pump that transferred gas from the tanks in the rear bomb bay. This pump was out of commission — and Sweeney, Tibbets, Kuharek and others had known this before we started the mission.

Those extra 640 gallons of gas in our rear bomb bay might as well have been back at Tinian. We couldn't pump them into our wing tanks and then to our engines. I knew our B-29 used about 400 gallons of gas each hour; and after "ginning around" Yakushima for about 45 minutes, I was sure we didn't have sufficient fuel left to get us back to Tinian — maybe not even enough for an emergency landing on Iwo Jima or Okinawa.

But then, I wasn't the one making decisions.

Finally Sweeney and Ashworth agreed to make one last bomb run on Kokura and, if this one was unsuccessful, fly straight to Nagasaki, drop "Fat Man," and hope we had enough fuel to reach Okinawa.

I say "Sweeney and Ashworth" made the decision. As Aircraft Commander, Sweeney was in complete command of the airplane. However, Ashworth was in charge of the Atomic Bomb, which apparently gave him quite a bit of authority. I did not hear much of their private discussions. Some were quite heated, as I recall.

As we came up for our third bomb run on Kokura, it was obvious to all of us in the cockpit that we wouldn't be dropping the "Fat Man." The clouds and smoke were just too heavy. When Beahan said for the third time, "No drop. No drop," Sweeney just shrugged his shoulders and turned "Bockscar" away from Kokura. He asked Van Pelt for a new heading — to Nagasaki.

11:32

Reducing power to save gas — wonder if the Pacific will be cold? Our chances for ditching are — good!!!
Bomb MUST be dropped for more reasons than one — Hope it goes off! It'll be a hell of a lot of sweating for nothing if it doesn't.

11:40

Boys getting jittery. Can't blame them.

I think for the first time during our mission I became concerned about making it safely back to Tinian. And I don't think I was alone. What made it even more difficult for me was the fact that I didn't have much to do — there was no real physical activity in which to immerse myself.

Sweeney and Albury were busy flying. Kuharek was scrambling with his gas consumption charts and trying to squeeze extra miles for every gallon of gas we had left. Spitzer had his radio to monitor. Jim Van Pelt was bent over his navigation charts, figuring the most direct route to Nagasaki. Barnes had his blinking red light to worry about, while Ashworth moved back and forth from Van Pelt's desk to the cockpit where he kept up a running conversation with Sweeney.

I don't know what the other members of our crew in the rear compartment were thinking about. But I was thinking about running out of gas, and of "Fat Man" with its explosive power of 20,000 tons of TNT that was set to go off if we dropped below 5,000 feet!

Chapter Sixteen

A THOUSAND SUNS

OVER NAGASAKI

11:50

*Target 8 min. off. Clouds still over this target, too —
making a radar run — it's our last pass — hoping for a hole
to drop visual — Bombing run down to 190 (MPH) to save
gas.*

Ahead of us, 30,000 feet below, I saw the coastline and the harbor area of
Nagasaki, appearing and then disappearing below a thick layer of clouds. Like
Kokura a half hour earlier, Nagasaki was heavily shrouded with clouds — what
we called nine-tenths cloud cover. I remembered seeing the aerial photos at our
briefing. A small mountain, more like a high hill, ran up from the ocean, dividing
the city into at least two sections. But I couldn't see it. And, if I couldn't see it, I
was sure Beahan couldn't either.

Jim Van Pelt brought us straight to our destination from Kokura, flying
directly southwest, right over several Japanese fighter bases. (None bothered to
come up after us). And now, minutes away from the IP. Someone had to make a
decision. Beahan would not be able to get a sight on the IP with his Norden Bomb
Sight. And our orders were to drop the bomb visually only!

I remember thinking about what was going to happen next: we could
abort the mission and drop the atomic bomb in the ocean or bomb Nagasaki by
radar.

But our orders were so specific about bombing visually. We were not to
use radar on the bomb run. In addition, we had never really practiced radar bombing. Buckley and Van Pelt had used radar during our "navigational" training
flights to pin-point targets, but we had never actually dropped a "Pumpkin" using
this electronic marvel.

I doubted it would happen, but hoped someone would opt for radar.

There was a third option I didn't want to think about: take "Fat Man"
home. We would have to refuel at Okinawa, then fly home to Tinian. But what if

we didn't make it back to Okinawa? In that case, we definitely would have to drop the atomic bomb in the ocean and then "ditch" our B-29 in the water. If we ever made it back to Tinian, I could imagine the ranting and raving. "You did <u>what</u>? That bomb cost millions of dollars!"

This last option was full of problems. Too many things could go wrong. Could Commander Ashworth disconnect whatever he connected just before we went up to 17,000 feet? Could "Fat Man" withstand the jolts and shock of landing? I, for one, didn't want to find out.

What happened next in the cockpit has been a controversial subject for over fifty years. In many accounts of our bomb run over Nagasaki, various authors have put words into the mouths of Major Chuck Sweeney, Commander Ashworth and others.

The best I can do is report what I saw and heard, not what other people say occurred. And I certainly cannot, and will not, try to delve into Sweeney's or Ashworth's minds, nor comment on their motives. Both did what <u>they had to do</u>!

All I remember is Sweeney telling the crew to set up for a radar run on Nagasaki. That was enough for me.

I went back and stood beside Jim Van Pelt as he and Buckley began working together as a team at their individual radar scopes — Buckley in the rear, Van Pelt in the forward compartment. They knew where we were, but to this day I am amazed that they could locate our Aiming Point in the downtown section of Nagasaki, right at the harbor and its shipyards. It was fascinating to watch and listen as they talked back and forth with Sweeney, Albury and Beahan giving compass headings and orienting the aircraft to the AP (Aiming Point). Several times Commander Ashworth joined me and peered at Van Pelt's radar scope. The radar scopes of 1945 had a diameter of about five inches and you had to get very close to see anything. I don't recall him saying anything to me personally.

Most of the time I stood between Sweeney and Albury, peering down at the city of Nagasaki, hidden by clouds below us.

11:56

No change in cloud coverage — It's radar all the way
so far — still hoping for visual sight of target.
Hope these glasses do the trick!

We had been issued welders' goggles to shield our eyes from the atom bomb's bright glare. I put mine on. My crewmates, who had all been on the Hiroshima mission, had warned me that an atomic bomb really lit up the sky and could possibly blind someone not wearing protective glasses. I didn't want to take any chances, and I think most of the crew also put on their goggles.

11:58

Bombs away! Bee (Beahan) had a 45 sec. bomb run visually — hope it's in!

I think I actually jumped when I heard Kermit Beahan shout, "I see it! I see it!" Immediately Van Pelt and Buckley ended their radar bomb run and relinquished control of "Bockscar" to Beahan. In less than forty-five seconds, Beahan calculated the proper drift and fine-tuned the orientation of the aircraft toward the AP. He worked fast. A normal bomb run took anywhere from three to five minutes, he did it in forty-five seconds that day. I recognize that Van Pelt and Buckley with their radar had put him on the right course, but Beahan proved he was one of the best bombardiers in the Army Air Corps on August 9th. He also saved our necks by dropping "Fat Man" visually — as ordered!

At 11:58 Beahan shouted in his Texas drawl, "Bombs away! Uh, that's bomb away."

"Bockscar" suddenly leaped upwards as the 10,000 pound "Fat Man" dropped away and began its long, curving path down through the clouds. I braced myself as Sweeney turned left into our well-rehearsed 155 degree hard turn and dive. I started counting the seconds ... one, two, three, four ... After about 45 seconds I began to wonder if "Fat Man" was a dud.

Suddenly, the light of a thousand suns illuminated the cockpit.

Even with my dark welders' goggles, I winced and shut my eyes for a couple of seconds. I guessed we were about seven miles from "ground zero" and headed directly away from the target, yet the light blinded me for an instant. I had never experienced such an intense bluish light, maybe three or four times brighter than the sun shining above us.

A few seconds later, "Bockscar" was buffeted by three sharp shock waves, the first hit with far more force than the last. We had been told to expect shock waves — I felt three. The first one was quite severe, and the aircraft shook violently. For a moment I wondered if any damage had been done to our B-29. Thankfully it just gave us a real jolt, and all we could do at the time was to look at each other and hope there would be no structural damage to the aircraft. Neither of the next two shock waves were as violent as the first, they just shook us up a bit.

I looked at the altimeter. It read 28,500. We had dropped 1,000 feet from our bombing altitude of 29,500, which I distinctly remember because I looked at the altimeter a second time, trying to imprint on my memory the exact altitude from which we dropped "Fat Man." For some reason, I thought it important to remember the number.

I quickly took off my welders' goggles and looked out over Sweeney's shoulder as he brought "Bockscar" through the left turn.

Jim Van Pelt joined us in the cockpit where he could get a better view of the city below us, now invisible under rolling clouds and fire. Jim turned to me and said with a great deal of relief in his voice, "God, Fred. I almost dropped it. I almost dropped it." I'll never forget those words.

I could understand Jim's feelings about being the one who almost sent "Fat Man" on its course. Earlier on the mission to Hiroshima, he had seen first-hand what an atomic bomb did to a city. Now, he — not the Bombardier — had been within forty-five seconds of being the hand to send an atomic bomb on its way to cause the same kind of destruction. It was an unsettling thought for Jim. I, too, wondered about what was going on below us in that terrible fire storm. But I quickly put it out of my mind. Our job had been to drop "Fat Man," which we did, and now I firmly believed the Japanese would have to surrender. I thought to myself, maybe this atom bomb will end it. Not even Japan wants to have its cities destroyed this way!

12:01

I've never seen anything like it! Biggest explosion I've ever seen. Those poor Japs. But they asked for it.

This plume of smoke I'm seeing is hard to explain. A great white mass of flame is seething within the white mushroom shaped cloud. It has a pinkish, salmon color. The base is black and is breaking a little way down from the mushroom.

12:04

Still circling plume of smoke. Damn thing is getting too close for comfort. It's goodbye if we're ever engulfed in it!

There have been many descriptions of what an atomic cloud looks like and I think all of them do justice to the sight. Some have said it must be like looking into hell, and maybe they're right. To me, the boiling pink, black and white multi-colored cloud was — awesome. That's the best word I can think of to describe it. It reached our bombing altitude in a matter of fifty seconds.

Although we were very low on gas, Sweeney kept "Bockscar" in a gentle left turn and began to circle the mushroom cloud. Our own aircraft, "The Great Artiste," which had dropped instruments attached to parachutes at the same instant we dropped "Fat Man," came up beside us on our right wing. Together we circled the mushroom cloud that quickly was boiling its way up to our altitude and then continued to climb into the noon sky to a height of 50 or 60,000 feet.

As we looked down, trying to see through the swirling smoke and fires that covered the city of Nagasaki, I heard Gallagher shout a warning over the intercom. The mushroom cloud was coming right at us. I immediately looked up and could see that he was right, the cloud <u>was</u> getting close to "Bockscar." We had been told <u>not</u> to fly through the atomic cloud because it was extremely dangerous to the crew and aircraft. Knowing this, Sweeney put "Bockscar" into a steep dive to the right, away from the cloud, throttles wide open. For a few moments we could not tell if we were out-running the ominous cloud or if it was gaining on us, but gradually we pulled away from the dangerous radioactive cloud before it engulfed us, much to everyone's relief. Had this occurred, I would not be writing this book. In time, the dangerous cloud would have done in the entire crew on board, causing death by radiation poisoning.

Sweeney turned south, away from Nagasaki. We had done our job. The "Fat Man" had exploded as planned, and had devastated a city with a force equal to 20,000 tons of TNT. We would have to wait for a photo reconnaissance plane to tell us how much damage had been done. But that could wait.

Right now, it was time to head for Okinawa and then Tinian.

"Thousand Suns Over Nagasaki"

12 December '84

A NOTE FROM: Kermit K. Beahan

Thoughts Concerning the Nagasaki A-Bomb Mission

August 9, 1945 is a day which I shall never forget, for it was the date on which I flew aboard the B-29 aircraft "Bocks Car" as the Bombardier on the second atomic bomb mission during World War II. Our takeoff from North Field on Tinian, a small island in the Marianas group in the W. Pacific, was uneventful. However, while climbing enroute to Japan, our Flight Engineer advised, that due to a fuel pump failure, 500 gallons of fuel in the rear bomb bay was trapped. At the time this did not seem to be a problem as the flight plan indicated that ample fuel would still be available. We proceeded to our rendezvous point, a small island off of the coast of Japan, where we effected a rendezvous with the instrumentation aircraft almost immediately - but we could not link up with the photographic aircraft both of which were to accompany us over the target. We circled the island for some length of time, consuming considerable fuel in the process. It was decided to proceed with the flight without the photographic aircraft. As

A NOTE FROM: Kermit K. Beahan

we approached what had been selected as the primary target, Kokura, site of the largest arsenal in Japan, to our dismay the target was completely obscured by clouds and industrial haze. We had strict orders that the bomb _must_ be released under visual conditions, that is, that the Bombardier must be able to sight the target through his bombsight. In any attempt to fulfill this requirement, we made three approaches to the target from different directions hoping to sight the target from a different angle of view. But to no avail -- fuel supply was now becoming a matter of concern. We proceeded to take a direct course to the secondary target, Nagasaki Japan. Enroute it was determined that only enough fuel remained for only one bomb run. Visibility over the Nagasaki area was very poor -- 8 to 9 tenths of cloud coverage prevailed. The decision was made that, if necessary, we would drop the bomb by radar in spite of the edict stipulating visual release only, as we had insufficient fuel to return the bomb to our home base

A NOTE FROM: Kermit K. Beahan

We proceeded on the bomb run under radar control until about 20 to 30 seconds from bomb release when I saw a hole developing in the clouds over the target area. I took over control of the bomb run and selected an aiming point in the industrial valley in Nagasaki. Fortunately the radar team had made an excellent initial bomb approach, and in the very brief time remaining I was able to synchronize the cross-hairs of the bomb sight on the target and released the bomb visually with "good" results being achieved. It was as if a great weight had been lifted from our shoulders since we did succeed in following the order "visual drop only!" Fuel was now critical and we made a bee line to our emergency landing site in Okinawa -- we had enough fuel left for one landing attempt. We landed OK and as we taxied up to the airfield ramp both outboard engines sputtered to a stop -- fuel starvation! It was really a "sweat job". After we finally returned to Tinian after being debriefed did I realize it was my 27th Birthday - We celebrate into the night.

Kermit K. Beahan
Bombardier - Nagasaki 9 Aug 1945

C
O
P
Y

WAR DEPARTMENT
CLASSIFIED MESSAGE CENTER
INCOMING CLASSIFIED MESSAGE

TOP SECRET
URGENT

From: CG, 313th Bomber Wing, Tinian

To: War Department

Nr: APCOM 5479   9 August 1945

T0.Groves personal from Farrell APCOM 5479 TOPSEC.

Strike and accompanying airplanes have returned to Tinian. Ashworth's message from Okinawa nr 44 is confirmed by all observers. Cloud cover was bad at strike and it will be necessary to await photographs to give exact point of strike and damage. Strike plane had barely enough fuel to reach Okinawa.

After listening to the accounts one gets the impression of a supremely tough job carried out with determination, sound judgement and great skill. It is fortunate for the success of the mission that its leaders, Ashworth and the pilot Sweeney were men of stamina and stout heart. Weaker men could not have done this job. Ashworth's small doubts reflected in his first strike report were resolved after checking at Okinawa with crews and observers from all 3 planes. He now feels confident that the bomb was satisfactorily placed and that it did its job well. Some detailed observations follow:

An observing plane reported that 20 minutes after explosion the southern edge of cloud was tangent to north and of Nagasaki harbor with southeastern part of city visible. There were scattered fires on west side of Nagasaki harbor. Boats were seen in harbor. Top mushroom of cloud broke off in a manner similar to cloud at Hiroshima.

CM-IN-9254   (9 Aug 45)

TOP SECRET

Chapter Seventeen

MAY DAY! MAY DAY!

12:06

We're on our way to Okinawa. It'll be close but I think we're in.
Sure hope so!

Jim Van Pelt once more turned to his charts and gave Major Chuck Sweeney a course for Okinawa and its Yonton airfield. Sweeney throttled back our B-29 engines and put "Bockscar" on the step — the maneuver we had practiced so many times before at Wendover — designed to obtain maximum range using a minimum amount of fuel. Sweeney, Kuharek and Albury were in constant communication as they figured out the speed, gas consumption, wind direction — all the calculations necessary for us to make it to Okinawa. I helped double-check their numbers. We could not afford a mistake.

Soon after we cleared the Japanese coastline, Sweeney told our radioman, Spitzer, to contact the "air-sea rescue" ships he knew had taken up positions between Japan and Okinawa. There was no response. Unknown to us, they had left their "stations" in the belief we were already half-way back to Tinian. I'll never know if they had left their positions, but I sure know we needed them if we had to "ditch" in the sea because of running out of gas.

For the first time in my brief flying career, I tightened up my "Mae West" life preserver jacket, wondering if it would work. I also started to rehearse in my mind our "ditching" procedures if we ended up in the ocean that was gradually getting closer and closer as we neared Okinawa.

13:00

Okinawa in sight. Passed over Ie Shima where Pyle was killed. Gas is low but we're sure of making Oki. Still 20 min. out —

As we neared Okinawa, Sweeney radioed Yonton airfield asking for emergency clearance to land. I only heard his end of the conversation, but his actions told me what was happening at the other end. <u>There was no reply</u>! He kept trying time after time to contact the Yonton tower before our gas was used up.

Our situation was critical. Kuharek told Sweeney, "Major, we're just about out. There's nothing left in the tanks!"

I think everyone in "Bockscar" started to sweat. This was a real emergency, and far more frightening than anything that had happened thus far on the mission.

Sweeney radioed his message three or four times. No response. We could hear the control tower talking to other planes over the field asking for landing instructions. They were in a landing pattern off the end of what we could see was the "active" runway. One by one, they were landing. Abe Spitzer checked his radio to make sure we were using the right frequency. We were.

By this time, Sweeney had brought "Bockscar" directly into the landing pattern where several B-24's circled, waiting their turn to land. Our altitude was about 1,000 feet. Either we landed on this runway at Yonton, or landed in the ocean which was directly off to the side of the runway.

13:20

Over Yon Ton but couldn't reach tower on V.H.F. There's heavy traffic but we're going in — we've got to — we have no choice — Firing all our flares to let them know we're coming in regardless.

Suddenly Sweeney turned to me and yelled, "Olivi! Start firing the flares. I'm declaring a "May Day!" We've got to get on the ground!" I didn't ask questions. And I didn't waste any time. I turned to the storage bin containing the flare gun and flares. It was located about two feet from where I stood. I grabbed the flare gun and took out a flare marked "Red." It meant "Wounded on board."

The procedure for firing a flare out of a B-29 was something we had all been trained to do back at Wendover. However, we had just <u>practiced</u> opening up the small, round hatch in the ceiling behind the pilot and co-pilot. We had practiced opening the flare gun, inserting a flare into the barrel, and finally pushing the gun up into the hole. But we never fired a real flare. It was considered too dangerous. We just rehearsed the procedure. But this was no rehearsal. This time I was doing it *for real!*

I grabbed the box of flares and held it steady between my feet. As soon as the "red" flare was fired, I reached down for another. To this day, I have no idea, other than that first one, which colors I fired. It was: stick the gun in the hole, fire, remove, reload — as fast as I could. Red — blue — pink — green — yellow — white — all the colors of the rainbow. One after the other.

The cockpit soon filled with smoke as I fired flare after flare into the afternoon sky. Some of the smoke reached the rear compartment of the airplane through the tunnel, causing great concern. Jake Beser thought we were on fire and wanted to know what was happening. I didn't really notice the choking sounds around me, I was concentrating on not "fouling up." In the back of my mind were gruesome stories of flares exploding in the cockpit and causing a fire and serious injuries to the crew. I went as fast as I could, but was careful to be sure to get the flare gun <u>locked</u> into the port hole <u>before</u> I pulled the trigger. I think I got off eight or ten flares warning those in the air around us, and on the ground, of our situation on board "Bockscar."

"Bockscar" must have looked like a flying Roman Candle as Sweeney swung on to the approach for a landing, cutting out other aircraft already on the approach for the active runway.

13:30

Landed just as No. 2 conked. We didn't get here a moment too soon. Landing was hot (150 MPH) Thought sure we were going to take a couple of B-24's with us after landing.

A B-29 is supposed to land at about 120 miles an hour. Sweeney hit the runway at 150! He was about one third of the way down the runway when we flared out and our tires hit. When the nose wheel came down and we were level to the ground, I could see that we were not properly oriented on the runway. We were veering to the left ; on the left side of the runway were parked B-24's. Sweeney hit the brakes and reversed the propellers, and somehow brought "Bockscar" back on line as we raced past the B-24's, gradually slowing down. We weren't in the middle of the runway, but we were straight.

The end of the runway was suddenly upon us. Our ground speed was still "hot," but Sweeney hit the brakes hard and turned into the taxi strip. It wasn't a "ground loop" and it wasn't pretty, but we were on the ground in one piece!

As we made the turn from the active runway, our inboard engine #2 twirled to a stop. No gas!

For several moments no one said a word. I think we were all caught up in our own thoughts about how close we had come to a fatal disaster. It was obvious to everyone in the cockpit area that Sweeney's skill as a pilot, and the use of the new reversible propellers, had saved our lives.

We soon were surrounded with fire trucks and various other "crash wagons" which had been alerted by our flares. (Someone had seen them!) A Jeep with a "Follow Me" sign appeared, we followed it to a hardstand, and switched off the other three engines.

Before we left the aircraft, I distinctly remember Sweeney saying, "Let's not mention where we came from or <u>anything</u> about what we did. They're not supposed to know anything about it. We're just a B-29 looking for gas to get home after a mission." Those may not have been his exact words, but he was very specific about maintaining security.

Later —
Hoppy and Bock are here too — orders from base —
guess they want us all together. Can't say much for Okinawa
— mud — heat — wrecked planes both ours and Japs. Going
to have some chow, while we gas up.
Ate Spam as I expected but it tasted good at that.
Cheshire, Jim and I sat at same table. Cheshire is very likable
in spite of being English. After dinner we walked back with
Cheshire. Told me all about Lancasters and Sterlings. He
seemed amazed at the speed of our 29 at high altitude — best
plane he says. That mission of his bombing the big dam in
Germany was no picnic either.

As soon as we climbed down from "Bockscar" we were asked a lot of questions by GI's who completely surrounded the plane. "How come you're here? How fast could the aircraft go? How high does it fly, etc., etc., etc." Lots of questions. I think most of them were in awe of the big B-29 since, apparently, it was the first B-29 that had ever landed at Okinawa. This made sense since Iwo Jima was the normal emergency field for B-29's. We just said we were out of gas after a mission and on our way back to Tinian.

We were hungry. A truck drove up and we got in, asking the driver to take us to the Mess Hall. I recall that Kuharek, and perhaps Gallagher too, stayed behind to handle the refueling and security. No one was permitted to get too close to "Bockscar," not until Colonel Tibbets changed his orders.

After we had washed up and relaxed a few minutes, we were joined by members of Bock's and Hopkins' crews who had landed soon after us. Both aircraft had not had any problems. Maybe all our flares and our "controlled crash landing" had alerted the Yonton control tower to the fact there were B-29's in the area.

Jim Van Pelt and two other men who happened to be from England — Professor William Penney, a professor of Applied Mathematics at London University, who was working with our scientists at Los Alamos, and Group Captain Leonard Cheshire of the Royal Air Force and winner of the Victoria Cross, Britain's highest award for valor, and a member of the British Military Mission to Tinian — joined me in the chow line. Penney and Cheshire were observers on Hopkins' B-29 which had stationed itself between Kokura and Nagasaki in hopes of joining up with us. Hopkins and his crew saw the towering mushroom cloud over Nagasaki and flew there, arriving over the city after we left. They took pictures, then radioed Tinian for orders. Tinian told them to head for Okinawa, re-fuel, and join us on the flight back to our home base.

I quickly found out that Cheshire was a high ranking officer, equivalent to a Colonel in the U. S. Army Air Corps. He had seen a lot of action with the British Bomber Command and led many dangerous missions over Germany. He was fascinated by our B-29 bombers, and said it performed at high altitudes and speeds not obtained by the British. He said he was totally surprised how our B-29 could operate at 30,000 feet.

Professor Penney didn't say what he did, only that he was a scientist working with our scientists at Los Alamos. I had heard of Los Alamos after the Hiroshima mission but had no idea what was done there. In fact, we did not talk about atoms or bombs, nor about our mission to Nagasaki. Our conversation was about American B-29's, and British Lancasters and Sterling bombers.

One of the Mess Hall's GI servers, noticing we were transients (not stationed at Yonton), said he had just learned the war was going to end — "real soon." He had it on good authority that a second bomb had been dropped on Japan and that the plane dropping the bomb was based here, at Yonton. The GI was excited. He said the bomb was the size of a golf ball and had been carried to Japan in a P-38 fighter.

I don't know how we managed not laughing out loud, but none of us even cracked a smile. We just nodded agreement and said something like, "Oh, is that right? That's great! Maybe it will end this war quicker." I think Professor Penney was very amused. I don't know where or how that GI got his information. *(I've always wondered if a crew member from one of our B-29's had provided him with this fantastic story as a joke, but I don't think I'll ever learn the answer.)*

Van Pelt, Cheshire, Penney and I walked back to our B-29's. The exercise felt good.

17:30

Gassed and ready for take off. It's our last lap home.

20:30

Everything going okay. No trouble so far. It's been a long trip. Continuing on course — three more hours till landfall.

23:25

Tinian in sight. It's a good feeling. Awfully tired now

I don't recall much in the way of chit-chat on our flight back to Tinian. I'm sure each of us was deep in his own thoughts. I don't think any of us had any regrets. We had done the job we were trained to do: fly an atomic bomb nicknamed "Fat Man" to a targeted city in the Japanese Empire, drop it, then return to our home base on Tinian.

It had been a very long day, and a very long and harrowing mission.

Certainly, it was a flight none of us wanted to repeat, but it wasn't over yet. Not until we landed at Tinian.

23:30

Landed okay. People here were a bit worried about us. Reports on raid are good. Tinian looks good. Real tired, but happy to be home safe.

This is the last entry in my diary. It marks the end of a momentous adventure for me. I had been a last minute addition to my own crew that flew someone else's B-29 on what turned out to be a very dangerous, yet successful, mission. I was glad it was over. I hoped we had helped end the war!

Our reception on Tinian, late at night on August 9th, was very different from Colonel Tibbets' return from Hiroshima the afternoon of August 6th, when he was awarded the Distinguished Service Cross for the Hiroshima mission by General Spaatz, and large crowds of well-wishers greeted the "Enola Gay."

Our arrival was met with very subdued enthusiasm, with a crowd made up primarily of our ground crews who exhibited great relief and joy on seeing us again. Yes, the generals and admirals were there, and they, too, exhibited general satisfaction that our mission had been a success. But there was no "hoopla" other than a lot of jokes and congratulations to Kermit Beahan. He had turned 27 on August 9th! What a birthday present!

An Air Corps staff photographer lined us up in front of the left wing and took a flash photo in the dark. When it was time for him to shoot the picture, I looked around and discovered that Commander Ashworth and Lt. Barnes were not present. I had no idea where they had disappeared to, but they are not in that first photograph.

Another was taken the two days later. All thirteen men who were on "Bockscar" were present, including Ashworth, Barnes and Beser. I think it was this latter photograph that was released to newspapers back in the States.

No one was aware that we had thirteen men aboard "Bockscar" until we lined up for the photo.

After the picture-taking session, we got in a truck that delivered us to the Quonset hut where our debriefing took place. This went fairly rapidly. Sweeney, Albury, Beahan, Van Pelt and I made our reports. The Intelligence officers asked questions, and got answers from the entire crew on board "Bockscar."

After the debriefing, I walked to the Mess Hall. After eating my first real meal in twenty-four hours, I headed for my quarters; but not before I asked Jim Van Pelt if I could borrow the Flight Log which I used to help recreate a minute-by-minute record of our mission.

Then I went to bed. It was almost 04:00 — 4:00 AM, and very late even for me.

HEADQUARTERS 509TH COMPOSITE GROUP
Office of the Group Combat Intelligence Officer
APO 247, c/o PM San Francisco, California

FINAL REPORT

1. MISSION NO. 16   DATE 9 Aug 19 45

2. TARGET ATTACKED: Nagasaki –

3. TIME OF TAKE OFF: First 081749 Z   Last 081751 Z

4. NUMBER OF AIRCRAFT AIRBORNE: 3

5. BOMB DATA:
        a. Bomb Load and Type: Special

            (1) Fusing: Special

        b. Disposition:
            3 Secondary – Nagasaki Urban Area
            A/C V77
                 V89
                 V90

        c. Method of Bombing: Visual X   Radar

        d. Time Bombs Away: First090158 Z   Last 090201Z

6. WEATHER: 7/8/10 Alto Cumulus. Bombed through hole

7. PRESSURE ALTITUDE: 28,900 feet

8. ENEMY AIR OPPOSITION: Nil

9. ENEMY ANTI-AIRCRAFT: A/C – V77 reports about 15 bursts from Yawata
   area all low – also 8 bursts level at 6 o'clock. MEAGER

10. OBSERVATIONS. 1 - large ship in Harbor at Nagasaki, numerous smaller
vessels in same area.

4 - R/SE at (35°15'N-132°00'E) low, circling

13 - U/SE at (30°25'N-130°38'E) 12 silver in color, 1 off color - 2 miles
east at 12/15,000 feet.

Near Sendai, SE coast of Kyushu, smoke was seen, very much like that observed
when special bomb explodes - intensity maintained until out of sight.

11. BOMBING RESULTS: Fair to Good

12. TIME OF LANDING: First 091306 Z Last 091339 Z

13. OTHER SIGNIFICANT INFORMATION:
90% of run was radar - Bombardier took over and made visual corrections in
last 10%. Bomb hit apporximately 500 feet so. of Mitsubishi Plant. Companion
ship observed after explosing, large whit smoke ring formed, red ball of fire,
covering ½ of area. Then column of smoke formed ½ mile wide, funneling upward
bottom dark brown in color, center amber color, top white. Column rose to
50,000 feet, rising to 30,000 feet in 1½ to 2 minutes. Many small bright
fires observed. Considerable smoke observed 175miles from area. Five shock
felt.

14. MISSION: Mission Effective.

A/C Victor 83 - stood by at Iwo Jima for emergency, but was not called
upon, returning this base 090910Z.

A/C Victor - 77 - 89-90 landed at Okinawa 090400 Z / 090404 Z, short of gas
took-off at 090703 Z / 090706 Z

TOP SECRET

10 AUGUST 1945

REPORTS

CONGENUSASTAF GUAM

INFO: CONGENUSASTAF (READ) WASH (URGENT) ATTN: GENERAL HORSTAD
INFO: 58MG 313 FOR 509TH GROUP (SAME PRECEDENCE AS ACTION)
AIMCR __5480__ SUBJECT IS CREW OBSERVATIONS FROM RECONNAISSANCE
PLANE ON CENTERBOARD 509TH SBM 16, FLOWN 9 AUGUST 1945.
APPROACH TO NAGASAKI BY PECCO PLANE WAS FROM THE SOUTH AT
32,000 FEET ALTITUDE. COLUMN OF SMOKE EXTENDED TO AN ESTIMATED
ALTITUDE OF 19,000 FEET WITH BLACK SMOKE COVERING MOST OF THE
CITY. APPROXIMATELY 20 LARGE FIRES WERE SEEN THROUGH THE SMOKE
IN THE CITY AREA WITH THE GREATEST CONCENTRATIONS IN AND AROUND
AIMING POINT LOCATED AT 113061 ON LITHOMOSAIC, NAGASAKI AREA,
MITSUBISHI STEEL AND ARMS WORKS, TARGET NO. 90.38-546. LARGE
EXPLOSIONS WERE VISIBLE AT APPROXIMATELY 084071 AND 094079 AS
RECCO PLANE PASSED OVER TARGET AT 090522 ZEBRA. NO APPARENT
DAMAGE TO INSTALLATIONS ON SOUTHWEST SIDE OF HARBOR AND TO THREE
LARGE AND THREE SMALL VESSELS ANCHORED IN HARBOR. CLOUDS AND
SMOKE IN THE NORTHERN AREA OF CITY PREVENTED FURTHER OBSERVATIONS.
NO TURBULENCE ENCOUNTERED OVER TARGET.

TOP SECRET

10 AUGUST 1945

REPORTS 091848 Z

X

X

COMGENUSASTAF GUAM

INFO: COMGENUSASTAF (REAR) WASH (URGENT) ATTN: GENERAL NORSTAD
AIMCR 5482 SUBJECT: FINAL REPORT, 509TH SBM 16, STRIKE
CENTERBOARD, FLOWN 9 AUGUST 1945.

1. TARGET ATTACKED: NAGASAKI

2. TIME TAKE OFF: FIRST: 081749Z LAST: 081751Z

3. NUMBER A/C AIRBORNE: 3

4. BOMB LOAD DATA: A. LOAD AND TYPE: SPECIAL

   B. FUSING: SPECIAL

   C. DISPOSITION: 3 SECONDARY NAGASAKI URBAN AREA

                   A/C VICTOR 77, VICTOR 89, VICTOR 90

5. METHOD OF BOMBING: VISUAL

6. TIME BOMBS AWAY: FIRST: 090158Z LAST: 090201Z

. WEATHER: 7-10/10 ALTO CUMULUS. BOMBED THROUGH HOLE.

. PRESSURE ALTITUDE: 28,000 FEET.

. ENEMY AIR OPPOSITION: NONE

TOP SECRET

11. OBSERVATIONS: 1 LARGE SHIP IN HARBOR AREA AT NAGASAKI, NUMEROUS SMALLER VESSELS IN SAME AREA. 4 UNIDENTIFIED SINGLE ENGINE AT 33/15 N 132/00 E, LOW, CIRCLING. 13 UNIDENTIFIED S/E AT 30/25 N 130/38 E, 12 SILVER IN COLOR, 1 OFF COLOR, 2 MILES EAST AT 12-15,000 FEET. NEAR SENDAI, SE COAST OF KYUSHU SMOKE WAS SEEN, VERY MUCH LIKE THAT OBSERVED WHEN SPECIAL BOMB EXPLODES, INTENSITY MAINTAINED TILL OUT OF SIGHT.

12. BOMBING RESULTS: FAIR TO GOOD.

13. TIME OF LANDING: FIRST: 091306Z   LAST: 091339Z.

14. OTHER SIGNIFICANT INFORMATION: 90 PERCENT OF RUN WAS RADAR, BOMBARDIER TOOK OVER AND MADE VISUAL CORRECTIONS IN LAST 10 PERCENT. BOMB HIT APPROXIMATELY 500 FEET SOUTH OF MITSUBISHI PLANT. COMPANION SHIP OBSERVED. AFTER EXPLOSION LARGE WHITE SMOKE RING FORMED, RED BALL OF FIRE COVERING 1/2 OF AREA. THEN COLUMN OF SMOKE FORMED 1/2 MILE WIDE, FUNNELING UPWARD, BOTTOM DARK BROWN IN COLOR, CENTER AMBER COLOR, TOP WHITE. COLUMN ROSE TO 50,000 FEET, RISING TO 30,000 FEET IN ONE AND ONE HALF TO TWO MINUTES. MANY SMALL BRIGHT FIRES OBSERVED. CONSIDERABLE SMOKE OBSERVED 175 MILES FROM AREA. FIVE SHOCK WAVES FELT.

15. MISSION EFFECTIVE.

16. REMARKS: A/C VICTOR 83 STOOD BY AT IWO JIMA FOR EMERGENCY BUT WAS NOT CALLED UPON, RETURNING THIS BASE 090910Z. A/C VICTOR 77, 89, AND 90 LANDED OKINAWA 090400Z - 090404Z, SHORT OF GAS, TOOK OFF 090703Z - 090706Z.

END...

TOP SECRET

WEATHER CAUSING DELAY IN RECEIPT OF PHOTOGRAPHY. ESTIMATE PRELIMINARY
DAMAGE ASSESSMENT REPORT READY AT 092100 ZEBRA DEPENDING UPON QUALITY
AND COVERAGE OF PHOTOGRAPHY.
END...

Crew Combat Missions
393rd Bombardment Squadron (VE) 509th Composite Group North Field, Tinian
July - August 1945
Supplied by Richard H. Campbell, 509th Historian

Crew	Msn	Date	Acft	Airplane Commander	Function	Target Area	Note
A-1	4	20 Jul	298	Taylor	Pumpkin	Toyama	
	5	24 Jul	298	Taylor	Pumpkin	Niihama	
	9	26 Jul	298	Taylor	Pumpkin	Yalzu	
	10	29 Jul	298	Taylor	Pumpkin	Ube	
	13	06 Aug	298	Taylor	Weather	Nagasaki	
	16	09 Aug	298	Taylor	Backup	Iwo Jima	1

A-2 No combat missions were flown by Crew A-2

Crew	Msn	Date	Acft	Airplane Commander	Function	Target Area	Note
A-3	4	20 Jul	299	Devore	Pumpkin	Toyama	
	5	24 Jul	299	Devore	Pumpkin	Niihama	
	9	26 Jul	303	Devore	Pumpkin	Osaka	
	14	08 Aug	299	Devore	Pumpkin	Abort	2
	17	14 Aug	299	Devore	Pumpkin	Nagoya	
A-4	6	24 Jul	300	Westover	Pumpkin	Robe	
	8	26 Jul	302	Westover	Pumpkin	Taira	
	14	08 Aug	300	Westover	Pumpkin	Tsuruga	
	17	14 Aug	300	Westover	Pumpkin	Nagoya	
A-5	3	20 Jul	354	Classen	Pumpkin	Nagaoka	
	8	26 Jul	354	Classen	Pumpkin	Hitachi	
	12	29 Jul	304	Smith	Pumpkin	Wakayama	
	-	09 Aug	346	Classen	-	To U.S.	3
B-6	3	20 Jul	303	Wilson	Pumpkin	Taira	
	10	29 Jul	303	Wilson	Pumpkin	Ube	
	13	06 Aug	303	Wilson	Weather	Kokura	
	14	08 Aug	303	Wilson	Pumpkin	Uwajima	
	-	09 Aug	303	Wilson	-	To U.S.	3
B-7	4	20 Jul	296	Price	Pumpkin	Toyama	
	7	24 Jul	296	Price	Pumpkin	Ogaki	
	9	26 Jul	296	Price	Pumpkin	Shimoda	
	15	08 Aug	296	Price	Pumpkin	Yokkaichi	
	17	14 Aug	296	Price	Pumpkin	Nagoya	
B-8	1	20 Jul	302	McKnight	Pumpkin	Otsu	
	7	24 Jul	302	McKnight	Pumpkin	Yokkaichi	
	10	29 Jul	302	McKnight	Pumpkin	Ube	
	13	06 Aug	354	McKnight	Backup	Iwo Jima	4
	16	09 Aug	347	McKnight	Weather	Nagasaki	
	18	14 Aug	302	McKnight	Pumpkin	Roroma	

Crew	Msn	Date	Acft	Airplane Commander	Function	Target Area	Note
B-9	6	24 Jul	292	Lewis	Pumpkin	Kobe	
	9	26 Jul	292	Lewis	Pumpkin	Nagoya	
	11	29 Jul	353	Lewis	Pumpkin	Koriyama	
	13	06 Jul	292	Tibbets	Little Boy	Hiroshima	5
	14	08 Aug	304	Lewis	Pumpkin	Tokushima	
B-10	1	20 Jul	304	Marquardt	Pumpkin	Taira	
	9	26 Jul	304	Marquardt	Pumpkin	Hamamatsu	
	13	06 Aug	291	Marquardt	Photo	Hiroshima	
	16	09 Aug	304	Marquardt	Weather	Kokura	
C-11	1	20 Jul	301	Eatherly	Pumpkin	Tokyo	6
	7	24 Jul	301	Eatherly	Pumpkin	Otsu	
	8	26 Jul	301	Eatherly	Pumpkin	Tsugawa	
	12	29 Jul	301	Eatherly	Pumpkin	Matzuru	
	13	06 Aug	301	Eatherly	Weather	Hiroshima	
	15	08 Aug	302	Eatherly	Pumpkin	Yokkaichi	

C-12 No combat missions were flown by Crew C-12

Crew	Msn	Date	Acft	Airplane Commander	Function	Target Area	Note
C-13	2	20 Jul	300	Bock	Pumpkin	Fukushima	
	5	24 Jul	297	Bock	Pumpkin	Niihama	
	11	29 Jul	297	Bock	Pumpkin	Tokyo-Musashino	
	16	09 Aug	353	Bock	Instruments	Nagasaki	
	18	14 Aug	298	Bock	Pumpkin	Koroma	
C-14	6	24 Jul	291	Ray	Pumpkin	Kobe	
	8	26 Jul	291	Ray	Pumpkin	Rashtwazaki	
	11	29 Jul	291	Ray	Pumpkin	Koriyama	
	16	09 Aug	354	Hopkins	Photo	Nagasaki	7
	17	14 Aug	304	Hopkins	Pumpkin	Nagoya	
C-15	2	20 Jul	353	Albury	Pumpkin	Abort	8
	6	24 Jul	353	Albury	Pumpkin	Kobe	
	9	26 Jul	297	Albury	Pumpkin	Yoyama	
	13	06 Aug	353	Sweeney	Instruments	Hiroshima	
	16	09 Aug	297	Sweeney	Fat Man	Nagasaki	
	18	14 Aug	301	Albury	Pumpkin	Koroma	

Notes:

1. On the Nagasaki atomic bombing mission, Crew A-1 was assigned the role of Iwo Jima standby airplane in the event the bombcarrying airplane (*297) encountered trouble and a switch of airplanes was necessary. Due to weather conditions, the mission flight path to Kokura and Nagasaki was far west of Iwo Jima and the standby airplane was not deployed.

2. On 8 August, Crew A-3 aborted a planned pumpkin mission to Osaka due to unknown problems. The pumpkin bomb was returned to Tinian.

3. On 9 August, two crews of the 509th were ordered to return to the United States in 509th B-29's to transport to Tinian the second Fat Man atomic bomb (509th Operations Order #41). Crew A-5 (Classen as airplane commander) in #346 and Crew B-6 (Wilson as airplane commander) in #303 left Tinian late at night on 9 August. After the crews and airplanes arrived in the United States and were preparing to load the components of the second Fat Man bomb, President Truman (through General Groves) gave the order to stop the shipment (the Japanese indicated they would surrender). The crews and B-29's did not return to Tinian.

4. On the Hiroshima atomic bombing mission, Crew B-8 was assigned the role of standby airplane on Iwo Jima, and would have been used if the bomb-carrying airplane (#292) had encountered difficulties. The standby airplane was not needed.

5. A modified Crew B-9 was used on the Hiroshima mission. The Hiroshima and normal crew members were:

Crew Position	Hiroshima	Normal
Airplane Commander	Tibbets	Lewis
Copilot	Lewis	McNamara
Navigator	Van Kirk	Rider
Bombardier	Ferebee	Williams
Flight Engineer	Duzenbury	Duzenbury
Radio Operator	Nelson	Nelson
Radar Operator	Stiborik	Stiborik
Tail Gunner	Caron	Caron
Asst Eng/Scanner	Shumard	Shumard
Weapon Officer	Parsons	-
Asst Weapon Off	Jeppson	-
Radar Counter-measures	Beser	-

6. On the first pumpkin mission on 20 July, Eatherly and Crew C-11 attempted to drop the pumpkin bomb on the Imperial Palace in Tokyo. The bomb actually hit a Tokyo railroad station.

7. Hopkins and Crew C-14 were to perform the photo airplane mission on the Nagasaki atomic bombing mission. For unknown reasons, they did not rendezvous with the bomb-carrying and instrument airplanes at the designated rendezvous point. Not knowing that the other two airplanes had proceeded to the primary target (Kokura) and then to Nagasaki (the secondary target), the photo airplane did not complete its mission.

8. On 20 July, Crew C-15 aborted a planned pumpkin mission to Fukushima due to an engine problem (overheating). The pumpkin bomb was jettisoned in the ocean at coordinates 29:52N / 141:36E.

509th Composite Group Crews and Aircraft
on Hiroshima and Nagasaki Missions, August 1945

Aircraft Commander	Crew	B-29: Victor No. and Informal Name	Principal Function	Notes
Hiroshima Mission, August 6, Msn No. 13, Opns Order 35				
Tibbets	B-9	82	Bomb delivery, Enola Gay	Weaponeer: Little Boy
(U235)	Parsons			
Sweeney	C-15	89 The Great Artiste	Blast measurement, parachuted gauges	Lead Scientist: Alvarez
Marquardt	B-10	91 Necessary Evil	Photography Fastax camera	No usable film obtained
Eatherly	C-11	85 Straight Flush	Advance weather report, Hiroshima	Primary target
Wilson	B-6	71 Jabit III	Advance weather report, Kokura	Secondary target
Taylor	A-1	83 Full House	Advance weather report, Nagasaki	Tertiary target
McKnight	B-8	90 Big Stink	Backup for V-82 at Iwo Jima	Not used
Nagasaki Mission, August 9, Msn No. 16, OPns Order No. 39				
Sweeney	C-15	77 Bockscar	Bomb delivery, Fat Man (Pu239)	Weaponeer: Ashworth
Bock	C-13	89 The Great Artiste	Blast measurement, parachuted gauges	Lead Scientist: Johnston
Hopkins	C-14	90 Big Stink	Photography, Fastax camera	No rendezvous with 77 & 89
Marquardt	B-10	88 Up an' Atom	Advance weather report, Kokura	Primary target
McKnight	B-8	95 Laggin' Dragon	Advance weather report, Nagasaki	Secondary target
Taylor	A-1	83 Full House	Backup for V-77 at Iwo Jima	Not used

509th Composite Group
Bomb Sorties on Japan
July - August 1945
Tinian North Field

The 509th flew 64 combat sorties in 18 missions against Japan during the July and August 1945 period. Bombs were dropped on 51 targets (including Hiroshima and Nagasaki) in these 18 missions. The sorties included:

51 sorties with pumpkin bombs (2 aborts)

2 sorties with atomic bombs (Hiroshima/Little Boy and Nagasaki/Fat Man)

11 sorties in support of the atomic bombing missions (photography, instrumentation, weather, and standby aircraft)

In July, the 509th flew 38 pumpkin sorties with one abort (the pumpkin bomb was jettisoned at sea) and 37 targets bombed.

In August, the 509th flew the Hiroshima and Nagasaki atomic bombing missions and 13 pumpkin sorties with one abort (the aircraft returned to Tinian with the pumpkin bomb).

The 509th sortie record was as follows:

20 Jul 45	10 pumpkin sorties (1 abort)
24 Jul 45	10 pumpkin sorties
26 Jul 45	10 pumpkin sorties
29 Jul 45	8 pumpkin sorties
6 Aug 45	Hiroshima atomic bomb mission (7 aircraft)
8 Aug 45	6 pumpkin sorties (1 abort)
9 Aug 45	Nagasaki atomic bomb mission (6 aircraft)
14 Aug 45	7 pumpkin sorties

Chapter Eighteen

IT'S OVER!

August 10, 11, 12, 13

After our harrowing experiences it was good to get a long rest, and our days were filled with swimming, playing softball, reading, sleeping or loafing, and generally just having a good time. The 509th did not fly any missions during this "off" period.

The main topic of every conversation at the Officer's Club, beach, Mess Hall, or Quonset hut was the end of the War. None of us could understand why the Japanese had not surrendered after Nagasaki. We couldn't understand what they were waiting for — another A-Bomb? Also, we wondered what effect Russia's entry into the war would have on the Japanese. The USSR declared war on Japan on August 9, 1945 — the same day we dropped our atomic bomb on Nagasaki.

I think most of us wondered why Russia had waited so long to join America, Britain and China in the war against the Japanese Empire. Maybe they wanted to make sure we had Japan beaten before they got involved. We had a great time discussing all the ramifications of peace, which seemed to be just around the corner, but still elusive.

It was not until several days after our mission, when good aerial reconnaissance photos became available, that we were informed of the damage "Fat Man" had done to Nagasaki. Although we had missed the original target identified at our briefing, our second atomic bomb had done substantial damage. It detonated 1,890 feet above the Urakami Valley.

The aerial photos revealed we were off by approximately one and a half miles. Instead of exploding over the heart of the city, the bomb detonated just north of the Mitsubishi Steel and Arms Works, located in the Urakami valley. These works were totally destroyed. It appeared that about three miles of factory buildings and other industrial plants located on the Urakami River, to the Mitsubishi Urakami Ordnance Plant, had been destroyed.

I remember that later General Jimmy Doolittle was reported to have said he was happy that we had not hit Nagasaki's downtown area in which many civilians were located. All in all, everyone considered our mission a success, and

General LeMay would be happy, too.

On either August 10th or 11th, I can't recall which, the crews of the "Enola Gay" and "Bockscar" were involved with a press conference. There were many reporters; and after we were introduced by name, home town and military duty, they started firing their questions. Colonel Tibbets, Major Sweeney and other ranking officers fielded most of their queries. I recall that several questions touched on highly secret subjects, but these were rebuffed with a quick, "No comment." I was glad when the "grilling" was over.

I think it was after this press conference that the last picture of our entire crew was taken by an Army photographer. We were all dressed up in our khaki uniforms, and this group photo included Ashworth, Barnes and Beser, who also were at the press conference. I never again did see these three men on Tinian, although in later years I have talked with Commander Ashworth on the telephone. He remained in the Navy and eventually became a Vice Admiral in charge of the 6th Mediterranean Fleet after World War II.

Following our mission to Nagasaki, rumors about peace filled Tinian Island. And there was some preliminary celebrating. I remember hearing the loud "bang-bang-bang" as guns were fired into the air by parties unknown, primarily late at night. I don't recall that anyone in the 509th was involved in these celebrations.

On August 14th, we were informed there was to be yet another mission to the Japanese Empire. Peace had not yet come to the Pacific, and apparently it was decided to let the Japanese know we still had a lot of bombs left.

All available B-29's in the 509th were scheduled to take part in this bombing strike. We were told it would be a "maximum effort," with B-29's flying from Guam and Saipan as well as from Tinian. The bombs used by the 509th would be the familiar "Pumpkins," filled with 10,000 pounds of Torpex.

At our briefing we were informed that the Japanese city of Koromo would be the target for "The Great Artiste." (Yes, we were back flying our own aircraft again!)

The general reaction of virtually every man in the 509th was, "What? Another mission? The War should be over — and now we've got to go out again!"

But we went — as ordered. Everyone hoped this would be our last mission.

North Field was alive with B-29's all afternoon and early evening as every available B-29 flew off to the Japanese Empire. Hundreds and hundreds of planes were involved, and the noise never seemed to end as they roared down the four runways.

The last B-29's to take off were from the 509th. Our operational orders had not changed. We still flew alone, not in formation with other aircraft.

On this mission to the Japanese Empire, Albury was back in the left hand seat as pilot, with me in the right seat as co-pilot. It felt good to be back in "The Great Artiste." Fred Bock's "Bockscar" was a great plane, and it got us home safe and sound even with the problems we had encountered on our mission.

Our flight to the Japanese Empire was smooth, and we were directed over Iwo Jima — our usual route — before heading for the main islands of Japan.

Jim Van Pelt again proved he was the best damn navigator in the 509th by putting us right on Koromo, where Kermit Beahan took over, dropping our "Pumpkin" dead on target.

We didn't see another B-29 going to, or returning from, the Japanese Empire until we were in the landing pattern at Tinian. I don't remember if we were the last of the B-29's that flew from Tinian to return to North Field, but we were close. All B-29's from the 509th returned safely from this mission no one wanted to fly. We all wondered, "Will this be the final mission? It's <u>got</u> to be the the last one!"

It is entirely possible that the very <u>last</u> bomb to explode on the Japanese Empire in World War II was delivered by a B-29 from the 509th Composite Group. I like to think it was.

August 15, 1945 — Peace!

On August 15th, we received news that the Japanese had surrendered — unconditionally!

I remember my immediate reaction to this announcement as being one of unbelievable relief. It was over! We had brought the Japanese Empire to its knees. It had taken four years, but we had won. As President Roosevelt promised after Pearl Harbor, we had won the inevitable victory.

The euphoria of knowing I would not have to put my life at risk flying another combat mission hit me pretty hard. I think it affected just about every other man in the 509th the same way.

Now, all those Marines and soldiers preparing for an invasion of Japan would not have to die in combat. All those fighters and bombers scattered on airfields across the Pacific could at last go home.

I was proud, truly proud to be an American.

SECTION FOUR

War's Aftermath

Chapter Nineteen

Tinian — after the War

As the celebrating continued, we discovered the U. S. Army still ran things "by the book;" and once again we were sent to school to sharpen our combat readiness. The 509th maintained its reputation as a separate, "secret organization" within the 313th Bomb Wing; and we were ordered not to disclose anything we did, not to talk about the atomic bomb other than in broad descriptive generalities, and not start any rumors.

Some of the men thought they were getting us ready for another war, but against whom? And why? It was just this kind of rumor the Army didn't want. I, for one, kept my mouth shut and did what I was told to do.

But it wasn't all spit and polish and drudgery. We had a lot of fun during the months of August, September and October while we waited to return home to the States. In fact, I was involved in several "stunts" that got a great deal of attention.

One involved the little auxiliary, gas-powered generators used to provide power for ground operations and to start the engines on a B-29. We called them "Putt-Putts." They made a terrible racket.

Two other Lieutenants and I acquired several of these "Putt-Putt's." Using the mechanical skills of several Navy SeaBees, we converted the "Putt-Putt's" into motor scooters. We paid for the SeaBee's labor with our hoarded fifths of liquor that we had obtained from the officer's liquor locker. They were happy. We were happy. None of us drank.

What a time we had with our scooters. Every day that we were not flying or had other duties, we'd race each other on the taxi ways in and around the parked B-29's. I think we were able to get up to a speed of 40 to 50 miles per hour. The scooters were noisy and tricky to handle at those speeds, but the thrill more than made up for the risks.

One of the "Putt-Putt" scooters was put aboard Captain Devore's B-29 for the flight home when we left Tinian in November, 1945. Lt. Locke Easton was the co-pilot and Lt. Leon Cooper the bombardier. These two also owned one of the fast scooters. But I didn't bring mine back to the States, although I thought of it. I didn't think Sweeney would have been receptive to the idea.

The "Putt-Putt's" also played a major role in another stunt. One night a flight engineer and another co-pilot and I used them to shake up the troops. The other two had had a bit too much to drink, which made them very brave with a "I don't give a damn" attitude. Me? I was just raising hell and having fun.

After everyone was asleep, about 2:00 am, we pulled the "Putt-Putt" around to each Quonset hut used by 509th officers, and started the machine. — it made a very loud popping noise when it started. We let it run for about three minutes, then shut it down, and moved on to another Quonset. The moaning, groaning and cussing that came from each Quonset made it all worthwhile. Luckily, no one came out, threw anything at us, or shot at us. Even the "high brass" Quonset, housing the VIP's — General Farrell, Admiral Purnell and Colonel Tibbets — got the same treatment.

On another occasion I finally had the opportunity to meet the enemy face to face. I laugh now at the escapade, but at the time I was just very surprised.

The War was over, but that didn't mean all the Japanese hiding on Tinian had decided to surrender. We were warned several times after August 15th not to stray too far into the countryside, especially the far southeast side of the island where a number of Japanese soldiers were suspected of hiding in the "jungle."

Dick McNamara, John Lundgren and I decided one day to sign out a Jeep from our Motor Pool and tour Tinian. We had not seen the upper part of the south end of the island, so we headed down "Broadway," never anticipating we would run into trouble. As we proceeded southward, we turned off the main road onto a very narrow dirt road with sugar cane fields on both sides. We waved to the natives working in the sugarcane, which was over six feet tall.

Suddenly, as we rounded a curve, we were face to face with three Japanese soldiers standing in the middle of the road. Their uniforms were frayed, and they didn't have any weapons that we could see. They just smiled broadly and bowed to us continually.

I don't know who was more surprised — the Japanese or McNamara and Lundgren and me. Maybe they wanted to surrender. I'll never know. We didn't wait to find out. We turned the Jeep around fast and raced through the sugarcane until we reached the main road. Then, we started laughing. It was a ticklish,

Tinian Island — Sept. 1945
A road, similar to the one shown right, led to the top of the island where the sugar cane fields were located. It was there that we encountered three Japanese soldiers coming out of the sugar cane field to surrender.

unsure moment when neither party knew exactly what to do and nothing did happen as we sped away. To this day, I often wondered about this incident and just how close we came to deciding to capture the three Japanese soldiers or completly ignore them as we did!

In October the 509th was alerted that we were going home, and soon the various support units were on a ship bound for the States. In early November, the air crews packed up, and with our ground crew again as passengers, "The Great Artiste" retraced its flight across the Pacific — destination: Roswell Air Force Base in Roswell, New Mexico, the new home of America's only self-contained "atomic" group.

Chapter Twenty
ROSWELL, NEW MEXICO

Back in the U.S.A.

There was a mad scramble after we returned to Roswell Air Force Base in early December. Every one of us was trying to be the first to get his paperwork completed, draw back pay, and get home. It took a few days, but soon I was on a train back to Chicago for my 45 day leave.

Pullman, Illinois, looked mighty good, even though it was December. My mother cried a lot, as mothers tend to do. She was proud of me, although I doubt she understood some of the wartime experiences I related. I remember she had to "show me off" to all the neighbors. Everyone wanted to know about the atomic bomb, what it was like to see one go off, and how much damage this strange new device really did. I answered their questions as best I could, although I am sure I disappointed a few when I had to say, "Gosh, I just can't answer that question. It's restricted information."

I remember we discussed my staying in the Army Air Corps. Mother didn't like the idea, and I don't think I ever convinced her that a career in the military was a good thing for her "Fradi." But she told me I should do what I wanted to do.

The 45 days went fast, too fast, and after a joyous Christmas, I headed back to Roswell and the 509th.

Our New York Gala

Soon after we all returned from our leaves, Colonel Tibbets invited the flight officers from both the "Enola Gay" and "Bockscar" to accompany him to a party to be held in New York City by a distant relative of his — a Neisa McMein. He indicated this was to be a real celebration of our missions to Hiroshima and Nagasaki, and we'd meet some famous people.

The pilots, co-pilots, navigators and bombardiers thought this was a great idea, and jumped at the opportunity. Off to New York went the eight of us for a

January 1946 — This is a candid photo of the "Atomic Bomb Party" hosted by Neisa McMein for the flight crews of the "Enola Gay" and "Bockscar." Playing "Charades, "clockwise from bottom left were: Bing Crosby, lighting his pipe; Capt. Lewis, Co-Pilot of the "Enola Gay", Colonel Tibbets, Pilot of the "Enola Gay;" an unknown actress; and Major Van Kirk, Navigator of the "Enola Gay." Facing the contestants wearing numbers were (back to camera), Adrian, the designer and husband of Janet Gaynor; myself in front of Lewis; an unknown actress; and Fredric March, actor, holding a piece of paper.

four-day holiday, all expenses paid, with Tibbets piloting one of the 509th C-54 transport planes.

And what a weekend party it was! Neisa McMein was what I called "a society lady." She lived in a big penthouse on Park Avenue and knew <u>everybody</u> who was anybody.

I am sure that I will never again meet so many famous people: Cole Porter, Elsa Maxwell, Bing Crosby, Fredric March, Joan Caulfield, Bennett Cerf, Adrian (the dress designer). And there were others, all equally famous movie stars, singers, stars of the Broadway stage, newspaper columnists, and radio personalities, but I can't remember all their names.

We were seated four to a table in this immense penthouse apartment. I ate dinner with Joan Caulfield and Mr. and Mrs. Bennett Cerf and actress Anne Shirley. After dinner, we played "Charades," a popular game at the time. I don't recall if my team won, but I sure had a good time.

The next night Colonel Tibbets took our group to a fancy nightclub. This was "heady" stuff for a poor, first generation Italian-American like me, but I have to admit it felt very good to be introduced to the crowd as an "American hero." I didn't feel much like a hero that night, and I still don't, but it was nice to hear all the applause for our two crews.

The <u>New</u> 393rd — and the New 509th Composite Group

When I had returned to duty at Roswell following my leave, it quickly became evident that most of the officers and enlisted men in the 509th had only one objective — discharge. However, Colonel Tibbets said he was working on one option, which he offered to the officers.

I remember Tibbets told us that he wanted to keep at least the pilots, co-pilots, navigators and bombardiers of the 509th intact as a unit. He felt very strongly that America was going to need a cohesive, self-contained air unit, prepared to go anywhere in the world to protect America's interests. I think a number of us seriously were considering making the Army a career; however, most men were "on the fence."

Colonel Tibbets said he was going to do everything possible in order to obtain regular commissions in the Army Air Corps for all the officers in the 509th, which was very important if one planned to make the Army a career. Most of us flyers during the war were not "regular" Army.

Tibbets flew to Washington, D.C. and visited the Pentagon to "sell" the idea. When he returned, he reported the Army "brass" had turned down his idea. For whatever reason, the generals in Washington didn't buy it.

When this word got around, most of the officers put in for a discharge. It didn't take long for the 509th I had known at Wendover and on Tinian to radically change. All the familiar faces, many of them close friends, were soon gone.

I faced a tough decision. I knew I didn't want to go back to work at the

Pullman Shops, not ever again. But what was I qualified to do? The Army had given me the opportunity to fly, had trained me and spent a lot of money on me. Besides, I loved flying. It was fun, and I could tolerate the military life, as long as I could spend most of my time flying.

Thus, a career in the Army Air Corps appeared to be the right and logical move. I was just twenty-four when I re-upped, signing a one year enlistment. I wasn't a "regular" Army Officer, but I hoped that would come in the near future.

Soon I was back flying B-29's again, making long navigational flights that took us from one coast to the other. The 509th was absorbed into the 313th Bomb Wing, and we flew when we could get enough gas to fuel the planes. It seemed that in the rush for peace, the Army Air Corps in 1946 had been allocated few dollars for such essential things as aviation fuel. We put up with the restriction and flew whenever the gas was available. It was a good life for a young man who loved to fly big airplanes.

Promotion

I got checked out as a First Pilot, left hand seat, at Roswell. In fact, it was the first thing I did after re-enlisting. This involved attending ground school and "shooting" landings, and was not difficult. I had finally reached one of my earliest goals: command of a B-29. I had achieved this goal on the B-24. It took me over a year to do it on a B-29. In June I was promoted to First Lieutenant.

Colonel Tibbets was promoted to a one star General and transferred to other duties. (*I didn't see him again until we met years later at a reunion of the 509th.*) He was replaced with a Colonel Cloyd, a veteran B-29 pilot. Colonel Cloyd and I "hit it off" really well, and it wasn't long before he asked me to fly with him to the many air shows being held all over America. From Roswell we would buzz an airfield at low altitude, circle, land, and then open up the B-29 for inspection by spectators. I especially liked showing young boys and girls around a B-29. They could hardly believe we had flown up that very day from New Mexico. The War had ended less than a year earlier and aviation's part in winning the War was still admired by almost everyone in America.

Before long I was made Assistant Intelligence Officer of the 393rd, and subsequently took over the command of the Third Aerial Photographic unit.

In August 1946, I got a big surprise. I was ordered to report for training as a Counter Intelligence Officer at Holabird Air Force Base near Baltimore, Maryland.

I went to see Colonel Cloyd, told him I had not requested this transfer, and asked if there was anything he could do to have my orders cancelled. I liked being with the 393rd, and I definitely did not want to leave. Cloyd tried, but was unable to change anything. I was told to report to Holabird in November.

September and October passed all too quickly. I could have flown, but I chose to go home by train for a short leave, and then on to Baltimore via the same ground transportation.

When I reported at Holabird I asked, "Why me? I didn't apply for this transfer." I was told that there was something in my background that qualified me for intelligence work, and I should be proud to have been selected for the top-secret, ten-month course. I asked about flying. I was informed there would be no flying involved with intelligence work. Regulations didn't permit it.

That did it. The Army was taking my Wings away from me. I said if I couldn't fly, I would resign.

Time to Get Out

I don't think the people at Holabird had expected such a reaction. I was told to "think about it" for a couple of days, and not to make a hasty decision I might regret later. But I had made up my mind. If I couldn't fly, I was getting out of the Army Air Corps!

I put in for a discharge immediately and waited for word to start my separation process from Active Duty. While waiting for discharge, orders came from Washington D.C. revoking my counter-intelligence orders and sending me back to Roswell, New Mexico.

Returning to Roswell AFB immediately, I found that everything was in a disturbing situation. Air Corp personnel were being discharged because the end of the war meant downsizing, a policy of a Reduction in Force or "RIF" as it is known in the military.

What I saw and heard disturbed me and I was very unhappy with the present situation. Many of my friends in the 393rd were involved with the "RIF" and didn't especially want to get out of the Air Corps. Flying programs were not the same as before and had many changes.

After much deliberation over the big changes, I decided the "handwriting was on the wall" and sought to seek my discharge from Active Duty. This consisted of being discharged from one side of the room and crossing to the other side of the room, to be sworn into the Air Corps Reserve.

Chapter Twenty One

CHICAGO, MY HOME TOWN

1947 - 1950

My first priority on returning home to Pullman was to apply for a position as a pilot with the airlines. I was not alone. I discovered there were hundreds of former Army Air Corps pilots and co-pilots ahead of me, trying to land the same kind of job.

I haunted the airline offices at Chicago's Municipal Field (now Midway Airport), and soon became a familiar face in the personnel offices at American, United, TWA, and all the other regional airlines flying from that busy location. Although I had over 1,500 hours flying time in four-engine airplanes, it was not enough. Every airline had a long list of applications from men who had flown over 5,000 hours during World War II. I was put on lists and told to wait at least four months before my name would come up as a "call back."

There was little to do but wait for the airlines to call. I had moved back home with my mother in the house on Langley Avenue, so I had a roof over my head. I took over the responsibility of maintaining the house, digging into the $5,000 I had saved in the Army Air Corps. In addition, I became a member of the "52/20 Club" — this meant I received $20 a week for 52 weeks from the U.S. Government. Most returning veterans I knew took advantage of the "52/20 Club," which I believe was intended to support a veteran while he looked for work.

Another fellow and I purchased a neighborhood candy store. This venture lasted only six months before I sold out. The long hours were ferocious — 7:00 am to midnight. My Uncle Fausto may have liked selling candy, but I soon discovered operating a retail store was not for me.

Air Force Reserve

I heard nothing from the airlines. But because I wanted to continue to fly, in 1948 I joined the 85th Troop Carrier Squadron, which was attached to the

2471st Air Force Reserve Training Center at Chicago's Orchard Airfield (now O'Hare Field). Fortunately, I had decided to remain in the Army Air Corps Reserves when I was discharged. When the Air Corps became a separate branch of the military services in 1947, and renamed the Air Force, my reserve status was not changed.

The 85th Squadron was assigned twin-engine C-46 "Commandos" and C-119 "Flying Boxcars" aircraft. We flew once a month, normally on the weekends. Several months we flew just enough hours to maintain our flight status (four hours a month). We flew cargo from one base to another and carried paratroopers from Camp Campbell, Kentucky, on their training exercises.

But I still didn't have a regular job. It was now 1950 and the airlines hadn't called me for employment. I was twenty-eight years old, still a young man, but I knew twenty-eight was over the limit for starting with the commercial airlines.

I had to find something to do. I was interested in using the G.I. Bill for a college education but I couldn't decide what I wanted to pursue as a career. My money was running out, and I began to wonder if I would have to return to the Pullman Works — something I did not want to do.

Bridges

One day, completely "out of the blue," Les Beck, the Democratic Committeeman of Chicago's 9th Ward, which included the Pullman neighborhood, asked me what I was doing. I had been introduced to Committeeman Beck at various political gatherings, but didn't know him personally. When I told him I was still looking for a job, Beck asked me if I knew anything about blueprints and drafting.

I told him I had had several years of mechanical drawing and machine shop at Pullman Tech and could still read blueprints.

That was enough for Beck. He introduced me to the Engineering Department of the Bridge Division of Chicago's Public Works Department. I was hired as a draftsman.

I'm sure some of my superiors thought I was just another political protégé who would not be able to meet their standards and leave quickly, but I fooled them. My education at Pullman Tech once again pulled me through. I had enough mathematics and engineering skills to do the work. In fact, I enjoyed the challenge. It was fun!

It didn't take long before I was given a temporary job status as Civil Engineer and went out into the field to work on the bridges. One of my first assignments was on the new Congress Street bridge over the Chicago River, where the new Eisenhower Expressway was to pass through the Chicago Post Office.

I was learning fast, and soon I was using a transit and calculating the tons of concrete being poured into the forms of the giant bascule bridge. (A bascule bridge is a bridge that is counterbalanced so that when one end is raised, the other is lowered . Concrete is used to balance the weight of the steel bridges. Chicago has more bascule bridges than any other city in America).

I began to move quickly up the ranks as a Draftsman, moving from Draftsman #1 to #3, as high as you could go. Although I was classified as a Draftsman, I believed I could do better. So based on my on-the-job experience, I decided to take the Civil Service examination for Civil Engineering. This required a great deal of study, but I "hit the books" and had to let my social life slide a bit as I prepared for the exam. Not too many people believed I could pass the difficult examination.

There was a lot of celebrating the day I got the test results. I was not surprised to find out I had passed the examination. I was able to work out a satisfactory solution to all the problems. But what did surprise me was the fact that my score qualified me to be a Civil Engineer II, not just an Engineer I.

Chicago, during the 1950's, and well into the 1970's, was a great place to be a young, energetic Civil Engineer. A building boom had hit the city, and there was always a new project in the planning stages or under construction. I continued with my studies and, after additional examinations, eventually was made a Civil Engineer IV. My immediate supervisor was a fellow Pullman Tech graduate, Edward Klausner. Working for him was a great experience. And since he had started with the City Bridge Division five years earlier, I learned a lot from him.

In 1973 I was promoted to Manager of Bridge Operations and Maintenance. This position made me responsible for the 200 to 400 people who maintained and repaired Chicago's fifty bascule bridges, as well as for the direct supervision of the 140 bridgetenders who operated these bridges. I was responsible for the expenditure of millions of dollars annually, not just for the bascule bridges but also for the repair and maintenance of 200 fixed bridges and viaducts carrying Chicago city streets over expressways and railroads. It was a big job and I enjoyed every minute of it.

My first bascule bridge over the Chicago River had been the one at Congress Street and the Eisenhower Expressway. My last was the Columbus Drive Bridge which was part of the reconstruction and relocation of The Outer Drive and its connection to Wacker Drive.

I retired in 1986, after thirty-six years with the City of Chicago.

No more flying in the Air Force Reserve

As I progressed up the ladder in the Bridge Division, I found myself flying fewer and fewer hours with the Air Force Reserve. This was not because I didn't want to fly; rather, it was because Congressional budget cuts were reducing the Air Force Reserves to a shadow of their former strength. I had been promoted to Captain, which was nice, but it seemed that every year meant another budget cut. By 1958, the 85th Troop Carrier Squadron could be disbanded for lack of funds.

I wanted to stay in the Air Force Reserves and looked around for another assignment. I learned there was an opening for a Liaison Officer to the Air Force Academy in Colorado Springs, Colorado. I applied, was accepted and, from 1962 through 1972, was assigned to the Air Force Academy. My duties included counseling and recruiting high school boys and girls from my Congressional District that covered the south side of Chicago and the southern suburbs.

I really enjoyed my years as a Liaison Officer for the Academy. I met many young people who went on to become Air Force Officers and pilots. Along the way, I rose from Captain to Lieutenant Colonel.

In 1972 I became fifty years old, and since I had not made the rank of full Colonel, the Air Force ruled I had to retire. I had been in the Air Corps, and then the Air Force, for thirty years, with twenty-five years in the Reserves. I hated to retire but decided it was for the best. I still had my career with the City of Chicago which was taking up more and more of my time.

Carole McVey

These memoirs would not be complete without including something about my wife, Carole.

Carole was my high school sweetheart and prom date in my senior year at Pullman Tech. She also attended this technical high school because her grandfather worked in the Pullman Shops. She was admitted to Pullman Tech's secretarial school where she had three years of intensive training in shorthand and typing, plus a lot of English grammar. A girl did not have to attend a business school after the rigorous studies at Pullman Tech. They were qualified as secretaries on the day they graduated.

Carole and I dated while I was in the Army Air Corps; in fact, she came down to visit me in Ada, Oklahoma when I was an Aviation Student at East Central State Teachers College. We continued to see each other off and on after I left the Air Force and went to work for the City of Chicago. I had an office on North LaSalle Street, she was located in the "Loop," which made it convenient for lunch and dinner dates to Chicago restaurants and nightclubs.

Carole lived with her widowed mother in Roseland, the neighborhood directly west of Pullman, and commuted daily on the Illinois Central Railroad to downtown Chicago where she was an executive secretary at AMSTED Industries for forty-four years.

I lived on Langley Avenue. When my mother died in 1956, my brother Mariano and his family moved back into the family house with me.

When Carole and I married, I moved in with Carole and her mother and we took care of this wonderful lady until her death in 1969. We then moved further west, but still in Chicago, to the area in which we now reside, Beverly Woods.

Our retirement years have been good to Carole and me. We have traveled the world with many trips to Europe, including Italy to visit my cousins and to Ireland to visit the land of Carole's ancestors.

One very enjoyable trip to Europe involved taking the Concorde, the supersonic jet that flies to Europe in three and a half hours. The return trip back to the States was unforgettable-- five days on the Queen Elizabeth II in luxurious comfort.

In addition, we have been very active with the Pullman Civic Organization and the Historic Pullman Foundation as we strive to restore the Pullman area as a historic district.

And I have not forgotten the 509th Composite Group and its significant role during World War II. I believe I have attended every reunion of the 509th. In fact, Carole and I acted as coordinators for the 509th's 1994 reunion which was held in Chicago.

Carole joins me at air shows all across the country,and makes sure I get to the many speaking engagements which occupy so much of my time.

Now, it's 1999-- fifty-four years after a very young Italian-American flyer flew to Nagasaki, Japan with twelve other American young men.

What we did there made history.

Today, in my mid-seventies, I look back on that August 9th with nostalgia, but no regrets. I firmly believe we helped end the war with the Japanese Empire, and thus saved thousands of lives--on both sides of the conflict.

It's a comforting thought.

SECTION FIVE

Appendix

THE MEN WHO BROUGHT THE DAWN

"Bock's Car" with post-mission markings

On August 8, 1945, Russia finally joined the Allies and declared war on Japan. Despite that and the atomic bombing of Hiroshima, the Japanese still did not surrender. By 10:00 that same night, a second atomic bomb was placed in a B-29 Superfortress named *Bock's Car*.

The flight was anything but routine. A fuel pump malfunctioned, trapping 600 gallons of fuel. At the rendezvous over Kyushu, one of the two aircraft that were supposed to join *Bockscar* was apparently at the wrong altitude; *Bockscar* wasted valuable time searching for her. Then the primary target of Kokura was completely obscured by cloud cover, forcing a change to the secondary target of Nagasaki. The cloud cover was thick there, too, but the bombardier finally found a hole in the clouds. With fuel running low, *Bockscar* released its atomic bomb shortly after 11:00 a.m., Nagasaki time.

On August 14, 1945, Emperor Hirohito personally said that Japan would surrender on American terms and broadcast his decision to the Japanese people. The formal surrender ceremonies took place aboard the battleship USS *Missouri* in Tokyo Bay on September 2, 1945. World War II was finally over.

CHARLES D. ALBURY

The pilot of *Bockscar* was born in Miami, Florida. After graduating from high school, he went to work and soon began flying lessons. In 1943, Albury entered the University of Miami as an engineering major. On a whim, he joined a group of students taking a U.S. Army Air Corps entrance exam. Three months later, he received orders to report to the classification center in Nashville, Tennessee.

After flight school, he was first assigned to B-17 and B-29 flight training; then to Alamogordo, New Mexico; and ultimately to Gulfport, Mississippi, where he waited three months without orders.

A call to the base commander in Alamogordo produced orders to report to Colonel Tibbets at Eglin Field, Florida, and Albury joined the special missions group that would deliver the only atomic weapons ever used in combat.

After the war, Albury – having received the Distinguished Flying Cross and Air Medal with two oak leaf clusters – joined Eastern airlines as a pilot and flew for 35 years. He then trained A-300 pilots in Toulouse, France; returned to Eastern Airlines; and put in two years of law school. During this time he also spent more that 20 years working with the south Miami Athletic League. Albury retired in 1989 to "enjoy my family, for which I am very thankful and very proud of."

FRED J. OLIVI

Bockscar copilot was born and raised in the picturesque Pullman section of Chicago's far south side. Olivi volunteered for Cadet Pilot Training in October of 1942 and was called to active duty in February 1943. After classification, he earned his pilot's wings and was commissioned as a second lieutenant on August 4, 1944. In January 1945, he was posted to the 509th Composite Group, 393rd Bomb Squadron, for training as copilot on B-29s. Seven months later, he flew as copilot of *Bock's Car* on the Nagasaki mission, receiving the Distinguished Flying

Cross as a result.

Olivi continued to serve until his discharge in 1947. He immediately joined the Air Force Reserve and spent 36 years working as a civil engineer for the city of Chicago. He retired in 1986 from his position of Manager of Bridge Operations and Maintenance, responsible for supervising the running and repair of Chicago's 50 bascule bridges and approximately 200 fixed bridges and viaducts.

During his retirement years Olivi has traveled extensively in the company of his wife, Carole, who was his high school sweetheart and senior prom date.

JAMES F. VAN PELT JR.

The navigator on *Bockscar* grew up in West Virginia and was graduated from Virginia Polytechnic Institute in 1940. He served in the Coast Artillery from 1940 until 1942, when he transferred to the U.S. Army air Corps. From 1943 to 1944, he instructed navigation at Walla Walla, Washington, before becoming a member of 509th Composite Group. He was awarded the Distinguished Flying Cross and Air Medal for his wartime service.

After the war Van Pelt entered Tulane University medical School, where he earned his medical degree in 1950. After special-izing in obstetrics and gynecology at Charity Hospital in New orleans, he continued his Air Force career, serving in England and rising to the rank of colonel in the Air Force Medical Corps. He retired from the military in 1965 and went into private practice, simultaneously serving on the staffs of the former Circle City and Corona Community hospitals.

Van Pelt retired in 1988 after 23 years of service and teaching in California. He was named professor emeritus by the University of southern California – Los Angeles County Medical Center, where he had taught surgery as a visiting clinical professor. He died in 1995 at the age of 76.

JOHN D. KUHAREK

The flight engineer of *Bockscar* was born in Pittsburgh, Pennsylvania. In 1931, in the midst of the Great Depression, Kuharek signed up for the military instead of returning to high school for his senior year. Choosing Coast Artillery over Infantry – those being the only branches open at the time – he soon found himself at Fort Sherman performing clerical duties.

He was discharged from the Coast Artillery in 1939 with the rank of corporal and enlisted in the U.S. Army Air Corps. By April 1941, he was a crew member on anti-sub patrols off Guatemala, the Galapagos Island, Venezuela, and Aruba. Kuharek returned to the United States in 1943, where he became crew chief on a YB-29 and eventually flight engineer on a B-29. In November of that year, he received orders to report to Colonel Tibbets, who made Kuharek part of his new unit.

After the war, Kuharek was attached to the Strategic Air Command at Walker Air Force Base in Roswell, New Mexico, where he stayed more than ten years. He was sent to Korea in 1956 and served a year there. In 1960, at the rank of senior master sergeant and having received the Distinguished Flying Cross, Air medal, Asiatic-Pacific Campaign Medal, and Armed Forces Longevity Service Award, among others, he retired from the military and went to work as an engineer at the University of south Florida. He retired at the age of 65 and still lives in Florida.

RAYMOND C. GALLAGHER

Bockscar's assistant flight engineer was born in Chicago, Illinois, one of ten children. Five of the six boys, of whom Ray Gallagher was the youngest, served in the military. "I thought for sure I would never go to war," he said, "after always going to one more school. But in September of 1944 my dream of flying came true." He was assigned to the 509th Composite Group. Less than a year later, he was part of the combat crew that flew right wing for the *Enola Gay* on August 6, 1945. Three days later his aircraft carried an atomic bomb to Nagasaki.

"The war came to an end fast," Gallagher remembers. "Those two missions changed my life when I came home." Having received the distinguished Flying Cross, two Bronze Stars, two air medals, the World War II Victory Medal, and the Asiatic-Pacific Campaign Medal, among other decorations, he went to work for the Illinois Bell Telephone Company and stayed with them for 38 years.

Gallagher and his wife, Mary, still live in Chicago and have been married for almost fifty years. "Even to this day," Gallagher says, "[people] enjoy hearing about the atomic bomb missions. [They seem] to think of us as heroes."

COMPANY E, 28th MARINES ASSOCIATION
(WORLD WAR II)
Post Office Box 1972
La Jolla, California 92038
(619) 459-0607

SPEARHEAD
DIVISION

TO THE ATOMIC BOMB "DELIVERY TEAM"--THE USS INDIANAPOLIS AND
THE 509th COMPOSITE BOMB GROUP, FROM AN IWO JIMA INFANTRY
COMPANY COMMANDER.

We were in the field on Hawaii participating in a Regimental training
exercise when we heard of the devastating attacks on Japan with the dropping of
two atomic bombs by the "Enola Gay" and the "Box Car" B-29 bombers, and the
subsequent surrender of the Japanese government.

I became aware that our efforts in capturing Iwo Jima had played more than
an ancillary part in this final attack on the Japanese by eliminating the threat of
Japanese fighter aircraft lifting from Iwo Jima to intercept our B-29 bombers.

About a month later I was in the general area of our intended landing
beaches in Japan and understood first hand how costly in lives our amphibious
attack would have been had we landed on those shores.

What a tragedy so many brave U.S. Naval personnel from the USS
Indianapolis did not live to realize the final results of their gallant efforts.

Dave E. Severance
Dave E. Severance
Colonel USMC (Ret)
Former Commanding Officer

FIFTH MARINE DIVISION
ONCE A MARINE - ALWAYS A MARINE

TO THE MEMBERS OF THE 509th COMPOSITE GROUP AND SURVIVORS OF THE U.S.S. INDIANAPOLIS:

"I FEEL SO PROUD AND MY HEART IS WITH YOU FELLOW VETERANS OF THE USS INDIANAPOLIS AND THE 509TH COMPOSITE BOMB GROUP, FOR YOUR EFFORT AND OUTSTANDING ACCOMPLISHMENTS IN BRINGING WORLD WAR II TO A DECISIVE ENDING.
DURING AUGUST 1945 I WAS ON OKINAWA WITH THE 1st MARINE DIVISION. HAVING LANDED THERE 1 APRIL 1945, THE BATTLE CONCLUDED THE LAST PART OF JUNE 1945. DURING JULY AND AUGUST WE WERE PLANNING AND TRAINING FOR THE FINAL BLOW TO JAPAN. WE KNEW THAT THE INVASION WOULD BE COSTLY. SO DURING JULY AND AUGUST WE WATCHED THE BIG BOMBERS MAKE THEIR DAILY RUNS TO JAPAN.
WE HOPED AND PRAYED THIS ACTION WOULD SOFTEN OUR OBJECTIVES.
THEN ON AUGUST 6 1945 PRESIDENT TRUMAN ANNOUNCED THAT AN A-BOMB HAD BEEN DROPPED ON HIROSHMA. ON 9 AUGUST 1945 THE 2ND A-BOMB CONVINCED ME THAT MY LIFE WAS SAVED AND THIS LONG STRUGGLE FOR OUR ARMED SERVICES (FROM PEARL HARBOR TO JAPAN) WAS OVER.

I THINK IT IS QUITE FITTING THAT A PORTION OF THE USS ARIZONA LIES WITHIN THE NATIONAL MEMORIAL OF THE USS INDIANAPOLIS. IN MEMORY OF THE FIRST AND LAST SHIP SUNK IN WORLD WAR II.

MAY I SAY TO YOU AND ALL OF AMERICA, THANKS!"

REMEMBER PEARL HARBOR.
HELP KEEP AMERICA ALERT AND STRONG

RUSSELL J. McCURDY Lt. Col. USMC (RET.)
ENLISTED MARINE SURVIVOR OF THE USS ARIZONA DECEMBER 7, 1941

171

TO THE MEMBERS OF THE 509th COMPOSITE GROUP AND SURVIVORS OF THE U.S.S. INDIANAPOLIS:

I JOIN IN SALUTING YOU FELLOW VETERANS FOR YOUR EFFORTS IN BRINGING ABOUT THE DEFEAT OF JAPAN DURING WORLD WAR II.

DURING THE LAST FEW MONTHS OF THE WAR, I WAS ASSIGNED TO THE STAFF OF FLEET ADMIRAL CHESTER NIMITZ, COMMANDER IN CHIEF OF THE PACIFIC FORCES. WHEN THE WAR STARTED, I WAS ASSIGNED TO THE U.S.S. ARIZONA (BB-39) WHICH SUFFERED 1,177 KIA, THE HEAVIEST LOSS OF LIFE ON ANY ONE SHIP IN THE HISTORY OF THE U.S. NAVY. MY SHIP WAS DESTROYED DURING THE ATTACK ON PEARL HARBOR ON DECEMBER 7, 1941 BEFORE WAR HAD BEEN DECLARED. THE ARIZONA WAS ONE OF THE FIRST SHIPS LOST DURING WW II. THE USS INDIANAPOLIS WAS THE LAST MAJOR CAPITAL SHIP SUNK DURING THAT CONFLICT. SHE SUFFERED 883 KIA, WHICH WAS THE SECOND HEAVIEST LOSS OF LIFE AMONG U.S. NAVY SHIPS LOST DURING ANY WAR.

DURING AUGUST OF 1945, OUR FLEET HAD FOR ALL PRACTICAL PURPOSES COMPLETELY ANNILATED THE JAPANESE FLEET. OUR SHIPS WERE ABLE TO GO CLOSE TO THE JAPANESE SHORE LINE AND BOMBARD THEIR CITIES INTO RUBBLE. ALSO THE ARMY AIR FORCES WERE FIRE BOMBING THE MAJOR CITIES OF JAPAN WITH RESULTANT HEAVY JAPANESE CASUALTIES.

IT WAS KNOWN THAT THE JAPANESE EXTENDED PEACE FEELERS THROUGH THE SOVIET GOVERNMENT; HOWEVER, MEMBERS OF THE JAPANESE IMPERIAL COUNCIL HELD THEIR POSITIONS AT THE PLEASURE OF THE ARMY AND MADE PRONOUNCMENTS WHICH WERE OPPOSED TO THE UNCONDITIONAL SURRENDER AS PROVIDED FOR BY THE ALLIED POWERS POTSDAM DECLARATION OF 26 JULY 1945.

THE B-29 ENOLA GAY WHICH TOOK OFF FROM TINIAN ON 6 AUGUST 1945 DROPPED THE FIRST ATOMIC BOMB ON HIROSHIMA AT 0915 THAT DATE. THE SECOND ATOMIC BOMB WAS DROPPED OVER NAGASAKI ON 9 AUGUST 1945, THE DATE RUSSIA DECLARED WAR ON JAPAN. THIS NEW WEAPON OF TERRIBLE DESTRUCTION RESULTED IN THE EMPEROR SPEAKING OUT AND OVERRULING HIS IMPERIAL COUNCIL. THE SURRENDER NOTIFICATION REACHED PRESIDENT TRUMAN ON 14 AUGUST 1945 (EAST LONGITUDE DATE). THE ALLIED POWERS PREVIOUSLY HAD RESPONDED POSITIVELY TO THE EMPERORS NOTE OF 10 AUGUST WHEREIN HE ASKED TO CONTINUE TO REIGN.

THE SURRENDER DOCUMENT SIGNED ON BOARD THE BATTLESHIP USS MISSOURI MADE IT UNNECESSARY TO CARRY OUT THE INVASION OF JAPAN. THE WILL OF THE JAPANESE TO FIGHT TO THE BITTER END HAD BEEN DEMONSTRATED IN THE MANY PRIOR ISLAND BATTLES. AT THE TIME OF THE SURRENDER THOUSANDS OF POWERFUL ALLIED SHIPS FROM THE UNITED STATES, GREAT BRITIAN, AUSTRALIA, THE NETHERLANDS, AND NEW ZEALAND WERE AVAILABLE PLUS A HUGE ARMADA OF AIRCRAFT. THE EMPERORS DECISION SAVED HIS COUNTRY FROM THE TERRIBLE DESTRUCTION AND LOSS OF LIFE THAT WOULD HAVE OCCURRED IF THE WAR HAD CONTINUED. IT ALSO SAVED LOSSES ON THE ALLIED SIDE THAT WOULD HAVE RESULTED FROM KAMIKAZE ATTACKS AND THE PLANNED INVASION OF THE JAPANESE HOMELAND.

Vincent "Jim" Vlach

VINCENT (JIM) VLACH, LCDR., U.S.N. (RET)
ONLY ENLISTED SURVIVOR FROM EXECUTIVE OFFICER'S
OFFICE,   USS ARIZONA, DECEMBER 7, 1941

REMEMBER PEARL HARBOR -
KEEP AMERICA ALERT
WEAKNESS INVITES ATTACK - KEEP AMERICA STRONG

**TO THE MEMBERS OF THE 509th COMPOSITE GROUP AND
SURVIVORS OF THE U.S.S. INDIANAPOLIS:**

I EXTEND MY THANKS TO YOU FOR YOUR GREAT CONTRIBUTION
TO BRING THE WAR TO A CONCLUSION WITH OUR VICTORY OVER
JAPAN. HAD YOU MEN NOT COMPLETED YOUR MISSIONS, I WOULD
NOT HAVE HAD THE "OPPORTUNITY TO KISS EDITH SHAIN" AND
END UP IN ALFRED EISENSTAEDT'S PHOTOGRAPH!

BEST WISHES,

August 17, 1962 — Chicago, Illinois. Members of the 393rd Squadron, 509th Composite Group, held its first reunion since the end of World War II at the Edgewater Beach Hotel. I'm not sure if I've got all the names, but to the best of my recollection, in the front row, from the left: DiJulio, Berman, Beser, Price, and David Lawrence, the reporter who flew with us to Nagasaki. In the back row, from the left: (unknown), Barsumian, Gackenback, Wey, Weatherly, Olivi, Bivans, Levy and Eidnes. (Photo courtesy of Kenneth L. Eidnes)

NAGASAKI -
SECOND ATOMIC BOMB TARGET

Nagasaki, one of Japan's principal shipbuilding, ordnance, and industrial centers with an estimated 1940 population of 252,000, was the target for the second 20th Air Force Atomic Bomb attack at 1100 on 9 August 1945 (Japan time).

Retuning crewmen of the 20AF B 29 aircraft participating in the mission reported that the bomb, dropped after a radar run corrected visually, hit 500 feet south of the Mitsubishi Steel and arms plant. The resulting explosions covered half of the urban area with a red ball of fire. Subsequently, a column of smoke, shading from dark brown through amber to white, rose to an altitude of 50,000 feet.

Resulting damage was assessed in post-strike photography of 10 August 1945.

Of an original area of 3.3 square miles, 30% was destroyed. Twelve industrial or transportation installations were destroyed in whole or in part.

STATISTICAL SUMMARY
Mission: SBM 16 Time of Attack: 090158Z
Organization: 20th Air force
Type of A/C: B-29
No. of Bombs Dropped: One
Method of bombing: 90% radar, 10% visual.
Target: NAGASAKI URBAN INDUSTRIAL AREA
Original Area: 3.3 sq.mi. Destroyed 0.98s q.mi.

Industrial Targets Destroyed or Damaged:
Mitsubishi Steel & Arms Works	
Mitsubishi-Urakami Ord. Plant	*30%*
Akunora Engine Works	*65%*
Nagasaki & Dejima Wharves & R.R.yds.	*25%*
Nagasaki Station & Freight yds.	*20%*
Gas Works & Power plant, each	*90%*

July 29, 1945, Pre-Strike aerial photo of Nagasaki, Japan, taken 11 days before our mission. The Nagasaki harbor is quite visible as the black area in the lower center of the photo. The "Fat Man" atomic bomb exploded part-way up the valley along the river shown in the left of the photo. (U. S. Army Air Corps photo)

A Brief Description
of the Implosion "Fat Man" Bomb
Dropped on Nagasaki, 9 August, 1945

It was sometime in 1939 that the German physicists Hahn and Strassmann carried out their spectacular experiments that showed that under certain circumstances Uranium 235, an isotope of Uranium-238, would fission, that is, if a neutron could penetrate the nucleus, the nucleus would split releasing two or three neutrons and a tremendous amount of energy. It took little imagination by a competent physicist to recognize the potential that this discovery offered for the manufacture of a specialized type of explosive if the release of these neutrons could be maintained in a chain reaction. When a sufficient amount of the material could be accumulated to "go critical" a chain reaction would be established. If the chain reaction would be controlled by draining off some neutrons it became a reactor. If the chain reaction went uncontrolled it became a bomb. It was this fact that prompted the beginning of our program to develop an "atomic bomb" .

Although U-235 occurs in natural Uranium 238 in about one part in one hundred forty, its separation from the natural uranium was not difficult because it became simply a matter of physically separating out the lighter isotope from the heavier parent material. With U-235 in hand the problem became one of trying to harness the fission process so that an explosion could be obtained. The Manhattan Engineer District then, had two goals immediately, first to create the engineering capability to accomplish the separation of the U-235 from the U-238, and second to establish and man with the required scientific talent a laboratory to

engineer a practical bomb. Oak Ridge comprised the first part of the solution and

the Los Alamos Laboratory the second.

At Los Alamos the first and logical approach to achieving a crit-

ical mass of U-235 was to attempt to unite two sub-critical masses together to

form a critical mass that would cause the nuclei to fission and thus attain a chain

reaction. The obvious approach was to use a gun to fire a projectile of the mater-

ial into a target of the same material at such a speed that the critical mass would

be achieved before the two parts were blown apart as a result of premature gener-

ation of neutrons. Experiments were carried out dropping a piece of U-235 down

a pipe, a portion of which was surrounded by a piece of U-235, and measuring the

generation of neutrons as the pieces passed one another. From these experiments

it was possible to determine the velocities that would be required to successfully

join the two parts of U-235. A gun barrel about ten feet long and with a bore of

six inches was built and a powder charge developed which would provide the nec-

essary velocity for the projectile to enter the target and "go critical". In the final

design the target was surrounded by a mass of Uranium 238 to act as a tamper and

contain the explosion as long as possible. This was the "Little Boy" bomb that was

used to attack Hiroshima.

While this was going on experiments in the accelerators at the

Radiation Laboratory at the University of California in Berkley under the direc-

tion of Ernest O. Lawrence were being carried on, out of which came the discov-

ery of Plutonium, a new element not found in a natural state. Further it was dis-

covered that plutonium, like U-235, was capable of fission. Of course the physicists at Los Alamos recognized the significance of this new discovery and embarked on a program to develop a system that could use Plutonium in a bomb.

The obvious first attempt was to utilize the same kind of a system for Plutonium as was being used for the U-238 bomb. It was quickly discovered however, that the natural neutron background of the Plutonium was such that, unless exceedingly high velocities were achieved, the system would blow itself apart before the two pieces of material could join to form the critical mass. It was estimated that velocities as much as thirty thousand foot seconds would be required, and to reach these velocities in a gun barrel, a length of nearly thirty feet would be required. Hardly a practical solution.

According to General Groves' book, <u>Now It Can Be Told</u>, Dr. Neddermeyer, a physicist at Los Alamos suggested that perhaps it might be possible to squeeze a mass of sub-critical Plutonium with sufficient force that it would become a critical mass and thus generate the desired chain reaction. Although the idea seemed to have merit there also seemed to be no conceivable way of generating sufficient force to accomplish the required degree of "squeeze". What ultimately was found to be required was to squeeze a sphere of Plutonium from the size of a soft ball to that of a billiard ball. Enter Captain, later Rear Admiral, William S. Parsons U.S.Navy, the Laboratory Deputy Director under Dr. Robert Oppenheimer.

Parsons was a naval ordnance expert without peer, probably the premier ordnance expert of the modern Navy. He decided that he and Dr. John Von Neumann, a world renowned theoretical mathematician also of the Laboratory, would closet themselves in an office of the Laboratory and not come out until they had solved' the problem of the Plutonium bomb.

The implosion process by the use of high explosive lenses was the result. This was the genesis of the Fat Man bomb used on Nagasaki.

They decided that it might be possible to generate, with the use of a properly designed high explosive system, a collapsing shock wave of such magnitude as to accomplish the force required to reduce the size of the Plutonium sphere to a critical mass. What was required would be a series of explosive lenses arranged in a large sphere surrounding the Plutonium. Thirty-two blocks of a pentagonal shape could be assembled into a sphere. Each block would be made of two separate explosive castings which would generate shock waves of different velocity, the outer casting providing a faster velocity than the inner so that the shock wave developed in the outer portion would overtake that developed in the inner portion with the result that, if properly designed, a concave spherical shock wave would result. Then, all that would be needed would be to detonate each of the thirty-two blocks of explosive simultaneously to form the complete collapsing spherical wave. Dr. George Kistiakowsky, a Harvard professor and high explosive expert also a member of the Laboratory staff, accomplished the engineering required to make the explosive lenses. It is interesting to note that there was no exact way to forecast the explosive force needed to make the squeeze, nor exactly how much force would be developed by the imploding shock wave. Therefore it could not be estimated how large the sphere of explosive should be made to accomplish the job. The solution was easy. It could be no larger than the bomb bay of the B-29 that ultimately would carry the bomb. This set the outside dimensions of the package at approximately five feet in diameter and ten feet long.

The next engineering problem was how to commence the detonation process in each of the thirty-two explosive lenses at exactly the same time. The timing was critical because any variation in the time of detonation of any one of the lenses would distort the collapsing shock wave and create jets rather than the desired perfect collapsing wave. Obviously a detonator for each lens would be required. The detonators chosen were small charges of a highly sensitive explosive actuated by an electric current. The source of the electric current would be a bank of four condensers charged to a voltage level of five thousand volts. Four condensers were chosen to provide the redundancy in the system determined to be required to achieve a failure rate of no more than one in ten thousand. They were connected together in such a way that any two could discharge to the detonators and start the detonation process. Since the co-axial cables leading from the condensers to each detonator were of varying length it was necessary to insert a delay mechanism in each cable of exactly the correct amount so that the electric current reached all detonators at precisely the same time. These were engineering problems of no small dimension and it was this phase of the development that required the most time to perfect and turned out to be the controlling factor for having the bomb ready for use in August as predicted by General Groves.

The fusing used in both bombs was essentially the same. Tail warning radars that were used in bombers to detect fighters attacking from astern provided the basic element of the fuse. Each radar was modified and adjusted to trigger when a certain range to the ground had been reached in order to provide the desired height of burst of the bomb. Again to achieve the reliability factor, four of the radars were used in the fusing system and so connected that any two could actuate the firing system that would send the proper signal to the condensers to release the electric current to fire the detonators.

Several safety factors were also designed into the bomb firing system. First, It was necessary to insure that under no circumstances could the bomb be accidentally detonated, through failure of some part of the system, so close to the delivery aircraft as to cause damage to the plane. Safe separation timers were provided to accomplish this. They were started to time by "arming wires" secured to the aircraft being pulled from the clocks as the bomb fell away from the bomb shackle in the bomb bay. Until these timers were started all power to the bomb electronic components was cut off so that nothing could cause a premature detonation. After fifteen seconds had passed after release of the bomb the clocks closed the power circuits required for the bomb fusing and firing circuits. Nine clocks were used in this system, and again for reliability, any three could close the appropriate switches.

Second, since the fuses were radar devices, it was recognized that they could easily be jammed if the enemy were to broadcast jamming signals on precisely the same frequency. Therefore it was necessary that the fuses start radiating at the latest possible time during the drop to reduce the vulnerability to jamming, should the frequency of the fuses have been compromised. Barometric switches were provided that would start the fuses radiating at about eight thousand feet above the ground. Again, there were nine of these switches so arranged that any three could start the process.

While the bomb was secured in the plane's bomb bay electrical power was provided from the aircraft electrical supply through an umbilical cord.

Upon release of the bomb this umbilical would be disconnected. To provide continuing power for the bomb's electronic components storage batteries were provided so that after release from the plane the bomb was completely self-contained and self-sufficient.

In order to preclude any spurious signals from entering the fusing and firing circuits safing plugs were provided mounted in the nose of the bomb. When the "green" plugs were inserted these circuits were completely isolated and therefore the bomb was considered to be in a "safe" condition. After takeoff, and well clear of any friendly territory, "red" plugs replaced the "green" plugs and the isolating circuits were removed. Thus the circuits were complete and permitted signals from the fuses to activate the firing system. This was as near as it was possible to "disarm" the bomb. It did not, of course provide the safety that was present in the "Little Boy" U-235 bomb by the removal of the powder charge from the gun feature of the bomb. An accident such as an aborted take off of the bomb carrying aircraft followed by a crash and fire could very well result in a "cook off" of the explosive lenses with the probable result of a low order detonation which would scatter toxic plutonium into a large area surrounding the disabled aircraft. Such an accident would certainly have put North Field on Tinian out of operation for many months.

Whereas the basic design of the "Little Boy" U-235 bomb lent itself to easy solution of the ballistic design problem, the basic spherical design of the "Fat Man" was a ballistician's night mare. To approach some kind of an acceptable ballistic shape it was decided to enclose the explosive sphere and the electronic components attached to it, inside an ellipsoid shaped case. This was suggested by the fact that having mounted the firing condensers, the fusing system, the storage batteries, the timers and barometric switches on opposite sides of the sphere the package became an elongated oval shape. Further, it was decided that the bomb should be protected from fifty caliber bullets should the delivery aircraft be attacked by enemy fighters. This required a half inch of special treatment steel formed into the ellipsoid shape, something that had never been done before by the armor plate industry. Small sections of the armor plate had to be formed into shapes with a compound curvature and then each section welded together to complete the case. Holding the proper shape during the welding process turned out to be an almost impossible job.

First, fins were tried to provide the stabilization in flight necessary to yield a reproducible trajectory, but without success. Wind tunnel test showed that perhaps a large box tail might solve the problem. But again, flight was erratic and reproducible trajectories were not achieved. At this point Captain Parsons, the ordnance expert, suggested placing baffles in the box tail to provide a parachute effect. Tests on the Navy's ballistic range at the Salton Sea in Southern California showed that this was the answer. Time of fall was reduced significantly and reproducible flight was achieved so that data could be obtained to calculate the bombing data inputs required by the Norden Mark XV bomb sight that would be used in the B-29.

During the winter of 1944 and the spring of 1945 tests of all the components of the bomb, both individually and in their final configuration, were being conducted at the Army Air Corps base at Wendover, Utah. As noted earlier, it was the firing system that was giving the most trouble and testing continued right up until the date of the drop of the first bomb on Japan. As a rehearsal for the operation with the Fat Man bomb, a complete bomb, was carried out off the island of Tinian. This was the first time that the bomb in its final configuration had ever been dropped out of an airplane. The next day, August 9, 1945, we attacked Nagasaki successfully. This was undoubtedly the shortest time between development and combat use of any ordnance in modern history. Less than two weeks later Japan surrendered unconditionally .

Reprinted with permission of Los Almos National Laboratory.

```
WESTERN UNION FSI
RENO, NEVADA 89502-2375
09AM
```

```
1-002742S343002 12/09/91 ICS IPMRNCZ CSP CBGB
1 3128810233 MGM TDRN CHICAGO IL 12-09 0127P EST
```

```
FRED J OLIVI
2535 W 117TH ST
CHICAGO IL 60655
```

```
THIS IS A CONFIRMATION COPY OF THE FOLLOWING MESSAGE:

 3128810233 POM TDRN CHICAGO IL 53 12-09 0127P EST
PMS PRESIDENT GEORGE BUSH
WHITE HOUSE DC 20500

MR PRESIDENT

AS COPILOT ON B-29 "BOCKSCAR" THAT DROPPED THE SECOND ATOM BOMB ON
NAGASAKI LET ME COMMEND YOU ON YOUR DECISION NOT TO APOLOGIZE TO
JAPAN FOR OUR WARTIME MISSIONS.

TO KNOW THE EFFORTS OF THE TWO FLIGHT CREWS INVOLVED IN ENDING THE
WAR WAS NOT WASTED, IS REASSURING AND GREATLY APPRECIATED.
 FRED J OLIVI
 2535 W 117TH ST
 CHICAGO IL 60655
```

```
13:26 EST
```

```
MGMCOMP
```

P.S. I never received an answer for this telegram to the President!!

To reply by Mailgram Message, see reverse side for Western Union's toll-free numbers.

Relayed

RGM V RGE NR 27 ███████ ROUTINE

FROM DEPCOMAF 20 POA 141000Z JUL 45

TO COMGENBOMCOM 21

NR 0162

THE FOLLOWING MESSAGE FROM WARCOS IS PASSED FOR YOUR INFORMATION AND
GUIDANCE. DESIRE YOU TAKE NECESSARY ACTION TO ADVISE COMMANDING OFFICER
509TH COMPOSITE GROUP.

"FROM: WARCOS

TO DEPCOMAF 20 POA, COMGENAAFPOA, COMGENPOA AND CINCAFPAC

INFO COMGENAAF 2 AND CGCAF

WARX 30245

SPECIAL PROJECT TO BE KNOWN AS CENTERBOARD HAS BEEN ESTABLISHED OF WHICH
THE 509 COMPOSITE GROUP NOW ASSIGNED TO THE 21 BOMBER COMMAND AND LOCATED
AT TINIAN IS THE PRINCIPAL PART IN THE THEATER. THE REAR ECHELON OF THIS
PROJECT IS IN THE 21. THE 320TH TROOP CARRIER SQUADRON IS ASSIGNED TO THE
ORGANIZATION TO PROVIDE NECESSARY TRANSPORTATION FOR PERSONNEL AND EQUIP-
MENT BETWEEN THE UNITED STATES AND THE MARIANAS. THE DEPUTY COMMANDER 20B
CIB FORCE POA IS AUTHORIZED TO TRANSPORT SUCH PERSONNEL AND EQUIPMENT BE-
TWEEN THE MARIANAS AND THE UNITED STATES AS MAY BE REQUIRED WITHOUT
FURTHER AUTHORIZATION OR CLEARANCE. THIS DOES NOT INCLUDE PERMANENT
TRANSFER OF PERSONNEL BUT MAY AUTHORIZE EXTENDED PERIODS OF TEMPORARY
DUTY AT EITHER LOCATION, THE ABOVE APPLIES ONLY WHEN SUCH PERSONNEL AND
EQUIPMENT ARE TRANSPORTED IN AIRCRAFT ASSIGNED TO THE CENTERBOARD PROJECT
ORDERS AND INSTRUCTIONS ISSUED HENCEFORTH IN IMPLEMENTING THIS DIRECTIVE
WILL EMPLOY THE DESIGNATION "CENTERBOARD" FOR THE PURPOSE OF IDENTIFY-
ING THE PROJECT AND INDICATING THE AUTHORITY HEREIN CONTAINED."

END

TOD:1117Z TB

ROGER NR 27 V RGM 1117Z LS

act — Plans
D/S oper
c/s

L-12-152

RGM V BEE NR 21 ▓▓▓▓▓▓—OPERATIONAL PRIORITY

FROM: COMGEN USASTAF 050420Z F V 6 45

TO : C.O. 509TH COMP GP (TINIAN)

INFO: COMGEN AAF 20

NR : 1326

   TO CLEAR UP ANY MISUNDERSTANDING THE FOLLOWIN PERSONNEL HAVE BEEN
CLEARED TO PARTICIPATE IN AERIAL COMBAT OPRATIONS IN CONNECTION WITH
CENTER BOARD PROJECT CMA IF REQUIRED TO DO SO IN THE PERFORMANCE OF
THEIR ASSIGNED MISSION COLON LAURENCE HOW JOHNSTON CMA TARE SLANT FOUR
WALTER GOODMAN CMA TARE SLANT THREE JAMES WIEBOLT CMA LOUIS ALVAREZ
CMA BERNARD WALDMAN CMA HAROLD MIKE AGNEW CMA CAPTAIN WILLIAM
SUGAR PARSONS UNCLE SUGAR NAN CMA COMMANDER FOX LOVE ASHWORTH UNCLE
SUGAR NAN CMA COLONEL PAUL WILLIAM TIBBETS JUNIOR CMA LIEUTENANT
COLONEL THOMAS JOG CLASSEN CMA MAJOR THOMAS WILLIAM FEREBEE CMA
MAJOR CHARLES WILLIAM SWEENEY CMA CAPTAIN KERMIT KING BEAHAN CMA
FIRST LIEUTENANT GEORGE ABLE KOESTER CMA SECOND LIEUTENANT PHILIP
MIKE BARNES CMA SECOND LIEUTENANT LEON DOG SMITH CMA SECOND
KIEUTENANT MORRIS ROGER·JEPPSON PD

END

CORR--- TEEING INSTRUCTIONS

-T- 20 AF, 509 COMP GP

TOD:0512 Z TB

ROGER NR21 0512Z JAW.

KY1V V RGM NR11 OPOP ███ ███

T - `CTU 94.11.1   CO AAF ??? FLT CONTROL CTR `AIPAN

FROM TWINING COMGENAF ??   0801572 AUG 45

TO COMGENU?A?TAF (GUAM)   COMGENU?A?TAF (REAR)

INFO 7TH FITER COM (OPOP)   CTU 94.11.3 (OPOP)   ISCOM IWO /RR/

CTF 94 /PP/ KK2U /OPOP/   INTERPRON 2 /RR/   CINCPOA ADV HQ /OPOP/

CINCPOA REAR /PP/   COM?USPAC /OPOP/   CTU 94.1.3 /PP/   CTU 94.4.1 /PP/

CTU 94.7.3 /PP/   CTU 94.1.2 /PP/   COAAF 20 COMBAT `TAGING CENTER

IWO /OPOP/   COM3RD FLT /OPOP/   CTU 94.1.1 /PP/   CTG 95.9 /PP/

CTU 94.11.1 /OPOP/   COAAF 20 FLIGHT CONTROL CENTER `AIPAN /OPOP/

COMAF 7 /OPOP/   FEAF OKINAWA /OPOP/   COMAF 8 /OPOP/   CTU 95.9.?

/OPOP/   ((AL INFO ADDEE? ?HOULD BE OP RPT OPP)

AIMCR 5347 SUBJECT: INTENTION? FOR 509TH BOMB GROUP STRIKE USING
SPECIAL MUNITION?.

THE 509TH BOMB GROUP, USING SPECIAL MUNITIONS, WILL STRIKE EITHER
KOKURA OR NAGASAKI AT APPROXIMATELY 091030K. MANDATORY THAT NO
FRIENDLY AIRCRAFT OTHER THAN THOSE DISPATCHED BY HEADQUARTERS 20TH
AIR FORCE IN CONJUNCTION WITH THI? MISSION FLY WITHIN 50 MILES OF THE?E
TWO TARGETS AREAS FOUR HOURS PRIOR TO THE INTENDED STRIKE TIME
AND SIX HOURS AFTER INTENDED STRIKE TIME. ANY AIRCRAFT FLYING IN
THESE TARGET AREAS AFTER THE SIX HOUR PERIOD SHOULD BE BRIEFED NOT
TO FLY IN ANY CLOUDS OR SMOKE NEAR THE TARGET AREAS. THE ROUTE WILL
BE: MARIANA BASES DIRECT YOKUSHIMA, DEPARTING THERE AT 090945K;
THENCE TO 132 DEGREES EAST 32 DEGREES 30 MINUTES NORTH AREA; THENCE
TO EITHER TARGET DEPENDING ON WEATHER; TO IWO; TO MARIANAS, AIRCRAFT
PARTICIPATING: TWO WEATHER SHIPS PRECEDING STRIKE AIRCRAFT BY ONE HOUR
TO ASSIGNED TARGET AREAS; ONE STRIKE AIRCRAFT ACCOMPANIED BY TWO
OBSERVER AIRCRAFT; TWO PHOTO AIRCRAFT PHOTOGRAPHING BOMBED TARGET.
AT APPROXIMATELY 091430K. END.

TOD....080325Z WW

ROGER V KY1V   FA:

PGE V RGH NR2S OPOP ~~████~~

T- CTU 94.11.3

FROM: COMAF 20   040741Z $A U G 45$

TO : CTU 95.9.2   CTU 94.11.3   313TH BOMWING   CONSUBPAC

INFO: CINCPAC ADV   COM3RD FLEET   COMGENFEAF ADV OKINAWA   CTU 94.11.1

AINCR 5155

SMALL FORCE B-29 A/C ATTACK HIROSHIMA ,KOKURA OR NAGASAKI DEPENDING ON
WEATHER DURING DAYLIGHT 6 AUGUST. ROUTES BASE TO IWO TO DEPARTURE POINT
33-36N 134-30E THENCE TO TARGET SELECTED EITHER DIRECTLY OR VIA OTHER
TARGETS IN ORDER ABOVE THENCE TO IWO TO BASES. TAKEOFF 060230K DEPARTURE
POINT 0915K TARGET BETWEEN 0945K AND 1040K. LIFEGUARD HULL NUMBER 388 AT
32-00N 132-00E COVERED BY 313TH BOMWINGS AIREDALES 1 AND 2 FROM 0915K
UNTIL COMPLETION RESCUES OR SAFE PASSAGE OF A/C. LIFEGUARD HULL NUMBER
221 AT 30 MILES BEARING 150 DEGREES FROM REFERENCE K-3 COVERED BY 313TH
BOMWINGS 3 AND 4 FROM 1000K. IN ACCORDANCE WITH CINCPAC ADVS 040257
CTU 95.9.2 REQUESTED TO COVER LIFEGUARDS WITH PLAYMATES 5 AND 7 RESPEC-
TIVELY FROM ABOVE TIMES AS XRAY TIMES. UNLESS WORD HAS BEEN RECEIVED OF
SAFE PASSAGE OF A/C IT IS REQUESTED THEY BE RELIEVED BY PLAYMATES 6 AND
8 RESPECTIVELY WHO WILL REMAIN TO PRUDENT LIMIT OF ENDURANCE UNLESS
SECURED EARLIER BY AIREDALES. AIREDALES WILL REMAIN UNTIL ALL PLAYMATES
ARE SECURED. AIRDALES, PLAYMATES AND LIFEGUARDS WILL UNDER NO CIRCUM-
STANCES APPROACH CLOSER THAN FIFTY MILES TO TARGET TO EFFECT RESCUE
UNTIL FOUR HOURS AFTER ATTACK, AND NOT CLOSER THEN FIFTEEN MILES FOR
TWO HOURS MORE, AFTER WHICH RESTRICTIONS ARE REMOVED. AIRDALES WILL
GIVE COVER TO LIFEGUARDS OR PLAYMATES IN MAKING RESCUE. CTU 94.11.3
AND CTU 94.7.3 REQUESTED TO PROVIDE PLAYMATE 61 AND BIRD DOG 61 AT
29-00N 136-30E FROM 1200K. CTU 94.11.1 ALERTED. REFERENCE POINTS K-3
AND S-1. A/C CALL WILL BE DIMPLES.

TOD:040833Z TAS.

████

ROGER NR 29(JB

Hypocenter; the point under which a nuclear blast occurs. Nagasaki looking east. Winter of 1945 - 46. Army Air Corps Photographer Sgt. William E. Jones.

Hypocenter of nuclear explosion.
Nagasaki looking south east. Winter of 1945 - 46.
Army Air Corps Photographer Sgt. William E. Jones.

Translation of the Leaflets Dropped on Japan

Between the Bombings of Hiroshima and Nagasaki

When one's home appears to be falling, one does not run away. Rather one repairs the bad places.

Japan is now facing a crisis. In other words, the Army is the source of decay within your country. That the Army is deceiving you regarding their strength is evidenced by the air raids that you have experienced recently. Remove your war leaders and save your country!

***

People of Japan!

A message from President Harry S. Truman of the United States of America.

Nazi Germany has been destroyed. You citizens of Japan will be made aware of the tremendous offensive might of the combined land, sea, and air forces of the United States. As long as your government officials and military leaders persist in their war efforts we will increase our offensive posture and destroy all facilities that provide support for your armed forces. Prolonging this war will only increase the suffering of the people. There is nothing to be gained for the people. However, we will continue our offensive until the Japanese army throws down its weapons and surrenders unconditionally. Surrender will destroy the power of the military leaders who have brought the people to the brink of disaster and untold suffering to the soldiers and sailors whom you love. Surrender will also permit them to return to their farms and workplaces. Surrender will not mean a life of slavery for you.

***

Long, long ago, there lived a maiden of unsurpassed beauty named Otoyo. Otoyo served Lord Bizen and was his favorite. One day the lord, waited upon by Otoyo, walked in the garden and remained there until sundown enjoying the lovely fragrance of the flowers. As they returned to the castle, they were unaware that they were followed by a large cat. Otoyo returned to her room and went to bed. When she was awakened in the middle of the night she saw the large cat beside her. As she screamed in fright, the cat leaped upon her and sank its fangs into her throat and killed her. After the cat buried Otoyo, it assumed her shape and commenced haunting the lord. The lord gradually became paler and weaker, and no medicine had any effect. Finally, a brave and loyal vassal named Itoh Suneta penetrated the disguise of this monster cat. The cat escaped to the mountain but was pursued by the crowd and was killed.

I imagine everyone knows this story. What is the moral of the story?

The monster cat is the army leaders who are sucking the blood of the people and causing the meaningless sacrifice of many thousands of young men. They are preventing the distribution of necessary food and medical supplies to the people and weakening the nation.

The lovely murdered maiden can be compared to the constitutional government destroyed by the army clique. The Army, in direct opposition to the law passed down by the Emperor Meiji, has meddled in politics. The Army has been responsible for the downfall of the nation rather than its protection.

Finally, the disguise of the monster cat was penetrated by the loyal vassal and it was pursued by the villagers and killed. To achieve peace and prosperity again, isn't it time to hope for the downfall of the military leaders who have brought suffering to the Emperor and the people of Japan?

***

To the Military Leaders of Japan!

Can you convince the people of Japan that you are capable of protecting the land, sea, and air of Japan?

***

These are the questions asked the people of Japan by President Harry S. Truman of the United States of America:

Didn't you swear to defend Guam, Tinian, the Philippines, Iwo Jima, and Okinawa as the final obstacles to reaching Tokyo? Didn't you swear that no American aircraft would sully the skies of Japan?

Were you able to keep your promise? The United States of America is determined to fight this war to the finish. We will achieve victory in spite of the costs in manpower and equipment Your future is in your hands. You can choose between the unnecessary loss of many soldiers or an honorable peace. The choice is yours.

***

You can understand the frightening reality by seeing the destruction caused in Hiroshima by one bomb.

By the use of the atom bomb we will destroy the Army, which is prolonging the war.

The United States hopes that you will plead with the Emperor to end this war so that it will not be necessary to use many atom bombs.

The President of the United States hopes that the thirteen articles will be approved quickly and that peace can come to the new Japan.

You must suspend armed opposition immediately. Otherwise, the United States will use the atom bomb in addition to the superior weapons available to permanently end this war.

Evacuate the city immediately!

***

NOTICE TO THE JAPANESE PEOPLE!

Evacuate the city immediately! What this leaflet contains is extremely important so please read carefully.

The Japanese people are facing an extremely important autumn. Your military leaders were presented with thirteen articles for surrender by our three-country alliance to put an end to this unprofitable war. This proposal was ignored by your Army leaders.

Because of this the Soviet Republic intervened.

In addition, the United States has developed an atom bomb, which had not been done by any nation before. It has been determined to employ this frightening bomb. One atom bomb has the destructive power of 2000 B29s.

***

—Translation by Toshiko Bradley
© copyright 1990 by Exceptional Books, Ltd.
Los Alamos, NM USA

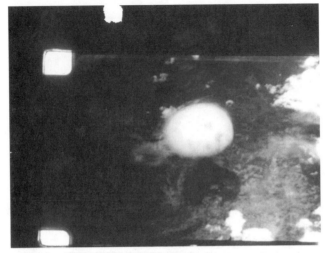

Here is a series of three photos taken at 11:58 am on August 9, 1945, as "Fat Man" exploded over Nagasaki, Japan. In the top photo, the mushroom cloud is just beginning to form.

In the middle photo, the mushroom cloud is climbing higher and higher.

In the bottom photo, the cloud is fully formed and rising above 50,000 feet.

(Photos courtesy Los Alamos Laboratory)

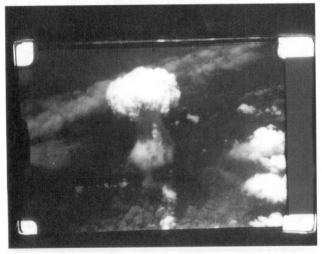

Aerial photograph of Nagasaki, taken several days after the bombing on August 9, 1945. Damage assessments of different areas are listed in the caption inset into photo. (Photo courtesy U. S. Army Air Corps)

These four photographs were taken in Nagasaki in September 1945, several weeks after the bomb strike on August 9, and show the damage at ground level. (Photo courtesy U. S. Army Air Corps)

This aerial photo of Nagasaki, Japan, looks north up into the Urakami Valley. The upper left arrow shows the approximate location where "Fat Man" exploded. The arrow in the lower right indicates (to be the best of my memory) the stadium which was the original target. (Photo courtesy of Sgt. William E. Jones)

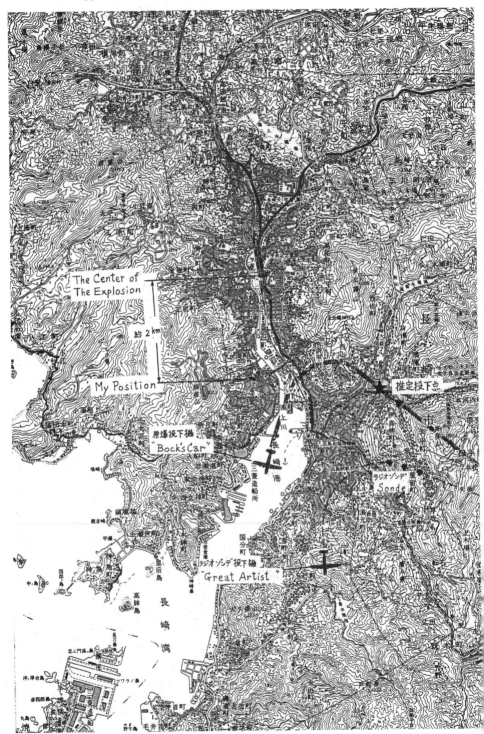

Courtesy of Takeshi Tanaka — Japan

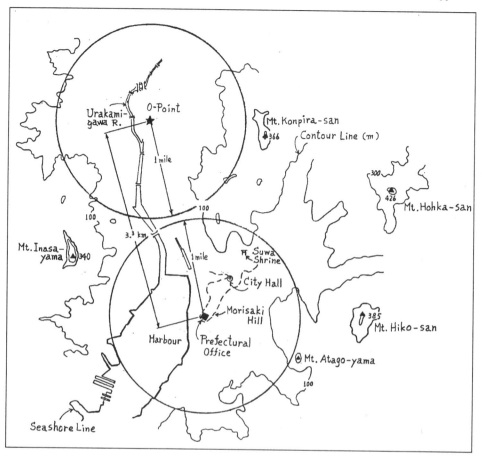

Courtesy of Takeshi Tanaka — Japan

These three pages (200 - 202) were sent to me by Takeshi Tanaka, a Japanese National, who did a lot of research on the Nagasaki Mission of 9 August, 1945.

You can locate Mr. Tanaka's position on page 200 on the left side of the page, regarding the Nagasaki Mission.

It is very apparent that he has had a great interest in the Nagasaki Mission. The result of his research information is extensive and informative.

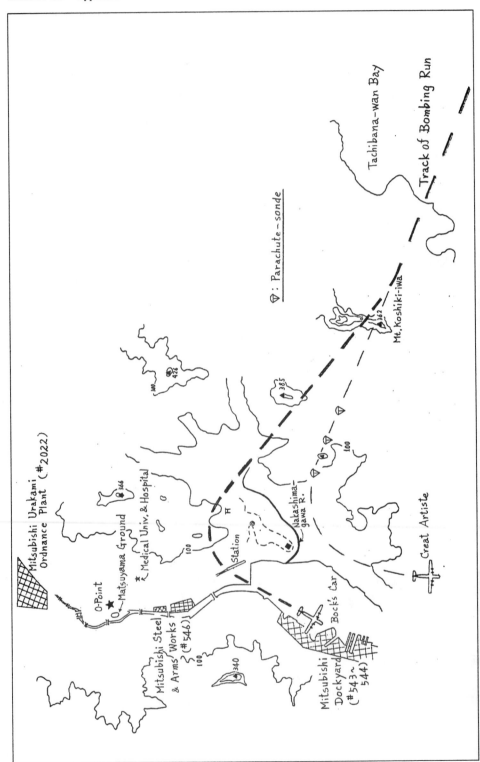

Courtesy of Takeshi Tanaka — Japan

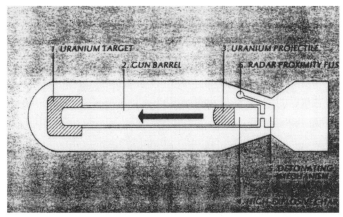

Figure 1
"Little Boy"

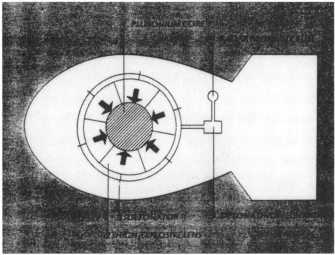

Figure 2
"Fat Man"

Drawings show method of starting the chain reaction in the two
atomic bombs that exploded over Japan.
Figure 1 - The "Little Boy" Bomb projectile was fired into the core
    of the uranium to cause the detonation.
Figure 1 - Chain reation was started from within the "Fat Man"
    Bomb by bombarding the plutonium core causing the
    explosion of the bomb.

RCC V RGM NRSQ URGENT ▬▬▬▬

T WCR AS FN-09-18

FROM TWINING COMGENAAF 20 GUAM 091843Z *A U G 45*

TO COMGENUSASTAF GUAM

INFO COMGENUSASTAF (REAR) WASHINGTON (URGENT) ATTN: GENERAL NORSTAD AFMCR 5482 SUBJECT: FINAL REPORT, 509TH SBM 16, STRIKE CENTERBOARD FLOWN 9 AUGUST 1945.

1. TARGET ATTACKED: NAGASAKI

2. TIME TAKE OFF: FIRST: 0817497 LAST 8817517

3. NUMBER A/C AIRBORNE: 3

4. BOMB DATA:

  A. LOAD AND TYPE: SPECIAL

  B. FUSING: SPECIAL

  C. DISPOSITION: 3 SECONDARY NAGASAKI URBAN AREA

    A/C VICTOR 77, VICTOR 89, VICTOR 90

5. METHOD OF BOMBING: VISUAL

6. TIME BOMBS AWAY: FIRST: 09015872 LAST: 090201Z

7. WEATHER: 7-10/10 ALTO CUMULUS. BOMBED THROUGH HOLE.

8. PRESSURE ALTITUDE: 28,900 FEET.

9. ENEMY AIR OPPOSITION: NONE

10. ENEMY ANTI-AIRCRAFT: A/C VICTOR 77 REPORTS ABOUT 15 BURSTS FROM YAHATA AREA, ALL LOW ALSO 8 BURSTS AT 6 O'CLOCK. MEAGER.

11. OBSERVATIONS: 1 LARGE SHIP IN HARBOR AREA AT NAGASAKI, NUMEROUS SMALLER VESSELS IN SAME AREA. 4 UNIDENTIFIED SINGLE ENGINE AT 33/15N 132/00E, LOW, CIRCLING. 13 UNIDENTIFIED S/E AT 30/25N 130/35E, 12 SILVER IN COLOR, 1 OFF COLOR, 2 MILES EAST AT 12-15,000 FEET. NEAR SENDAI, SE COAST OF KYUSHU SMOKE WAS SEEN, VERY MUCH LIKE THAT OBSERVED WHEN SPECIAL BOMB EXPLODES, INTENSITY MAIN-TAINED TILL OUT OF SIGHT.

12. BOMBING RESULTS: FAIR TO GOOD.

13. TIME OF LANDING: FIRST: 091506Z LAST: 891339Z.

14. OTHER SIGNIFICANT INFORMATION: 90 PER CENT OF RUN WAS RADAR, BOMBARDIER TOOK OVER AND MADE VISUAL CORRECTIONS IN LAST 10 PER CENT. BOMB HIT APPROXIMATELY 500 FEET SOUTH OF MITSUBISHI PLANT. COMPANION SHIP OBSERVED. AFTER EXPLOSION LARGE WHITE SMOKE RING FORMED, RED BALL OF FIRE COVERING 1/2 OF AREA. THEN COLUMN OF SMOKE FORMED 1/2 MILE WIDE, FUNNELING UPWARD, BOTTOM DARK BROWN IN COLOR, CENTER AMBER COLOR, TOP WHITE. COLUMN ROSE TO 50,000 FEET, RISING TO 30,000 FEET IN ONE AND ONE HALF TO TWO MINUTES. MANY SMALL BRIGHT FIRES OBSERVED. CONSIDERABLE SMOKE OBSERVED 175 MILES FROM AREA. FIVE SCHOCK WAVES FELT.

15. MISSION EFFECTIVE.

16. REMARKS: A/C VICTOR 83 STOOD BY AT IWO JIMA FOR EMERGENCY BUT WAS NOT CALLED UPON, RETURNING THIS BASE 090918Z. A/C VICTOR 77, 89, AND 90 LANDED OKINAWA 090480Z - 090404Z, SHORT OF GAS, TOOK OF 090763Z - 090706Z.

END

TOD 091906Z FER

ROGER 091903Z ER

RCE V RGH NR54 URGENT URGENT

T- COMGENUSASTAF (REAR) AS FN-06-16

FROM: COMGENAAF 20 GUAM 0613182 AUG45

TO: COMGENUSASTAF GUAM

INFO: COMGENUSASTAF (REAR) WASHINGTON (PRECEDENCE SAME AS ACTION)

AIMCR 5260 SUBJECT: FINAL REPORT, 509TH GP SPECIAL BOMBING MISSIO
13, TARGET HIROSHIMA URBAN INDUSTRIAL AREA, FLOWN 5 AUGUST 194

1. MISSION NO: 509TH SBM 13

2. TARGET ATTACKED: HIROSHIMA URBAN INDUSTRIAL AREA

3. TIME OF TAKE OFF: 0516452 0516472 0516492

4. NO. OF A/C AIRBORNE: 3

5. BOMB DATA: A. LOAD AND TYPE: SPECIAL. (1) FUSING: SPECIAL.
   B. DISPOSITION: 3 A/C PRIMARY: HIROSHIMA URBAN INDUSTRIAL AR
   C. METHOD OF BOMBING: VISUAL
   D. TIME BOMBS AWAY : 0523152 - 0523172

6. WEATHER: 2/10 CLOUD COVERAGE TO TARGET AREA.

7. ALTITUDE: 30,200 FEET.

8. ENEMY AIR OPPOSITION: NIL.

9. ENEMY ANTI-AIRCRAFT: 1 A/C REPORTED 20 BURSTS OF FLAK 10,000
   FEET BELOW A/C AT MISCHA.

10. OBSERVATIONS: NONE

11. BOMBING RESULTS: EXCELLENT.

12. TIME OF LANDING: 0604582 0605272 0605352

13. OTHER INFORMATION: NONE

14. MISSION RESULTS: EXCELLENT

15. REMARKS: 4 SUPERDUMBO A/C WERE AIRBORNE FOR THIS MISSION.

FINAL REPORT, 509TH GP SPECIAL BOMBING MISSION NO. 13 (WEATHER AIRCRA
TARGETS HIROSHIMA, KOKURA, AND NAGASAKI, FLOWN 5 AUGUST 1945.

1. MISSION NO: 509TH SBM 13 (WEATHER AIRCRAFT)

2. TARGETS OBSERVED: HIROSHIMA, KOKURA, AND NAGASAKI.

3. TIME OF TAKE OFF: 0515372 0515402 0515462

4. NO. A/C AIRBORNE: 3

5. BOMB DATA: NONE CARRIED.

6. WEATHER: HIROSHIMA 2/10 CLOUD, KOKURA 4/10 TO 7/10 CLOUD, NAGASAI
   CAVU.

7. ALTITUDE: 28,000 FT.

8. ENEMY AIR OPPOSITION: NIL

9. ENEMY FLAK: NIL

10. OBSERVAIONS: 4 S/E A/C ON MIYAZAKI A/F. 12 T/E ON UNIDENTIFIED
    A/F AT 32/00 N 132/00E. CONSIDERABLE SMOKE OVER INLAND SEA AREA
    COMING FROM SOUTHWEST TIP OF SHIKOKU, EXACT LOCATION UNOBSERVED.

11. TIME OF LANDING: 0604252 0604452 0603552

12. OTHER INFORMATION: FURNISHED DATA FOR STRIKE A/C.

13. MISSION SUCCESSFUL.

END

TOD. 261348 DM K
ROGER 0613482 KH

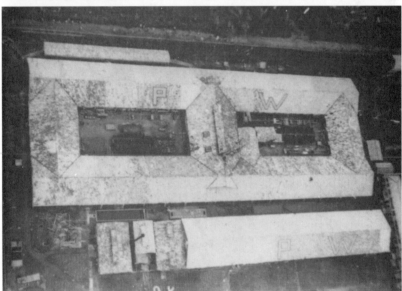

Photos courtesy of James Pittman

These remarkable aerial photos of the POW camp located in Nagasaki (but not in area damaged by "Fat Man"), were taken by James Dittmar, Central Fire Control gunner, with the 871st Bomb Squadron of the 497th Bomb Group, which was based on Saipan, soon after the Japanese surrender. In the top photo parachutes carrying food supplies into the camp can be seen. In the lower photo, taken directly over one of the buildings, you can read the letters "P.O.W." that were painted on the roof by the American prisoners to direct the B-29's on their mission of mercy.

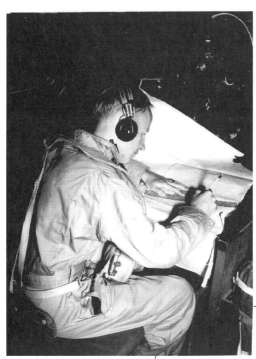

1945 - Tinian Island. Lt. Stanley Steinke, Navigator on Crew C-14 (Lt. Norm Ray - Aircraft Commander) accompanied "Bockscar" - Nagasaki Mission. Major Hopkins flew aircraft V-90 "Big Stink" as the photographic aircraft for the mission because of illness of Lt. Ray.
Letter was written to Fred J. Olivi in response to questions about Nagasaki Mission.

Stanley G. Steinke, C.P.C.U.
4 Crooked Road   Feasterville, Pa
ELmwood 7-3569

Life, Fire and Casualty Insurance

Dear Fred,   July 18, 1972

It was a surprise hearing from you and you do tax an old man's memory.

I did not make any note during the Nagasaki flight or did I jot any items down after the flight so you can see what it is doing to me.

As I recall — we reached the I.P. cruising at 30,000 feet. We were on radio silence so there was no way of communicating. We did not make visual contact, so we were - 't in 'formation. We cruised the I.P. point for 15 or 20 (??) minutes. During that time I spotted a 29 at our altitude flying in the opposite direction to ours. Our tail gunner also reported the sighting but no one else in the crew made the sighting.

Sometime (?) after that it was decided to head toward the primary target to make contact.

I don't know the time frame when the radio operator intercepted the message that the drop had been made. We made a quick visual check of the results and headed for Okinawa as radio contact had been established and those were the orders.

Sorry that I can't give you a more accurate and specific report but as I mentioned I had made no personal notes or reminders.

"FAT MAN" BOMB

Used with permission of Frederick L. Ashworth, Vice Admiral, U.S.Navy (Ret)

Weaponeer on B-29 "Bockscar" - Nagasaki Mission, 9 August 1945

The Fat Man Bomb did not contain "six (6) fuses", all of which were to activate at 1890 feet.

The Fat Man Bomb contained a bank of nine (9) safe separation timers that would close 15 seconds after release of the bomb and several thousand feet below to insure that a "premature" detonation would not harm the dropping aircraft. There was a bank of nine (9) barometric switches that had been calibrated to close at eight thousand (8,000) feet above the ground to start the modified tail warning radars, any two (2) of which would activate the firing system when they sensed an altitude of, say, 1,890 feet above the ground.

A full-scale dress rehearsal for the Nagasaki operation and the bomb that was used in the test was a full-scale and complete Fat Man Bomb configured exactly as would be the bomb to be dropped in Nagasaki the following day. Of course, there was no nuclear material loaded into the core for this test. The explosion of the high explosive in the bomb marked its successful operation.

Nuclear weapon of the "Little Boy" type, the kind detonated over Hiroshima, Japan, in World War II. The bomb is 28 inches in diameter and 120 inches long. The first nuclear weapon ever detonated, it weighed about 9,000 pounds and had a yield equivalent to approximately 14,000 tons of high explosive. The atomic material used in making the Hiroshima bomb was Uranium.

Nuclear weapon of the "Fat Man" type, the kind detonated over Nagasaki, Japan, in World War II. The bomb is 60 inches in diameter and 128 inches long. The second nuclear weapon to be detonated, it weighed about 10,000 pounds and had a yield equivalent to approximately 20,000 tons of high explosive. The atomic material used in this bomb was Plutonium and made the Hiroshima Bomb obsolete. It was an implosion type bomb that started the chain reaction to explode the bomb.

1945 - Mysterious Black Box Installed in B-29 "Bockscar" Nagasaki (Kokura Mission) North Field - Tinian Island.

The mysterious Black Box installed in the Navigator's Compartment was used to monitor the plutonium atom bomb ("Fat Man") in the front bomb bay of the aircraft dropped on Nagasaki, 9 August 1945.
The "Fat Man" bomb was continually monitored by Lt. Phil Barnes, Weapon Test Officer, one of two persons responsible for the bomb while on the aircraft. It was his duty to see that the bomb was working properly while on board. Any departure from the norm would be detected immediately and corrected if <u>possible!</u>
A little red light blinked slowly if all was well - <u>if not</u> it would begin to blink <u>very</u> fast indicating a malfunction had occurred and the atom bomb was in <u>danger</u> of exploding in the bomb bay!!
Sometime during the flight this did happen and scared <u>hell out of all of us</u>!! Lt. Barnes and Commander Ashworth started looking into the problem immediately by checking the wiring and other things that could possibly go wrong. It was discovered that a wire had been installed <u>backwards</u> - causing the fast blinking and much worry to the crew. The problem was rectified at once and everything returned to normal – much to the relief of everyone on board!
COURTESY OF LOS ALAMOS LABORATORIES

1945 - Tinian Island.
L to R: Lt. Commander Fred Ashworth U.S. Navy Academy graduate and Weaponeer that armed
the plutonium atomic bomb "Fat Man" on-board "Bockscar" Nagasaki Mission. Don Mastick -
Asst. to Ashworth. Bob Server from Project Alberta.

The success of the operation against Nagasaki in the face of the difficulties that I have related
prompted many commendatory notes and citations for all of us in the crew of Bockscar. I was
awarded the Silver star by the Army which was presented to me personally by General Arnold in
ceremonies in his office. Many months later General Groves gave me a copy of his book, "Now It
Can Be Told" and I am particularly proud of the note he inscribed in it.

> "To Admiral F.L. Ashworth – Without your sound judge-
> ment and courageous decisions the Nagasaki Bombing
> Flight might not have been a success – You fully justified
> the confidence I had in you – With the very best Wishes."
>   Leslie R. Groves

Frederick L. Ashworth
Vice Admiral U.S.N.(Ret.)

The active component of the Fat Man came by special C-54 transport. The HE components of two Fat Men arrived in two B-29s attached to the 509th Group, which had been held at Albuquerque for this purpose. In all cases, the active components were accompanied by special personnel to guard against accident and loss.

The first Fat Man was scheduled for dropping on August 11. At one time, the schedule called for August 20, but by August 7, it was apparent that the date could be advanced to August 10. When Parsons and Ramsey proposed this change to Tibbets, he expressed regret that the schedule could not be advanced two days instead of only one, because good weather was forecast for August 9 and bad weather for the five succeeding days. It was finally agreed that Project Alberta would try to be ready for August 9, if all concerned understood that advancing the date by two full days introduced a large measure of uncertainty. All went well with the assembly, however, and the unit was loaded and fully checked late in the evening of August 8. The strike plane and two observer planes took off shortly before dawn on August 9. Major C. W. Sweeney piloted the strike ship "Bockscar," Captain K. K. Beahan was bombardier, Commander Ashworth was bomb commander, and Lieutenant Phillip Barnes was electronics test officer.

It was impossible to "safe" the Fat Man by leaving the assembly incomplete during takeoff as for Little Boy. The technical staff realized that a crash during takeoff would risk contaminating a wide area on Tinian with plutonium scattered by an HE explosion, and even risk a high-order nuclear explosion that would do heavy damage to the island. These risks were pointed out to the military with the request that special guarding and evacuation precautions be taken during the takeoff. The Air Force officer in command decided that such special precautions were not necessary, and as it turned out, the takeoff was made without incident. This mission was as eventful as the Hiroshima mission was operationally routine.

Mission 13: Hiroshima, Japan Atomic Bomb Attack, 6 Aug 1945.
Twentieth Air Force

COMPOSITION OF FORCE: 1 B-29 "Enola Gay" (pilot: Col Paul W. Tibbetts);
2 B-29 photography and observation aircraft "The Great Artiste"
(pilot: Maj Charles W Sweeney) and "No. 91" (pilot: Capt George
W Marquardt).

DEPARTURE: "Enola Gay" at 0245 hours, followed at 0247 and 0249 by
other two B-29s.

PRIMARY TARGET: Hiroshima Industrial Area and City

SECONDARY TARGET: Kokura Arsenal and City

TERTIARY TARGET : Nagasaki Mitsubishi Steel & Arms Works and City

AIMING POINT: 063096, Litho-Mosaic Hiroshima Area

FLIGHT ROUTE:
North Field, Tinian

Iwo Jima (Rendezvous Point)

Departure Point (3337N-13430E)

Initial Point (3424N-1330530E)

Target Area (Bomb dropped at 0915 /0815 Japan Time/; detonation
50 seconds later).

Breakaway (turn of 150 degrees, 3400N-13334E)

Iwo Jima

North Field, Tinian ("Enola Gay" landed at 1458, followed within
the hours by the two other B-29s.

Mission 16: Nagasaki, Japan Atomic Bomb Attack, 9 Aug 1945.
Twentieth Air Force

COMPOSITION OF FORCE: 1 B-29 "Bock's Car" (pilot: Maj Charles W Sweeney);
2 B-29 photography and observation aircraft "The Great Artiste"
(pilot: Capt Frederick C Bock) and "Full House" (pilot: Maj
James I Hopkins). Hopkins lost contact with the others.

DEPARTURE: "Bock's Car" at 0347 hours, followed at intervals by the
two other B-29s.

PRIMARY TARGET: Kokura Arsenal and City

AIMING POINT: 104082

CHECK POINT: 3243N-13233E.

SECONDARY TARGET: <u>Nagasaki Mitsubishi.Steel and Arms Works and City</u>

FLIGHT ROUTE:

    North Field, Tinian

    Iwo Jima

    Yakoshima (3020N-1303E) Rendezvous Point; Arrived 1900 hours,
           "Bock's Car" circled awaiting arrival of the other
           B-29s; only "The Great Artiste" showed up. After
           circling, departed at 0950 for Primary Target of
           KOKURA.

    Kokura (Arrival at Initial Point, 3343N-131380E, at 1044 and began
           bombing run; target obscured by smoke and clouds;
           Failed to sight aiming point in two further bombing
           runs. After c. 45 minutes proceeded on to Secondary
           Target, NAGASAKI.

    Check Point 3225N-13141E

    Nagasaki (Arrival at Initial Point, 3238N-13039E, at 1150; began
           approach by radar;) After 20 second visual bombing
           run dropped bomb at 1158; detonation about one
           minute later.

    Breakaway - Left turn of 150 degrees, 3137N-13128E, then, after
           circling smoke column, departed at 1205 hours for
           Okinawa.

    Yontan Fld, Okinawa ("Bock's Car" landed at 1351. After refueling
           proceeded to home base on Tinian.)

    North Field, Tinian ("Bock's Car arrived 2339 hours.)

FLAK ON BOTH MISSIONS: nil

From — The Manhattan Project : A Documentary Introduction to the Atomic Age - Michael Stoff
Temple Univ. Press 1991

234   **Document 79** Account of Drop on Nagasaki. August 9. 1945

C
O
P
Y

WAR DEPARTMENT
CLASSIFIED MESSAGE CENTER
INCOMING CLASSIFIED MESSAGE

TOP SECRET

URGENT

Page - 2-

From: CG, 313th Bomber Wing, Tinian

Nr : APCOM 5479   9 August 1945

Pilot Sweeney who took an observing airplane on
Hirosnima mission reported that flash was brighter and
bumps greater than Hiroshima. He was however, somewhat
closer to burst today. Weather over target was 7 to 8
tenths cloud.

Bombadier believes his point of aim at time of strike
was about 500 feet south of south end of Mitsubishi steel
works. He and others report 3 bumps and compared with 2 at
Hiroshima. One crew member reported 3 shock waves as visible.
Several reported the cloud as brighter than Hiroshima. It
was a bright orange color with the top mushroom definitely
luminous of orange and pink colors. Cloud moved up faster
and went higher than Hiroshima. Cloud burned away the ex-
isting clouds. Base cloud of dust and smoke was smaller in
area than Hiroshima. Fires were seen on both east and west
sides of cloud.
                                          End

Note: Received by TELECON as msg nbr FN-09-17

ACTION: Maj Derry

INFO: Gen Arnold, Gen Hull, Gen Bissell, Cofs

CM-IN-9254   (9Aug 45)   DTG: 091500Z   ngr

TOP SECRET

```
RGM V KQ1J  NR51    OPOP

-T- WAR

FROM COMGENAAF 20 BY KIRKPATRICK  OPOP                    0612402 AUG
TO   COMGENUSASTAF (REAR) WASHINGTON FOR NORSTAD, PASS TO CONFERENCE
     (SEND VIA TELECON ONLY)
BT

APCOM 5271
THIS MESSAGE FROM SCALE TO RELIEF
TWO PHOTO RECONNAISSANCE AIRPLANES RETURNED AT 0611002 FROM A TRIP OVE
THE TARGET WHICH THEY VISITED FOUR HOURS AFTER THE STRIKE. THEIR OBSER
ATIONS FOLLOW COLON ON ARRIVAL AT THE TARGET THERE WAS A HUGE CLOUD TO
A HEIGHT OF FORTY THOUSAND FEET OVER A WIDE AREA PD ONLY THE SEA ENDS
THE DOCKS WERE VISIBLE PD THE HIGHER PART OF THE CLOUD HAD A BLUISH TI
AND THE LOWER PART WHICH APPEARED TO BE LARGELY SMOKE AND DUST WAS
BROWNISH YELLOW PD THERE WERE SEVERAL FIRES VISIBLE NEAR THE DOCK AREA
PD BECAUSE OF THE DENSE SMOKE IT WAS IMPOSSIBLE TO DETERMINE MAGNITUDE
OF FIRES PD WITHIN HALF AN HOUR THE CLOUD OR SMOKE FLATTENED OUT
TO A HEIGHT OF TWENTY THOUSAND FEET PD ONE OBSERVER COMMENTED THAT
IT WAS SO SOLID ONE COULD WALK ON IT PD ANOTHER SAID IT WAS FAR WORSE
THAN NAGOYA AFTER A FOUR HUNDRED PLANE STRIKE PD THE CLOUD WAS FIRST
VISIBLE FROM A DISTANCE OF TWO HUNDRED FIFTY MILES PD ALL WERE IMPRESS
WITH THE EXTREME DENSITY AND SOLIDITY OF THE SMOKE CLOUD PD THE PHOTO-
GRAPHS ARE NOT EXPECTED TO SHOW ANY OF THE CITY EXCEPT THE EXTREME OUTI
ENDS OF THE DOCK AREA WHICH WAS CLEAR PD
PARA. ONE PHOTOGRAPH TAKEN BY A TAIL GUNNER IN STRIKE AIRCRAFT VERIFIES
DESCRIPTION OF EARLY CLOUD GIVEN IN MY EARLIER MESSAGE PD THE TOP
MUSHROOM HAD BEEN SEVERED FROM THE COLUMN AND A NEW ONE WAS FORMING PD
PARA. A REQUEST IS BEING MADE FOR ADDITIONAL PHOTOS OF TARGET AS SOON A
POSSIBLE PD
PARA JUDGE AND YOKE WILL VISIT CURFEW TOMORROW TO DESCRIBE OPERATION TO
>CARVE PD+YOKE AWARDED DSC BY SPAATZ ON STEPPING FROM AIRPLANE ON RETURN
PD ERRANT IS STILL THRILLED BY THE OPERATION WHICH WENT FROM START TO
FINISH WITH CLOCK LIKE PRECISION PD JUDGE'S PERFORMANCE WAS OUTSTANDIN
CMA INCLUDING HIS PERSONAL LOADING OF THE GUN IN FLIGHT TO INSURE SAFET
AT TAKEOFF PD THE THREE AIR FORCE CREWS WITH THE PRIMARY MISSION ALL
PERFORMED SUPERBLY PD OUR ENTIRE EFFORTS ARE
NOW DIRECTED TO FM SCHEDULED AS YOU WERE PREVIOUSLY ADVISED PD
BT 0612402
C/JLK

TOD 13252 LB
ROGER V RGM JG
```

Michael W. Kurgh J. Cox   Glenn A. Morgan Bym 3/c   Robert M. McQuiggan G/M

TO FRED BEST OF HEALTH

TO FRED:
WE CARRIED the Bomb From the States
You CARRIED IT to JAPAN.

This photo of the USS Indianapolis was given to me in 1995 by several survivors of this ill-fated ship - the one that carried the core of our atomic bomb – "Little Boy" from California to the island of Tinian in late July 1945. After leaving Tinian, and halfway between the Philippines and Guam, the Indianapolis was torpedoed by a Japanese submarine. Of the 1,197 men who sailed on that fateful voyage, only 317 survived.

1996 — Grisson Air Force Base, Peru, Indiana. L to R - Bob McGuiggan and Mike Kuryla, surviving crew members of the cruiser, Indianapolis, sunk in the Phillipine Sea, after delivering Uranium material used in the "Little Boy" Atom Bomb dropped on Hiroshima, Japan on 6 August 1945.

L to R - Bob McGuiggan and Mike Kuryla, John H. Wassell Jr., son of 509th Historian John Wassell, Fred J. Olivi co-pilot "Bockscar" Nagasaki Mission 9 August, 1945.

1944 — Photo of my brother, Emil, on his graduation from the University of Illinois Dental School, commissioned a Lt. (JG) in the U.S. Navy. Emil served as a dentist with "SACO" — Sino American Cooperative Organization — that operated behind enemy lines in the China/Burma/India theater. One of its missions was to supply weather information to the 20th Air Force which was flying B-29's bombing the Japanese Empire.

*North Field, Tinian Island - South Pacific —
Me flying our crew airplane, "Great Artiste"
on a flight over Tinian Island during
July, 1945*

*November 1945 — Roswell Air Force Base,
New Mexico. I'm finally back home in the U.S.*

219

1945 — North Field - Tinian Island.
This is Lt. Locke Easton sitting in his scooter made by the CBs (Construction Battalion) on
Tinian. My scooter was also made by the CB and Lt. Easton and myself, along with Lt. Cooper,
used to have great fun racing each other all over the island. It was something we enjoyed very
much and wanted to prove which scooter was fastest!

"Next Objective Crew"
L to R - 2nd Lt. Franklin B. Wimer, Navigator.
2nd Lt. William T. Hulse, Flight Engineer.
2nd Lt. Locke J. Easton, Co-pilot.
2nd Lt. Leon Cooper, Bombardier.

August, 1945 — North Field, Tinian Island, South Pacific. L to R - Lt. Ralph Devore, Aircraft Commander of Crew A-3 and B-29 "Next Objective," Major Charles Sweeney 393rd Sqd. Commander and Aircraft Commander of Crew C-15 B-29 "Great Artiste" before take off for 2nd atomic bombing of Kokura - Nagasaki Mission of 9 August, 1945.

1945 — Wendover AFB, Utah. Crew #A3. L to R Standing: 1st Lt. Devore - Airplane Commander; 2nd Lt. Easton - pilot, 2nd Lt. Leon Cooper - Bombardier; 2nd Lt. William Hulse - Flight Engineer; 2nd Lt. Frank Wimer - Navigator. L to R Kneeling: Enlisted men of Crew.

August 1945 — 393rd Combat Crew briefing prior to bombing missions over Japan.

1. *Wimer*	6. *Bontekoe*	11. *Devore*	16. *Dulin*
2. *Gruning*	7. *McKnight*	12. *Godfrey*	17. *Wey*
3. *Collinson*	8. *Bednorz*	13. *Widowsky*	18. *Barsumian*
4. *Taylor*	9. *Carrington*	14. *Eatherly*	
5. *Hoey*	10. *Westover*	15. *Allen*	

1945 — Wendover AFB, Wendover, Utah. Crew Briefing for practice bombing missions over Muroc Desert, California.
1st Row: Lt. McKnight. 2nd Row L to R: Lt. Weatherly - Co-pilot, Capt. Eatherly - Airplane Commander. 3rd Row L to R: Lt. Easton -
Co-pilot, Capt. Devore - Airplane Commander. 4th Row L to R: Unknown, Lt. Ferguson - Co-pilot, Lt. Levy - Bombardier, Lt. Godfrey -
Navigator, Lt. Widowsky - Navigator, Capt. Bock - Airplane Commander. 5th Row L to R: Lt. Norm Ray - Airplane Commander.

1945 — Wendover AFB - Crew C-11 "Straight Flush."
Kneeling, L to R - Sgt. Bivans, Sgt. Niceley, Sgt. Baldasarro, Lt. Grennan-
Navigator.
Back row, standing, L to R - Major Eatherly - AC Commander, Lt. Weatherly - Co-
Pilot, Lt. Wey - Bombardier, Capt. Thornhill - Navigator, and Sgt. Barsumian.
This crew almost dropped a Pumpkin Bomb on the Imperial Palace of Japan, as a
target of opportunity - against orders!
"Straight Flush" was one of the Weather aircraft that took off 1 hour before the
"Enola Gay", carrying the first atomic bomb dropped on Hiroshima, to report the
weather to the bomb carrying aircraft flying to the primary target.

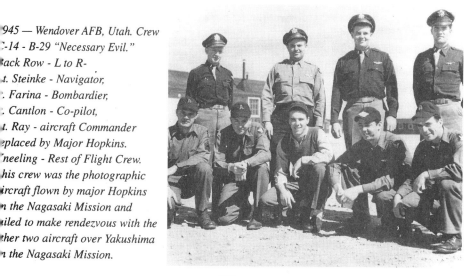

1945 — Wendover AFB, Utah. Crew
C-14 - B-29 "Necessary Evil."
Back Row - L to R-
Lt. Steinke - Navigator,
Farina - Bombardier,
Cantlon - Co-pilot,
Lt. Ray - aircraft Commander
replaced by Major Hopkins.
Kneeling - Rest of Flight Crew.
This crew was the photographic
aircraft flown by major Hopkins
on the Nagasaki Mission and
failed to make rendezvous with the
other two aircraft over Yakushima
on the Nagasaki Mission.

Crew # A-2 - Wendover AFB, Utah. L to R Standing: Costello - Airplane Commander; Davis - Co-Pilot; Brumagin - Flight Engineer; Petrolli - Navigator; Downey - Bombardier. Kneeling: Enlisted flight crew.

Crew C-13 and "Bockscar" 509th Composite Group

Crew C-13 of the B-29 named "Bockscar." This crew, switched aircraft with our crew and flew our B-29, "The Great Artiste." They carried instruments that were dropped over Nagasaki on August 9th. L to R: Sgt. Curry, Lt. Levy, Sgt. Stock, Capt. Bock, Sgt. Belanger, Lt. Godfrey, Sgt. Barney, Lt. Ferguson, and M/Sgt. Arnold. (Photo courtesy U.S. Army Air Corps)

"Enola Gay" Crew 1945 — Tinian Island - Marianas. Back Row L to R — Col. Porter; Major Van Kirk, Navigator; Major Ferebee, Bombardier; Col. Tibbets, Aircraft Commander and 509th Composite Group Commander; Capt. Lewis, Copilot; Lt. Beser, Radar Countermeasure Officer. Front Row L to R — Sgt. Stiborik, Radar; Sgt. Caron, Tail Gunner; Cpl. Nelson, Radio Operator; Sgt. Schumard, Asst. Flight Engineer; T/Sgt. Duzenbury, Flight Engineer.

1945 Tinian Island - Marianas. Crew of Capt. George Marquardt, Aircraft Commander - Part of three-ship strike force on Hiroshima Mission, 6 August 1945.
Back Row - L to R - Sgt. Corliss, Sgt. DiJulio, Sgt. Bierman, Sgt. Capua, Lt. Gackenbach.
Front Row - L to R - Lt. Anderson, Capt. Marquardt, Sgt. Coble, Capt. Strudwick.

1945 Tinian. Crew of Enola Gay waiting for take-off on Hiroshima Mission - North Field.
L to R - Back to Camera - Major Ferebee, Bombardier; Major Van Kirk, Navigator.
L to R - Facing Camera - Col. Tibbets, Acft Commander; Capt. Lewis, Co-pilot.

1945 Tinian Island — Crew B-7 of B-29 "Some Punkins," taken on Tinian. In the front row L to R: Madrid, Josefink, Crotty, Meyers, Miller, and Carrigan (ground crew). Kneeling L to R: Compronio (ground crew); members of the Flight Crew: Byrd, F. Brown, Atkins, J. Brown and Byson. Standing, L to R, Collinson (Navigator), Price (Aircraft Commander), Costa (Bombardier), and Bednorz (Co-Pilot). (Photo courtesy U. S. Army Air Corps)

1945 Roswell AFB - Roswell N. Mex.
Left - Aircraft Commander of crew B-7 "Some Punkins" - Capt. Price
Right - Co-pilot Lt. Everest Bednarz.

Lt. Richard McNamera was probably my best friend in the 509th. He was my classmate in Pilot Class 44G and we both were assigned to duty with the highly secret 509th Composite Group at Wendover. This photo was taken at North Field, Tinian. Mac was the regular Co-Pilot on the "Enola Gay," but did not go on the mission to Hiroshima.

Combat Crew Members

393rd Bombardment Squadron (VH)
509th Composite Group
Tinian North Field - 1945

Crew	Member	Function
A-1	Ralph R. Taylor	Aircraft Commander
	Raymond P. Biel	Copilot
	Fred A. Hoey	Navigator
	Michael Angelich	Bombardier
	Frank M. Briese	Flight Engineer
	Theodore M. Slife	Radio Operator
	Nathaniel T. R. Burgwyn	Radar Operator
	Robert J. Valley	Tail Gunner
	Richard B. Anselme	Asst Eng/Scanner
A-2	Edward M. Costello	Aircraft Commander
	Harry B. Davis	Copilot
	Robert J. Petrolli	Navigator
	John L. Downey	Bombardier
	Thomas H. Brumagin	Flight Engineer
	David Purdon	Radio Operator
	James R. Bryant	Radar Operator
	Carleton C. McEachern	Tail Gunner
	Maurice J. Clark	Asst Eng/Scanner
A-3	Ralph N. Devore	Aircraft Commander
	William J. Easton	Copilot
	Franklin B. Wimer	Navigator
	Leon Cooper	Bombardier
	William T. Hulse	Flight Engineer
	Lee E. Palmert	Radio Operator
	Michael B. Bohon	Radar Operator
	Glenn S. Allison	Tail Gunner
	Clarence E. Britt	Asst Eng/Scanner
A-4	Joseph E. Westover	Aircraft Commander
	William J. Desmond	Copilot
	John W. Dulin	Navigator
	Louis B. Allen	Bombardier
	Robert M. Donnell	Flight Engineer
	James H. Doiron	Radio Operator
	William J. Cotter	Radar Operator
	Walter A. Spradlin	Tail Gunner
	Samuel R. Wheeler	Asst Eng/Scanner
A-5	Thomas J. Classen	Aircraft Commander
	William M. Rowe	Copilot
	William E. Wright	Navigator
	Bobby J. Chapman	Bombardier
	Floyd W. Kemner	Flight Engineer
	Omar G. Strickland	Radio Operator
	George A. Weller	Radar Operator
	Alfred A. Lewandowski	Tail Gunner
	Lee E. Caylor	Asst Eng/Scanner

Crew	Member	Function
B-6	John A. Wilson	Aircraft Commander
	Ellsworth T. Carrington	Copilot
	James S. Duva	Navigator
	Paul W. Gruning	Bombardier
	James W. Davis	Flight Engineer
	Glen H. Floweree	Radio Operator
	Vernon J. Rowley	Radar Operator
	Chester A. Rogalski	Tail Gunner
	Donald L. Rowe	Asst Eng/Scanner
B-7	James N. Price	Aircraft Commander
	Everist L. Bednorz	Copilot
	William J. Collinson	Navigator
	Thomas F. Costa	Bombardier
	James A. Adkins	Flight Engineer
	Robert H. Byrd	Radio Operator
	Joe R. Brown	Radar Operator
	Clyde L. Bysom	Tail Gunner
	Frederick E. Brown	Asst Eng/Scanner
B-8	Charles F. McKnight	Aircraft Commander
	Jacob Y. Bontekoe	Copilot
	Jack Widowsky	Navigator
	Franklin H. MacGregor	Bombardier
	George H. Cohen	Flight Engineer
	Lloyd J. Reeder	Radio Operator
	William F. Orren	Radar Operator
	Roderick E. Legg	Tail Gunner
	Donald O. Cole	Asst Eng/Scanner
B-9	Robert A. Lewis	Aircraft Commander
	Richard McNamara	Copilot
	Harold J. Rider	Navigator
	Stewart W. Williams	Bombardier
	Wyatt E. Duzenbury	Flight Engineer
	Richard H. Nelson	Radio Operator
	Joseph S. Stiborik	Radar Operator
	George R. Caron	Tail Gunner
	Robert H. Shumard	Asst Eng/Scanner
B-10	George W. Marquardt	Aircraft Commander
	James M. Anderson	Copilot
	Russell E. Gackenbach	Navigator
	James W. Strudwick	Bombardier
	James R. Corliss	Flight Engineer
	Warren L. Coble	Radio Operator
	Joseph M. DiJulio	Radar Operator
	Melvin H. Bierman	Tail Gunner
	Anthony D. Capua	Asst Eng/Scanner

Crew	Member	Function
C-11	Claude R. Eatherly	Aircraft Commander
	Ira C. Weatherly	Copilot
	Francis D. Thornhill	Navigator
	Frank K. Wey	Bombardier
	Eugene S. Grennan	Flight Engineer
	Pasquale Baldasaro	Radio Operator
	Albert G. Barsumian	Radar Operator
	Gillen T. Niceley	Tail Gunner
	Jack Bivans	Asst Eng/Scanner
C-12	Herman S. Zahn	Aircraft Commander
	Gilbert B. Dickman	Copilot
	Henry Deutsch	Navigator
	Francis R. Ormond	Bombardier
	James K. Elder	Flight Engineer
	Leander J. Baur	Radio Operator
	Gerard F. Clapso	Radar Operator
	Raymond E. Allen	Tail Gunner
	Neil R. Corey	Asst Eng/Scanner
C-13	Frederick C. Bock	Aircraft Commander
	Hugh C. Ferguson	Copilot
	Leonard A. Godfrey	Navigator
	Charles Levy	Bombardier
	Roderick F. Arnold	Flight Engineer
	Ralph D. Curry	Radio Operator
	William C. Barney	Radar Operator
	Robert J. Stock	Tail Gunner
	Ralph D. Belanger	Asst Eng/Scanner
C-14	Norman W. Ray	Aircraft Commander
	John E. Cantlon	Copilot
	Stanley G. Steinke	Navigator
	Myron Faryna	Bombardier
	George L. Brabenec	Flight Engineer
	Francis X. Dolan	Radio Operator
	Richard F. Cannon	Radar Operator
	Martin G. Murray	Tail Gunner
	Thomas A. Bunting	Asst Eng/Scanner
C-15	Charles D. Albury	Aircraft Commander
	Fred J. Olivi	Copilot
	James F. Van Pelt	Navigator
	Kermit K. Beahan	Bombardier
	John D. Kuharek	Flight Engineer
	Abe M. Spitzer	Radio Operator
	Edward K. Buckley	Radar Operator
	Albert T. Dehart	Tail Gunner
	Raymond G. Gallagher	Asst Eng/Scanner

Note - All assigned Co-pilots on designated crews of the 393rd Bomb Squadron were all checked out as First Pilots on our other 4 engine bombers B-17 s or B-24 s. They could assume command of their B-29 should circumstances dictate the need for this during a bombing mission against Japan.

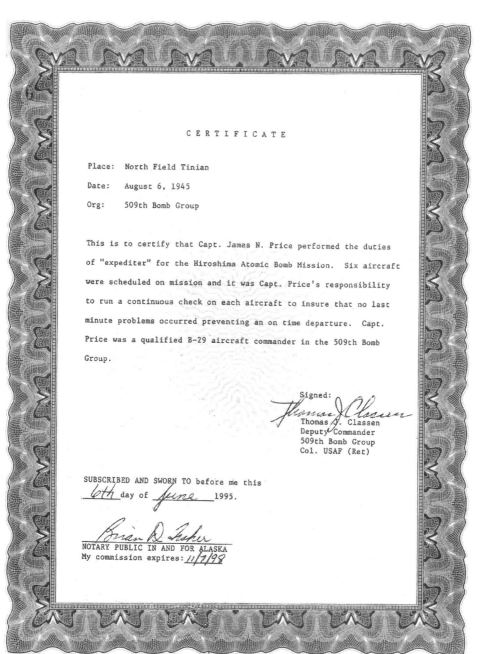

C E R T I F I C A T E

Place: North Field Tinian

Date: August 6, 1945

Org: 509th Bomb Group

This is to certify that Capt. James N. Price performed the duties of "expediter" for the Hiroshima Atomic Bomb Mission. Six aircraft were scheduled on mission and it was Capt. Price's responsibility to run a continuous check on each aircraft to insure that no last minute problems occurred preventing an on time departure. Capt. Price was a qualified B-29 aircraft commander in the 509th Bomb Group.

Signed:

Thomas J. Classen
Deputy Commander
509th Bomb Group
Col. USAF (Ret)

SUBSCRIBED AND SWORN TO before me this

_6th_ day of _June_ 1995.

NOTARY PUBLIC IN AND FOR ALASKA
My commission expires: 11/7/98

1945 — North Field - Tinian Island. B-29 "Great Artiste" plane assigned to Crew C-15 flew on both atomic missions to Hiroshima and Nagasaki as the instrument carrying aircraft on the 6th and 9th of August, 1945. Plane was named for our Bombardier Capt. Beahan. Capt. Bock flew the "Great Artiste: that dropped the instrumentation on the Nagasaki Mission.

Tinian — Mid-August 1945. Major Charles Sweeney, Aircraft Commander of "The Great Artiste," being decorated for his participation in the Hiroshima mission by General Davies . Waiting to be decorated are Capt. Van Pelt, Navigator, and Capt. Beahan, Bombardier. (Photo by Dick Campbell)

September, 1970 — Air Force Academy, Colorado Springs, Colorado. I'm on the right with a Cadet at the Academy. By now a Major in the Air Force Reserves, I served as a Liaison Officer from 1962 to 1972. (Photo courtesy U. S. Air Force)

24 May 1980 - Midway Airport, Chicago, Illinois.
Lt. Col. Fred J. Olivi sitting in co-pilot's seat of B-29 "FI FI" during visit to Chicago
Midway Airport.

August, 1980 — Washington D. C. Members of the 509th gathered at Bolling Air Force Base in
the Officer's Club for our 35th anniversary reunion

August, 1984 — Philadelphia, Pennsylvania. This snapshot was taken at our reunion that year. Left to right: Joe Papalia, New York City, Historian of the 509th Composite Group; Kermit Beahan, Bombardier; and myself.

1988 — Boston, Massachusetts. We visited Boston for the 43rd Anniversary Reunion of the 509th. I'm in the middle, joined (on the left) by Don Rehl, AC Commander, and (on the right) Don Albury, Pilot of "The Great Artiste."

1989 — Columbus, Ohio. The cockpit crew of "Bockscar" on August 9, 1945. I'm on the left. In the middle of the photo is our Aircraft Commander, Charles Sweeney, Major General USAF (Ret), on the right is Don Albury, Pilot of "The Great Artiste," and a retired pilot with Eastern Airlines.

This is a photo of the cockpit of the B-29 "Bockscar," now on exhibit at the Air Force Museum, Wright-Patterson Air Force Base, Dayton, Ohio. "Bockscar" is the only B-29 currently on permanent display in America. Every year thousands of visitors see this historic aircraft which was actually flown to Wright-Patterson. (Photo courtesy of Wright-Patterson Air Force Museum)

1989 — I often visit the Air Force Museum in Dayton. And on every trip I make sure to give a "thank you pat" to the side of "Bockscar" for bringing us home safely on our mission to Nagasaki, Japan.

On display at the Air Force Museum, close to "Bockscar," are many of my personal effects from World War II, including my gloves, goggles, flare gun, "dog tags," wrist bracelet, medal and ring. The Distinguished Flying Cross seen at the lower right hand corner was given to me for the Nagasaki Mission.

1989 — November, North Field, Tinian Island. Forty-four years after the end of World War II, men from the 509th visited the site of the Bomb Loading Pit used for loading "Fat Man" into the B-29 "Bockscar" for its mission to Nagasaki. Left to right: Don Albury, Pilot of "The Great Artiste" pilot on the mission; Richard Nelson, Radio Operator of "Enola Gay" on its Hiroshima mission; Charles Sweeney, Aircraft Commander of "Bockscar" on the Nagasaki mission; and Fred Bock, Pilot, for whom "Bockscar" was named but who flew "The Great Artiste" to Nagasaki.

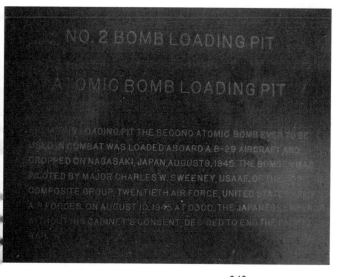

August 1990 — Wendover, Utah. Crew members of the B-29's "Enola Gay" and "Bockscar" gathered under the hot Utah sun in 1990 to dedicate this monument to the 509th Composite Group during our 45th Anniversary Reunion. Left to right: Jacob Beser, Ted Van Kirk, Tom Ferebee, Richard Nelson, General Paul Tibbets, General Sweeney, Don Albury, and me. Kneeling (L to R): George Caron and Jim Van Pelt.

Monument erected at Wendover, Utah, in honor of the 509th Composite Group.

Tinian Island in 1989

Runways #1 and #2 are still visible today and are used occasionally. However, Runways #3 and #4 (at the right) are covered over by jungle growth. (Photo courtesy Professor Anderson Giles, University of Maine)

The site of the Headquarters area of the 509th on Tinian is completely hidden by jungle. I've put an "X" at the approximate location. I was interested to see that what we called "8th Avenue Traffic Circle" is still visible and looks like it's being used today. (Photo courtesy Professor Anderson Giles, University of Maine)

In May 1994, with our wives and families, members of the 509th met for lunch at River Farm in Alexandria, Virginia, once owned by George Washington. Front row (L to R): Tom Ferebee, Mary Ann Ferebee, Bob Caron, Don Albury, Ray Gallagher, Mary Gallagher. Second row (L to R): Jim Van Pelt, Roberta Albury, Jean Van Kirk, Ted Van Kirk, Susie Van Pelt, Mrs. Bill Phillips, Artist Bill Phillips, and Artist Craig Codera. In the back row (L to R): Fred Olivi, Carole Olivi, Nancy Nelson, Dick Nelson, Charlotte Kuharek and John Kuharek.

August 1992 — 20th AF Reunion, Seattle Washington. L to R - Fred Olivi, Carole Olivi, Charles Sweeney.

September 1995 — Whiteman Air Force Base, Missouri. Carole and I visited this base, now the home of the newly activated 393rd Bomb Squadron - 509th Bomb Wing, and posed in front of the B-2 Stealth Bomber. I was very proud to see that our old "organization" has been re-born and now flies a fantastic new aircraft in a far different world than what we knew in 1945.

1980, Chicago — Chief Engineer Louis Koncza (Left) and Commissioner Jerome Butler, Dept. of Public Works, City of Chicago, at Rededication of the Rehabilitation of one of Chicago's oldest movable bridges on Cortland Street, build in 1902 over the north branch of the Chicago River. It was declared a historic civil engineering landmark by the American Society of Civil Engineers in 1982. Because of its 52 Movable Chicago designed Bascule Bridges over the three branches of the Chicago River, Chicago became known as "Venice" of Chicago.

1980 — Chicago. This photo was taken while the Chicago Bureau of Engineering, Bridge Division, was replacing the old Randoph Street bridge over the Chicago River. Left to right are: Henry Ecale, Chief Bridge Engineer; me, Manager of Bridge Operations and Maintenance; and Ted Kaczkowski, Assistant Chief Bridge Engineer.

November 2, 1995 — Minneapolis, Minnesota. How strange "Fate" is — here I am, meeting for the first time, Bernard FitzPatrick, at a presentation of "A Gathering of Eagles." FitzPatrick was an American Prisoner of War in a camp located in Kokura, Japan, on August 9, 1945. During our conversation we both agreed he is alive today only because Kokura was hidden by smoke and clouds. FitzPatrick told me he remembers hearing two B-29's that day, but doesn't recall giving it much thought. Little did he know what kind of bomb we carried! It gave me a great feeling to meet a man who remembers that day and who lived to tell about it — only because we couldn't see the ground!

POW E.E. Laporte, Sgt. Major USMC (Ret)

23 Sept 97

Dear Col. Olivi

Thanks for the information on the book.

Here is a retirement photo. If there is any made during the war, the Japanese have it.

I was surprised to know that in Wash D.C. where documents are/were held in secret but now available, is an order from the Japanese high command, and had 29 Aug 45 to execute all POW'S, CIVILIAN INTERNEES – IN ANY CAMP THEY HAD THEM, IN ANY COUNTRY THEY HAD THEM.

You beat them by 20 days and again we can all say a hearty "Thanks"

I'll be looking forward to your book,

Sincerely

Laporte

E.E. LAPORTE Sgt-Maj Retired
1969 12th St. N.E.
Hickory, North Carolina 28601

Col. Zahn,   21 July 94

Recently I read in one of the military magazines where a Mr Evans - a school teacher from San Antonio Texas, was requesting news items, paper clippings from WWII to be sent to him, to be used by interested parties, individual historians etc. I had many from the 1940's which I sent to him. Some went to the Admiral Nimity museum in Texas, some to class room studies and individuals.

There was several which dealt with the US Air force and bombing raids.

In Oct 1994 chairman for a in Springfield of War, 23 Dec 1941. address and him, he thought a letter would be in order.

5-9 Oct I am a reunion to be held Mo. for the ex Prisoner captured on Wake Island. Mr Evans gave me your due to what I had written to the Doolittle group

It was not until the war was over that we found out things that had happened around us, which we never knew was going on.

We were in a Prison Camp at Kiang Wan China which is about 10 miles from Shanghai. And we were there for 3 years. In our camp there were several aviators - shot down, B25 + P40 personnel & later some P51 pilots. One of those P40 pilots was a

Capt Bishop of the Flying Tigus who later escaped by jumping off a train in North China.

But the story that we learned after the war about some Doolittle flyers really hit most of us hard.

We knew of the Doolittle raid and the Japanese were only too willing to talk about it.

They did in fact publish photos in their news showing captured personnel in Tokyo.

But the ironical thing is, Lt Farrow, Lt Hallmark and Sgt (?) Spatz — ? were executed just down the road from our camp. We did not know it, We did not see them. Only one of our men told of seeing something one day which he described as follows: He saw 3 men, with Gunny socks over their heads reaching to their waist and these men's hands were tied behind their back & the Jap holding the end of the rope. This was the humiliating way of the Japanese who were no better than animals.

Anyway — our witness — a Marine who is now deceased said the men were walked up & over a small hill — which was later to be found to be a Cemetery. He stated that Chinese puppet police were with them also & after a short time they all came back from that locality without the 3 men and he only assumed there had been an execution. He could not tell by the clothing of these 3 men if they were aviation personnel but their size denoted that they were not oriental.

But this story does not at all compare to the Japanese version. They state the prisoners were driven to the grave site. There were 3 crosses in the ground with shallow graves dug.

The three men were made to kneel a small thin cloth put around the head with Jap sun showing. Two Jap rifle men were assigned to each POW and on signal they shot their respective POW through the head.

The 3 men were pushed into the grave but later brought to a crematorium, cremated and the ashes stored. However after the war ended they tried to cover up their deed by putting other names on the containers.

I realize I have written what anyone can find out through books, but regardless of the circumstance of the execution, it seemed really ironical to us to have been so close to those 3 men and not knowing it. The one witness I have mentioned, well we will never know what he saw or who it might be. We had seen atrocities against Chinese that was so severe it was hard to imagine any thing human could have done such acts.

In 1945 - June - we were moved from Shanghai to North China - around Peking. En route 4 Marine officers & the aforementioned Capt Bishop - flying tigers - escaped and One Wake Island Civilian.

We were taken thereafter through Manchuria and down to Pusan Korea and later on, taken to Shimonoseki on Honshu, 2 July 1945. The Japs put blankets over our windows on the train They did not want us to see the results of the B-29 fire bombing - the childish idiots they were, was a sad thing. But we looked anyway. It was like opening the curtains to see the greatest show on earth

We laughed - secretly of course - it was pay back time - we had seen treatment of women in children in China and now they were getting it.

We also knew there was no way out for us, and we were going to pay the price. They did not send us all the way, to have a picnic. So we watched the burned out cities and in Tokyo at night on 3 July 1945 we saw the red fiery glow of other cities getting the baptism of fire. Great.

But there was a way out of this mess, after all, and the US Air force has got more admirers than they probably know about, because they dropped the atomic bomb and we all know, without it we would surely pay the price.

There are many who say the bomb was not necessary, but for us who lived in that country and saw the preparations being made for invasion, with little kids practicing grenade throwing and women practicing bayonet fighting, plus the Jap guards & civilians getting meaner by the day there was no way of subduing them except by extreme measures.

So I can truthfully say I owe my life to the dropping of the bomb. I can also say I owe a lot just for the laughs & pleasure I got out of seeing the burned out cities and those folks living like the ones they had persecuted. Thanks from all of us.

Semper Fi

Laporte

U.S.S. Grenadier (SS 210) crew
15 September 1945 Prisoners of
War at Fukuoka Camp No. 3
located northeast of Yawata
between Tabata and Kokura.
Camp in background of coal
fired power plant.

Back Row (L to R):
Dean B. Shoemaker, Ben H.
Fulton, Randolph J. Garrison,
Miner B. Pierce, John H.
Gunderson, Bernard W. Witzke

Center Row (L to R):
William H. Keefe, Charles (n)
Roskell, Henry W. Rutkowski,
Rex R. Evans, Lyle L. Sawatzke,
Charles H. Whitlock, Charles E.
Johnson

Front Row: Joseph A. Minton,
John E. Simpson, Riley H.
Keysor, Virgil A. Ouillette,
Thomas J. Trigg.

24 September 1997

Dear Fred Olivé,

Enclosed is a photo of some
of the crew of the USS Grenadier SS 210 who
were Prisoners of War in Fukuoka Camp No. 3
which was located a few miles from downtown
Kokura. The camp in the background was 500 yards
from a coal fired power plant with 6 smoke
stacks 100 ft high. The area around the power
plant was never bombed, altho the Yawata
steel mills where we worked, 6 miles away, was
bombed a number of times. The City of Yawata
and the steel mill was burned out two days
before the Nagasaki bomb was dropped.

B-29's flew over the camp day after day
and we thought the power plant was a landmark
for the bombers on the way to Tokyo. We did not
know until years later that our area was the
primary target for the 2nd atomic bomb. The
steel mill area of Yawata was still burning two days
later and I believe this saved the 1200+ POW's at
our camp.

The photo was taken by an Army photographer
15 September 1945. We had received a number of air drops
and had gained weight. We were moved out the next
day to Nagasaki

B. K. Wilfle
LT USN Ret.

5743 Antigua Blvd.
San Diego, CA 92124
1 October 1996

Dear Sir:

I got your address at my 55th High School reunion from Tony Rericha, a classmate, who said he has met you. He told me you are writing a book on the Nagasaki A-Bomb.

I was a Prisoner of War, crew member of the USS Grenadier SS210, at Fukuoka Camp 3 in the vicinity of KoKura. Our camp was next to a large coal fired power plant with six large smoke stacks, the most visible object in the area. B-29's flew over us day after day but never bombed the area, so we thought it was a land mark on the way to Tokyo. The Yawata Iron works, where we worked, was bombed a number of times and burned out 2 days before you tried to wipe us out on 9 August '45.

All the stories I've read about Bock's Car always said you couldn't see the target, but none actually stated what you were looking for. I've been wondering if the coal fired power plant was part of the land mark. I did not know about KoKura and the bomb until 1969 when I read the short story in February '69 True magazine.

I'll be looking for your book when it comes out. I am glad you didn't see the target. The picture enclosed was taken by a photographer with the US Army before we left camp for Nagasaki on 17 September 1945.

Very respectfully,
Bernard W. Witzke
LT USN Ret.

258

5743 Antigua Blvd.
San Diego, CA 92124
15 October 1986

Dear Col. Olivi,

I was glad to hear that Bock's Car
could not find the target at Kokura. There were
1200 prisoner of war there, 42 were from the
USS Grenadier (SS210), 4 of which died of malnutrition,
another 300+ prisoner were at Moji a short distance
north of Kokura. The area around the camp was
never bombed and we thought the Power Plant with
the six smoke stacks was a land mark, as the
B-29's flew over us day after day. The Yawata
steal mill, where the prisoners worked, was bombed
a number of times. The last time being 2 days before
the Nagasaki bomb, 50 years later I learned the area
was not bombed so the Atomic bomb destruction could
be measured.

The men in the picture had all gained weight as the
result of air drops for nearly a month. The Japanese
stole most of the Red Cross food and supplies. I went
from 165 lbs to 110 lbs, I was 6'2" tall. An entry in my
diary 2-21-44 - 97 men died so far this winter.

Photo by a Photographer with the U.S. Army
repatriation Team.

Very respectfully,
Bernard W. Wkizl
LT USN Ret

*Millard E. Hileman,
POW stationed in
Kokura 1945.*

Primary target — Kokura

Millard E. Hileman, Ex P.O.W.

O n August 6, 1945, a lonely B-29 approached the city of Hiroshima, unchallenged by an impotent Japanese airforce and almost unnoticed by the city's inhabitants. The Bomb bay opened and an object was dropped from the monster's silver belly.

As it fell toward earth, a parachute opened. It descended to an altitude of 1,500 feet. Instantly a giant flash illuminated the sky. A blinding glare, ranging from a blue-white to a deep orange color, released fantastic forces equal to an earthquake, hurricane, and flood combined.

Three days later an even more powerful bomb was dropped on the city of Nagasaki, resulting in the loss of 30,000 lives and the complete destruction of 18,000 buildings.

It could have been worse. The second mission was hampered by confusion and adverse weather conditions. Nagasaki had been chosen in desperation as an alternate target, and even then the target area had been missed by almost three miles.

Sixty miles south of Hiroshima and about the same distance north of Nagasaki was the city of Kokura. A beautiful, quiet residential city of 130,000 people, it lay nestled in the low coastal hills of northern Kyushu Island. Kokura was also the location of a Japanese prison camp, Fukuoka Camp #3.

I first arrived at Camp #3 on a hot August day in 1944, after the Japanese freighter NISSYO MARU quietly slipped into Moji to unload her cargo of 1,500 American prisoners of war.

All were quickly unloaded and forced to wait in the hot sun for three hours. Divided into two sections, the first group was marched to a depot where they boarded electric cars for an unknown

destination. Our group sat under the relentless rays of the hot summer sun for an additional two hours before we, too, were herded from the park area to a string of electric cars.

The noisy, clanging cars ground to a halt about an hour later. We were pushed through the doors and quickly lined up for roll call.

The order was given to count off, the counting to be done in Japanese. One slip in counting gave the guard in charge the right to punish the offender with a knee to the groin, the butt of a rifle to the Adam's apple, or a resounding thump under the nose.

We were not required to stand in any designated order, so a prisoner's number changed with each roll call. It was advisable to stay alert during the count.

Finally, we were marched to a stockade, complete with barbed wire and guard towers. Two large gates swung open and we got our first look at Camp #3, our residence until the war's end.

The streetcar trip from Moji to Kokura had followed the coastline. The crowded conditions in the cars had somewhat hampered our view, but the natural beauty of the green, lush landscape was a welcome change from the ugliness we had experienced in the hold of NISSYO MARU.

All along the coast of Kyushu the land rose from the sea in gentle contours, unblemished by busy highways and billboard advertising. As the street cars entered the outskirts of Kokura, it was apparent the city was mostly residential, and very delightfully situated among the low terraced hills so characteristic of Kyushu Island.

Like most Japanese cities in 1944, the war had not actually reached Kokura. Isolated air raids had taken place in some

areas, more for psychological reasons than anything else, such as Doolittle's first raid on Tokyo in 1942. As yet, however, the Americans had not been able to

position themselves to mount a concentrated barrage on the heart of Japan's heavy industry.

Yawata, three miles away, was

➡

WORLD WAR II TIMES — 9

the heart of Japanese heavy industry on Kyushu. Sugar and oil refineries, chemical plants, paper and flour mills, glass factories, and various metal industries were located there. It was also the home of the enormous government-owned Yawata Steel Works, where we would be forced to perform slave labor during our incarceration.

Each day we would board a small train that carried us to the work area of the mill. A short distance from Kokura the train entered a tunnel, then emerged abruptly into the confines of the vast industrial complex. Each evening we returned to the more serene surroundings of Kokura.

The morning of August 9, 1945 dawned hot and humid, not unlike every morning that summer. However, on this morning the sky was overcast and there was the smell and feel of rain in the air.

As we finished breakfast and prepared for work call, everyone seemed to sense that this day would be different.

"COUNT OFF!" The command caught everyone unaware. Being preoccupied with thoughts of the weather and what the future held, everyone had neglected to precount his position. But for some unknown reason that morning, the guards seemed oblivious to minor mistakes. The gates of the stockade swung open and the march to the train began.

The sudden grinding squeal of the brakes was like a signal which changed the preoccupied minds to the reality of the day. The train had emerged from the tunnel and stopped at its usual place in front of the Yawata Steel Works business office.

Once again everyone lined up for roll call, the never-ending ritual some enterprising GI had dubbed "Japanese roulette."

Making the silent trek to the work area, everyone looked forward to the 10:15 break. Then we would look forward to the half hour lunch period, and so on, dividing the day into short segments of endurable time.

As the haggard group made the silent trek to their work stations, a B-29 was already airborne, carrying a single bomb: Primary Target — Kokura!

By 8:30 A.M. clouds were already rolling in from Tsushima Strait. The sky darkened and we all breathed a sigh of relief. Kokura was our haven and in a few hours we would be there. At this moment, however, an unscheduled plan of fantastic circumstances was beginning to unfold.

It was three minutes before smoke break, when the first bomb crashed into the area with shattering force. If there had been an air-raid warning, no one had heard it amidst the clattering air hammers and the screaming of high-speed equipment, and the noise of approaching aircraft had gone unnoticed.

As the first explosion rocked the area, all the air hammers stopped. Switches went out, stopping the compressors. In the silence that followed, the drone of heavy bombers could be heard. How high or how many it was impossible to determine.

One of our guards, a big, strong heavy-bearded fellow, called out, "B-29s!"

Moments later the entire area was chaos. Guards, civilian workers with men and women, were running in every direction. We dropped our tools and headed for the exit, with only one thought in mind—the nearest shelter. The clouds were so low it was impossible to see any aircraft, but the boom of heavy demolition bombs could be heard in the distance.

Then there was a tremendous roar of low-flying planes overhead, and a screaming shower of incendiary bombs began to hit everywhere, burning their way through the metal roof, spewing deadly streams of white phosphorus in all directions. Ironically, even in that atmosphere of bedlam and confusion, every American found reason to smile. For the first time, the pompous Japanese guards were in utter panic.

The acrid smell of phosphorus, gasoline and oil fumes, burning buildings and even the smell of burning flesh filled the air. Inside the tunnel confusion reigned as close friends tried to locate one another. It was ascertained, however, that all Americans were present and accounted for. Had the hope, faith and prayers been a factor?

Kokura was quiet, with no war, no ugly smells, or burning buildings. Only the green, lush countryside greeted our horror filled eyes.

A feeling of freedom seemed to overwhelm us as we neared the camp's gates. Suddenly we felt released from the fears and uncertainties that had, for so long, been a part of our lives.

The last act of the miracle was beginning to unfold as we heard the drone of a single airplane. But there was no worry. One plane could harm no one, and besides weren't they now within the friendly and untouchable confines of the city of Kokura?

The roar of the engines died out, and again all was quiet. Then again, there was the drone of a single airplane, but it passed and quiet returned. It made a third approach, then once again faded into the distance.

Everyone listened, bewildered.

The miracle was now complete. Aboard the high-flying aircraft someone had shouted, "Kokura socked in! Try Nagasaki." Clouds covered Nagasaki, but not as densely as those which covered Kokura.

The "Bomb" had been destined for Kokura, but unforeseen, inclement weather made it impossible to deliver.

It rained on Kokura that day, preserving its beauty and tradition for generations to come, and saving its 1,200 prisoners of war from complete and utter annihilation.

Used with permission of
Mrs. Milldred E. Hillman

343rd C.T.D. Albuquerque New Mexico - Reunion - 20 May, 1995

Sitting (L to R) - Felzer, Olivi, Carole Olivi, Anita Cunningham

1st Row (L to R) - Sue Clifton, Shirley Mesirow, Lucille Clark, Bobbie Luckenbach, Mildred McLenny, C. McLenny, Jackie Meketa, A. Cunningham

Back Row (L to R) - L. Marks, Paula Abramson Clifton, Deering, Helen Deering, Sam Clark Luckenbach, Johnnie Elsberry, R.G. Elsberry, Dorthy Dobbins, B. Dobbins, Chuck Meketa.

The men attended East Central State Teaches college in Ada, Oklahoma after completing Basic Training at Sheppard Field AFB, Wichita Falls, Texas in 1943. They started training as Aviation Students with 10 hrs of Dual Flight Instruction in a Piper Cub as the beginning of their flying careers hoping to win their Wings as qualified Military pilots. Most were successful!

Dallas, Texas — May 1, 1992
Reunion of Aviation Students from C.T.D. Classmates at East Central State University Ada,
Oklahoma in 1943.
L to R - Jack Gorbette, Charlotte Gorbette, Fred Olivi, Bobie Lukenbach, Guenther Luckenbach.

Chicago, Illinois — 509th
Reunion, September 9, 1994
509th Composite Group Reunion
with 393rd Bomb Squadron Crew
Members flying B-29 during
WWII
L to R - William Hulse - Flight
Engineer, Jake Bontekoe - Pilot,
Fred J. Olivi - Pilot

October 1990 —
Fred J. Olivi (left) and Edward Klausner worked for the Bridge Division - City of Chicago. Ed Klausner was in charge of repairs and rebuilding of Chicago's Bascule Bridges after the War. He was my Boss and Best man at my wedding. Both retired, we have a total of 72 years of service between us, working for the City of Chicago. We have remained good friends through the many years and have traveled to Europe and other places on vacations with our wives.
Klausner passed on May 31, 1997 and I've lost a great friend who's company I enjoyed very much!

Chicago, Illinois — Family of my Cousin Angelo Bianchini
First Row - Sitting - L to R - Angelo, Dolores, Jean, Bernice Bianchini
Standing - L to R - Clarice, Marcella, Ed, Loretta, Irene
Since I was related to Angelo, I spent a lot of time, visiting with the family and becoming good friends. I also worked quite a bit in the family grocery store in Pullman doing and learning the many things required to work with the public. Bernice was a hard worker and tough task master - she expected nothing but the best work possible from you!
Ed and I were childhood chums and played together - Cowboys and Indians in our youth - what else!
The years spent during my formative years with the family were enjoyable and rewarding and was an important part of my life.

1990 - Chicago, Illinois
L to R - William Payes, President of Builders Chicago, Fence Contractor
Henry Ecale, Chief Bridge Engineer
Fred Olivi, Manager Bridge Operations and Maintenance
Employees of City of Chicago.

October 26, 1991 - AF Museum, Dayton, Ohio
509th Mini-Reunion
L to R - Petrolli, Garner, Bruenger, Wasz, Griffin (Kneeling), Olivi, Felchlia, Norris

June 1997 - Reading, Pennsylvania Air Show L to R - Linda Morgan, Col. (Ret.) Robert Morgan Pilot of B-17 "Memphis Belle", Chris Dialictos, Fred J. Olivi - Lt. Col. (Ret) Co-pilot of B-29 "Bockscar", Carole Olivi. We make a lot of Air Shows and Military Shows with the Morgans and have become great friends!

Attending Rose Festival in Thomasville, Georgia - April 1988 while visiting Cadet Classmate A.B. Paul - Class 44G
L to R - Fred J. Olivi, Carole Olivi, A.B. Paul, Miriam Paul, Barbara Wallace, Dempsey Wallace
A.B. Paul and Fred Olivi were 44G Pilot Classmates and remain good friends today.

RANGERS

The above photo is of some of the veteran Rangers of the 2nd and 5th Battalions that landed on Omaha Beach on 6 June 1944 in Normandy, France.

Some of these men carried out the most desperate and dangerous mission of the entire invasion. They were to assault the perpendicular cliffs of Point du Hoc. Under intense machine gun, mortar and artillery fire, they destroyed a large German gun battery that would have wreaked havoc on the landing troops and Allied Fleet laying offshore. I visited Point du Hoc on one of my visits to Normandy and saw firsthand the courage each Ranger needed and displayed in taking the heights from the Germans.

I have become an Honorary Member of this fine group of Chicago Area Rangers who meet every other Thursday for a breakfast gathering and get-together. It's an honor for me to be accepted by these men and associate with them. Their valor will never be forgotten and I will always be proud of my being able to talk and be with them. Their personal courage in achieving their objective should always be remembered!

Rangers – Left to Right –

Jack Summers

Steve Zaher

Randy Brown

Ed Zaino

Ray Alm

Les McKie

Lloyd Pollard

Donald McCormick

Harold (Jesse) James

George Zanta

Andy Stojak

Henry Kandziorski

Tom O'Shea

The 509th Composite Group Hx.

Spring/43 Tibbets returns to US to participate in the B-29 program.

Spring/43 Los Alamos laboratory opens under Dr. Oppenheimer

7/1/43 Received word to report to Wichita, Kansas for B-29 program.

Training took place at Smokey Hill Airfield near Salina, Kansas.

Reassigned to Grand Island, Nebraska to start a training school for B-29 pilots.

Went to Alamogordo, New Mexico to work with E.J. Workman a UNM physics professor to study the vulnerability of the B-29 to attack.

Flew a stripped bomber for the first time during testing, and found that it handled better than a fully equipped plane. 7000 lbs lighter.

Fall/43 The Army Air Force decided to use the B-29 to deliver the A-Bomb

2/28/44 393rd BMS was created.

3/11/44 393rd was activated as part of the 504th Bombardment Group.

4/27/44 Lt Colonel Thomas Classen was chosen as commander of the 393rd.

General Henry "Hap" Arnold hand picks Tibbets to command the new project.

9/1/44 Flew B-29 to Colorado Springs in response to a call from General Uzal G. Ent, Commander of the Second AF.

Introduced to Cpt. William Parsons and Norman Ramsey, Ph.d, a professor at Columbia University.

Was asked to organize a combat force to deliver a new type of explosive that was so powerful, it's full potential was unknown. Ramsey then explained the secret of the bomb.

Required to devise a way to increase the distance between the bomber and the blast of at least 8 miles.

Bomb bay would have to be modified to carry the bomb.

15 B-29s, and approximately 1800 support personnel would be assigned to the new group.

Tibbets and Albury flew to Wendover Field (formerly a P-47 training base) and chose it as training base.

Gen. Ent offered Tibbets the 393rd Bomb Squadron, which was completing it's training in the new B-29 at Fairmont Army Air Field, as the nucleus of the new outfit.

Tibbets became the commander of the 393rd, and Lt. Col. Tom Classen Squadron Commander became Tibbets deputy commander.

9/8/44 Tibbets set up headquarters at Wendover Field.

9/11/44 393rd personnel arrived. 15 B-29s with crews and ground crew.

Tibbets personally chose the following:

Bombardier - Tom Ferebee
Tail gunner - George Carron S/Sgt
Navigator - Dutch Van Kirk
Flight Engineer - Wyatt Duzenbury
Pilot - Bob Lewis (formerly involved with B-29 program)
Pilot - Charles Albury
Pilot - Charles Sweeney
Navigator - James Van Pelt
Bombardier - Kermit Beahan
Radar Specialist - Jacob Beser

11/25/44 393rd was reassigned from the 504th BG to the Second Air Force.

12/9/44 509th Composite Group was constituted.

12/17/44 509th officially activated, and became the new higher headquarters for the 393rd BMS. (41st anniversary of the Wright Bros first flight at Kitty Hawk).

Tibbets held a meeting at the base auditorium and said: "You have been brought here to work on a very special mission. Those of you who stay will be going overseas. You are going to participate in an effort that could end the war!"

Tibbets had all of the armament removed except for the tailguns on each B-29.

Original 393rd B-29s were replaced with new ones direct from the assembly lines, modified to Tibbets specifications.

3/6/45 The 1st ordinance Squadron, Special, Aviation joined the 509th-CG.

NOTES ON MISSION

It would be unsafe to drop the bomb at an altitude of less than 30,000 ft.

The mission to Japan and back to Tinian would take about 14 hours.

It would take the B-29 two minutes to fly 8 miles.

It takes the bomb 43 seconds to drop from 31,000 ft to the point of detonation at about 2000 ft.

Shock waves travel at 1,100 ft/sec. 40 sec to travel 8 miles.

Plane would be 6 miles away vertically when the bomb detonated.

The most effective maneuver for increasing the distance would be to make a sharp 155 degree turn after releasing the bomb.

Practiced dropping bombs from 30,000 ft at a target 400 feet in diameter.

Initially practiced with conventional bombs.

Soon employed "PUMPKINS", which were the same size and weight as the bomb they would eventually drop.

Tibbets realized that there would be a problem transition from flying over water, to flying over land.

Received permission to fly training missions from Batista Field in Havana, and used entire Caribbean for practice missions.

5 planes were sent out at a time on 10 day training missions over the Caribbean.

Sweeney frequently accompanied Tibbets as co-pilot to his Los Alamos meetings, flying into Kirtland AFB at Albuquerque, New Mexico.

"The Green Hornet" line was the name used when shuttling back and forth from Los Alamos to Wendover.

"When the 509th was organized, it was assumed that the outfit would be divided, with one unit going to Europe, and the other to the Pacific. ...By summer, our lone enemy was Japan." Pg 179

Tinian Island became known as the Manhattan in the Pacific, because it resembled Manhattan.

509th was assigned to the Columbia University District.

Tinian was an island in the Marianna's, which also included Guam and Saipan.

5/6/45 1200 people sailed to Tinian on the troopship SS Cape Victory from Seattle, WA.

5/18/45 Advance air echelon arrived on Tinian.

5/29/45 Troop ship arrived at Tinian.

6/11/45 B-29s began arriving at Tinian. 18 planes were sent to the island. (3 more B-29s were added to the group)

Upon their arrival, 509th became part of the 313th BW of the Twentieth AF.

The 509th lived in relative isolation on the island, near North Field.

Four of the islands runways extended 8,500 feet.

509th consisted of the following:

1) 393rd Bomber Squadron
2) 320th Troop Carrier Squadron
3) 390th Air Service Group
4) 603rd Air Engineering Squadron
5) 1027th Air Material Squadron
6) 1st Ordinance Squadron (responsible for arming the bomb)

By mid June, plans were being drawn to transfer up to two million men to the Pacific for Operation OLYMPIC. Olympic would put 800,000 soldiers on the island of Kyushu by November of 1945.

A second operation called CORONET was scheduled to take place in April 1946. Soldiers would land on the island of Honshu.

TARGETS

Kyoto, Hiroshima, Yokahama and Kokura were on the first list of targets. Each was chosen because of it's importance as a war industry, and military center.

Kyoto was rejected by Secretary of State Stinson because it was an important historical center containing many shrines.

Later, Niigata replaced Kokura, and Nagasaki replaced Kyoto as targets.

In early July, Tom Ferebee sent an urgent message to Tibbets advising him to return to Tinian.

General Curtis LeMay had decided that the 509th would not drop the bomb.

LeMay had informed his Chief of Operations, Colonel William Blanchard about the bomb, and Blanchard had said the 509th was not qualified to deliver the bomb.

Upon his return, Tibbets flew to Guam where he met with Lemay and suggested that if Blanchard or anyone else on LeMays staff wanted to fly a practice mission with the 509th, they would be welcome.

Blanchard was then assigned to fly on a training mission to Rota, an Island that was still held by the Japanese.

Tibbots was the pilot, Bob Lewis was the co\pilot, and Blanchard flew in the jump seat.

After dropping a pumpkin on the target, Tibbets turned the plane into a 155 degree dive, and Blanchard was pinned to the seat.

On the same day that Tibbets had met with LeMay, he received a message that the A-bomb test at Alamagardo had been a success.

July turned out to be a tough month for the men of the 509th. To the others on the island, the crews of the 509th were pampered and only flew an occasional dangerous mission, dropping a single bomb.

Eventually, word got out around the island that the 509th was involved in something special, but when time went on and nothing happened, they came under suspicion.

During their first two or three weeks on Tinian, the 509th was involved in many training missions, dropping conventional bombs.

By July, they began dropping pumpkins (orange color and shape) loaded with high explosives on targets in Japan. By the end of the month, 12 pumpkins had been dropped on Japan.

Precision bombing would help accustom the Japanese to seeing daylight flights of 2 or 3 B-29s over a single target.

7/20/45 509th flew it's first mission over Japan, followed by more missions on the 20, 24, 26, 29, using groups of 2 to 6 planes, practicing precision rather than area bombing.

7/25/45 The war department issued orders to General Spaatz, Commanding General of the US Army Strategic AF, reading the 509th for action.

7/26/45 The Indianapolis dropped anchor off Tinian and unloaded a 15 foot wood crate which contained the firing mechanism for the bomb. A bucket which contained the first slug of Uranium 235 was also on board. Each was brought to the bomb assembly hut.

The second piece of Uranium was sent from Hamilton AFB by a B-29, along with two more pieces (on two B-29s) for the second bomb.

7/29/45 General Spaatz arrived on Guam, and brought an order from General Groves authorizing the dropping of the first SPECIAL BOMB on one of the four targets, Hiroshima, Kokura, Niigata or Nagasaki after August 3rd.

8/3/45 General Groves sent "Special Bombing Mission #13", (the twelve previous were the pumpkin missions). designating Hiroshima as the target. The secondary target was Kokura, and the third target was Nagasaki.

Hiroshima was chosen as the primary target because it was an important military and industrial center, and there were no known POW camps located in the city.

"PLAYERS"
"CENTERBOARD" was the code name for the first mission.

A total of 7 planes were involved in the actual mission.

Three weather planes would fly ahead to report weather conditions at the primary and secondary targets.

Straight Flush - Hiroshima
Jabbitt III - Kokura   FINGER CREWS
Full House - Nagasaki

Planes left Tinian at 01:37, more than an hour before the Enola Gay and headed for the target cities.

The Great Artiste would be flown by Major Charles Sweeney, and was assigned to drop the three instruments used to measure the effects of the bomb.

#91 flown by Capt George Marquardt would fly reconnaissance role, and carry scientists.

Top Secret piloted by Chuck Knight was the standby AC, and it was flown to Iwo Jima in the event mechanical problems arose with the Enola Gay.

Enola Gay was flown by P. Tibbets, and carried the bomb "Little Boy".

CREW

Pilot - Colonel Paul W. Tibbets
Co-Pilot - Captain Bob Lewis
Navigator - Dutch Van Kirk
Bombardier - Tom Ferebee
Tail Gunner - Bob Carron
Weaponeer - Captain William Parsons
Weaponeer - Commander Fred Ashworth

In order to make the planes conform with others on Tinian, the 509th tail insignia was replaced with an R, The same change was made on the rest of the planes involved in the mission.

"Little Boy"

The bomb was 12 feet long, and 28 inches in diameter. It weighed 9,000 pounds, and was painted a dull gun metal color.

8/5/45 Little Boy was taken by trailer from the ordinance hut at noon, and placed in the loading pit.

1400 General Lemay officially confirmed that the mission would take place on August 6.

After seeing numerous B-29 crashes during take-off, Parsons suggested arming the bomb in flight, inserting the uranium slugs and the explosive charge during the early stage of the mission while flying at low level.

Parsons arrived as soon as the bomb was loaded onto the plane, and began practicing arming it using the Double Plug system. He emerged 2 hours later confidant he could arm the bomb in flight.

"MISSION"

8/4/45 1500 Shortly after evening mess, the seven crews that would participate in the mission were gathered for a pre-flight briefing, which included discussions on routes, altitudes, radio frequencies and weather report.

Radio call was changed from VICTOR to DIMPLES.

The first leg would be flown at 5000 feet in order for Parsons to arm the bomb in flight.

Submarines and surface ships would be spaced 1700 miles apart along the route to Japan in case of problems.

23:00, the briefing for the three crews that would actually fly the 13 hour trip to the target began.

Although the film of the Alamogordo test was not shown, Parsons told the group about the bomb. The word ATOM was not mentioned.

Enola Gay would drop the bomb and bank 155 degrees to the right. Sweeney would drop the instruments at the same moment and bank 155 degrees to the left. Marquardt in the photo plane would fly behind the others to be out of immediate danger from the blast.

8/6/45 00:00 the final preflight briefing was held.

01:37, the weather planes left Tinian.

02:45 Enola Gay lifted off weighing 65 tons, (15,000 lbs overweight) with a crew of 12, 7,000 gallons of fuel and the 9,000 pound bomb.

02:47 The Great Artiste lifted off from Tinian.

02:49 #91 left Tinian.

Top Secret was flown to Iwo Jima in case of mechanical problems with Enola Gay.

02:53 Parsons and Jeppson descended into the bomb bay and began arming the bomb, with Jeppson holding the flashlight and Parsons putting it together.

02:55 Enola Gay crossed the northern tip of Saipan. Communication between Parsons and Tibbets was made possible by an intercom.

Parsons began by confirming that the green plugs blocking the firing signal and preventing accidental detonation were in place.

Parsons then removed a rear plate, and an armor plate beneath, exposing the cannon breech and unscrewed the breech plug. He then inserted the 4 pieces of cordite into the breech, then replaced the breech plug. He then connected the firing line and reinstalled the two metal plates.

Little Boy was not armed until the charge had been loaded.

Coded messages were sent back to General Farrel, indicating Parsons progress. Each step was reported until the last when the plane was out of range.

<u>03:18</u> 25 minutes later, Little Boy was armed.

No formation was attempted during the first leg of the mission.

The rendezvous was scheduled to take place over Iwo Jima, and the mission would be completed as a group.

The three planes were in radio contact throughout the trip.

Throughout the journey, Parsons and Jepson were electronically monitoring the bomb.

<u>05:34</u> Tibbets ascended from 4600 ft to 5500 feet. 20 minutes later, they had reached a cruising altitude of 9300 feet.

<u>05:52</u> Enola Gay approached Iwo Jima and began climbing to 9,300 feet to rendezvous with the other planes.

<u>05:55</u> arrived at Iwo Jima. Top Secret landed.

<u>06:07</u> after rendezvousing with other planes, they headed for Japan, a little more than three hours away, still unsure of their target.

<u>07:10</u> The undercast sky began breaking up.

<u>07:30</u> Parsons again entered the bomb bay and exchanged the bombs GREEN plugs for RED, thus activating the bombs internal batteries. He then declared the bomb was armed and ready.

The planes slowly climbed to 30,700 feet for the rest of the trip.

<u>08:30</u> Straight Flush radioed that Hiroshima had cloud coverage of < 3/10 at all altitudes.

Sweeney and Marquardt also received this message and there was no reason to break radio silence.

After studying Hiroshima, the crew knew every feature.
Once the city was identified, the IP (Initial Point) was
located. The "T" shaped bridge.

Once the target had been located, Tibbets instructed the
crew to prepare their goggles for use.

09:12:17 the three minute bombing run began. Ferebee
began adjusting the plane.

09:13:47 Tibbets turned control of the plane over to
Ferebee for the rest of the run.

09:14:17 Ferebee flicked the switch that activated a high
pitch tone which would ring for one minute before the
bomb was released. This tone was heard on each of the
three planes, as well as the weather planes which were
already more than 200 miles away.

09:15:17 The bomb was released from the Enola Gay, and
the instruments were dropped by parachute from the Great
Artiste.

After releasing the bomb, EG and GA each turned into the
155 degree turn, loosing 1700 feet of altitude in the
process.

The crew members each put on their dark glasses and prepared for the blast.

09:16:00 the bomb exploded at an altitude of 1890 ft.
above the target. Yield was equivalent to 12,500 tons of
TNT.

At the moment of the blast, a taste of lead caused by
electrolysis occurred. This was due to the radioactive
forces affecting fillings.

The shock wave took about 1 minute to reach the planes
which were now 9 miles away.

The results of the blast were radioed back to the Great
Artiste, the instrument plane.

Caron saw the first shock wave coming toward the plane at
1100 ft/sec.

A second shock wave (echo effect) hit the planes with less intensity.

The crew was shocked and full of disbelief when they saw the damage that had occurred.

A coded message was sent to General Farrell on Tinian declaring the successful bombing.

The atomic cloud remained visible for 90 minutes as the plane flew southward from Hiroshima. It could be seen until the planes were almost 400 miles away.

"It had been an easy mission, one of the most routine I had ever flown...." Quote from P.W. Tibbets

As the planes approached Tinian, Sweeney and Marquardt reduced speed allowing the Enola Gay to arrive well ahead.

<u>14:58</u> the "Enola Gay" touched down on Tinian.

Silver stars were presented to each man involved in the mission.

Tibbets received the Distinguished Service Cross.

Formal debriefing was done by Hazen Payett, a lawyer in civilian life and Intelligence Officer.

Before sitting, each crew member was given a quick medical checkup.

The interviewers were skeptical of the descriptions of the bombing.

"NAGASAKI"

Washington decided to drop the second bomb soon after
Hiroshima to bring a quick end to the war.

Two photo-recon planes flew over Hiroshima 4 hours after
the bombing. They reported that it was impossible to
obtain clear pictures of the damage due to the dense
blanket of smoke covering the ruins, a result of the
fires burning everywhere.

8/7/45 President Truman announces that an atomic bomb had
been dropped on Hiroshima, Japan.

Radio Saipan began broadcasting surrender appeals while
airplanes with loudspeakers flew over Japan carrying the
message of atomic destruction.

The office of War Information printed several million
leaflets and a newspaper containing Sgt. Carrons picture
of the atomic cloud rising over Hiroshima.

"Fat Man"

The second bomb was altogether different in looks and
content.

It was the familiar pumpkin shape.

Plutonium (an artificial substance derived from uranium)
was the new material.

The bomb consisted of two hemispheres of plutonium that
when joined formed a ball of plutonium that fell short of
critical mass. Inside the ball was an activator, and surrounding the plutonium sphere were 64 cloverleaf lens
molds that were wired together so that all would fire at
the same time, therefore putting pressure on all sides of
the sphere, and compressing it into critical mass.

8/7/45 The decision to drop the second bomb was made on
Guam. It's use was calculated to indicate that we had an
endless supply of the new weapon for use against Japan.
The third bomb would not be ready until September 1945.

Fat Man F31 (a Fat Man with high explosives and a nuclear
core) was assembled by Commander Ashworth. In the rush to
complete the bomb, the firing unit cable was installed

backwards, requiring B.J. Okeefe to cut the connectors
and reinstall them at the last minute.

8/8/45 1400 Word was sent out that a briefing would occur
at 2300.

2200 Fat Man was loaded onto Bock's Car, fully armed!

2300 Briefing was,held, among other things discussed was
the naming of Yakushima as the rendezvous due to bad
weather over Iwo Jima.

8/9/45 Prior to take off, flight engineer Kuharek notices
the fuel pump for one of the reserve tanks on Bock's Car
is not functioning. The crew deplanes while the situation
is discussed. The decision is made to carry on with the
mission as planned.

03:49 Bock's Car, piloted by Major Charles "Chuck"
Sweeney left Tinian and headed for Japan.

03:51 The Great Artiste, piloted by Captain Fred Bock
left Tinian.

03:53 Lt Colonel Hopkins left Tinian flying the recon AC.

09:00 Bock's Car and the Great Artiste arrive at the rendezvous and wait 45 minutes for Lt. Col Hopkins.

09:40 Sweeney heads Bock's Car northward toward Kokura.

10:44 Bock's Car arrives over Kokura.

Captain Beahan indicates that he can see enough landmarks
to drop the bomb visually. At the last moment, his vision
was obscured by clouds and the drop was terminated.

Sweeney circled around again, making a second and third
bomb run over the target. Each time Beahan was unable to
see the aiming point.

After 50 minutes over the target, Sweeney conferred with
Ashworth, and the decision was made to fly on to
Nagasaki, 95 miles to the north.

Upon reaching Nagasaki, there was 70% cloud cover, and the aiming point was hidden from view.

Faced with the possibility of aborting the mission, the decision was made to drop the bomb by radar, rather than visually as they had been instructed.

Ashworth agreed with Sweeney, so a few minutes before 11, BC was over the target with the navigator and the radar man in control.

At the last minute, clouds opened up, and Beahan shouted that he had the city in view. Control was returned to Beahan and the bomb was dropped visually. The aiming point was a stadium in the city.

11:01 Fat Man was released from "Bockscar".

Sweeney then put the plane into a sharp 155 degree turn to the left to escape the effects of the blast.

11:02 Fat Man explodes 1,840 feet above Nagasaki with an estimated yield of 22 Kilotons. Three aftershocks were felt by the crews of the BC and the GA.

8/10/45 General Spaatz proposes dropping a third bomb on Tokyo

114 B-29s are sent on another incendiary mission.

8/14/45 11:00 Emperor Hirohito assembles his ministers and informs them that he favors the Allies ultimatum.

More than 1000 bombers participate in a raid that destroyed half of the city of Kumagaya, and one sixth of the city Isezaki.

8/15/45 Hirohito broadcasts the Japanese surrender to 100 million subjects.

9/2/45 Japan signs an unconditional surrender on the battleship Missouri.

10/17/45 509th returned to the United States.

11/7/45 509th arrived at Roswell Army Air Field, New Mexico.

1/22/46 Colonel Tibbets turned the Command of the 509th over to Colonel Wm. Blanchard.

<u>Enola Gay</u> Crew
Hiroshima Mission (Little Boy)
August 6, 1945

A. Aircraft used: B-29 serial number 45-MO-44-86292.
Victor No. 82 (call sign used for
this mission was Dimples 82.

Aircraft delivered from Martin
plant in Omaha (Nebraska) on May
18, 1945.

B. Basic crew:

Aircraft Commander	Paul W. Tibbets, Jr.	Living
Copilot	Robert A. Lewis	Deceased
Navigator	Theodore J. Van Rirk	Living
Bombardier	Thomas W. Ferebee	Living
Flight Engineer	Wyatt E. Duzenbury	Deceased
Radio Operator	Richard H. Nelson	Living
Radar Operator	Joseph S. Stiborik	Deceased
Tail Gunner	George R. Caron	Deceased
Asst Eng/Scanner	Robert H. Shumard	Deceased

C. Added crew:

Weapon Officer	William S. Parsons	Deceased
Weapon Test Officer	Morris R. Jeppson	Living
Radar Countermeasures	Jacob Beser	Deceased

Bockscar Crew
Nagasaki Mission (Fat Man)
August 9, 1945

A. Aircraft used: B-29 serial number 35-MO-44-27297.
Victor No. 77.
Aircraft delivered from Martin
plant in Omaha
(Nebraska) on March 19, 1945.

B. Basic crew:

Aircraft Commander	Charles W. Sweeney	Living
Pilot	Charles D. Albury	Living
Co-Pilot	Fred J. Olivi	Living
Navigator	James F. Van Pelt	Deceased
Bombardier	Kermit K. Beahan	Deceased
Flight Engineer	John D. Kuharek	Living
Radio Operator	Abe M. Spitzer	Deceased
Radar Operator	Edward R. Buckley	Deceased
Tail Gunner	Albert T. Dehart	Deceased
Asst Eng/Scanner	Raymond G. Gallagher	Living

C. Added crew:

Weapon Officer	Frederick L. Ashworth	Living
Weapon Test Officer	Philip M. Barnes	Deceased
Radar Countermeasures	Jacob Beser	Deceased

Summary History
Assigned B-29 Aircraft
509th Composite Group

Tail No.	Victor No.	Name	Delivery Date	Msns	Disposition Date
296	84	Some Punkins	19 Mar 45	5	Scrapped Aug 46 (Kirtland AAF)
297	77	Bockscar	19 Mar 45	4	AF Museum Sep 46
298	83	Full House	20 Mar 45	7	US Navy Nov 56
299	86	Next Objective	20 Mar 45	4	Scrapped Jul 49 (Biggs AFB)
300	73	Strange Cargo	2 Apr 45	4	Scrapped Aug 57 (Brize Norton UK)
301	85	Straight Flush	2 Apr 45	6	Scrapped Jul 54 (Davis-Monthan)
302	72	Top Secret	2 Apr 45	6	Scrapped Jul 54 (Davis-Monthan)
303	71	Jabit III	3 Apr 45	5	Scrapped Apr 46 (Chicago Mun AP)
304	88	Up An' Atom	3 Apr 45	6	US Navy Nov 56
353	89	The Great Artiste	20 Apr 45	5	Scrapped Sep 49 (Goose Bay)
354	90	Big Stink	20 Apr 45	4	Scrapped Feb 60 (Davis-Monthan)
291	91	Necessary Evil	18 May 45	4	US Navy Nov 56
292	82	Enola Gay	18 May 45	3	A/S Museum Aug 46
346	94	Spook	15 Jun 45	0	Scrapped Jun 60 (Naha Japan)
347	95	Laggin' Dragon	15 Jun 45	1	Scrapped Jul 60 (Naha Japan)